Dummies 101: Word Perfect® 8 For Windows®

CHEAT SHEET

S0-BZK-902

Opening, Printing, and Saving

When You Want to	Do This
Open a document	Choose File⇨Open from the menu bar, press Ctrl+O, or click the Open button on the toolbar
Save a document	Choose File⇨Save from the menu bar, press Ctrl+S, or click the Save button on the toolbar
Print a document	Choose File⇨Print from the menu bar, press Ctrl+P, or click the Print button on the toolbar
Close a document	Choose File⇨Close from the menu bar, press Ctrl+F4, or click the document Close button in the upper-right corner of the document window
Close WordPerfect	Choose File⇨Exit from the menu bar, click the Close button in the upper-right corner, or double-click the control menu box in the upper-left corner of the WordPerfect window

Mouse Droppings

When You Want to	Do This with Your Mouse
Select (highlight) text	Click at the beginning of the text, hold down the mouse button, and drag to the end (in a straight line)
Select a word	Double-click the word
Select a sentence	Click in the left margin
Select a paragraph	Double-click in the left margin
Move text	Select it and then click and drag it to new position
See a QuickMenu	Press the right mouse button

Cutting and Pasting Text

When You Want to	Do This
Copy something to Clipboard	Select what you want to copy and then click the Copy button on the toolbar or press Ctrl+C
Delete something but save it on Clipboard	Select what you want to delete and then click the Cut button on the toolbar or press Ctrl+X
Paste contents of Clipboard	Move your cursor to the spot where the information should appear and then click the Paste button on the toolbar or press Ctrl+V

☑ Progress Check

Dummies 101®: WordPerfect® 8 For Windows®

CHEAT SHEET

Fixing Mistakes

- ▸ If you see a menu or dialog box that you don't want, press Esc a few times.
- ▸ If you delete something and want it back, press Ctrl+Shift+Z.
- ▸ If you want to undo your most recent action, press Ctrl+Z or click the Undo button. Repeat to undo more actions (up to 300).

Formatting Tricks

To Get This Effect	Do This
Boldface	Select text and then press Ctrl+B or click the Bold icon on the toolbar
Italics	Select text and then press Ctrl+I or click the Italics icon on the toolbar
Underlining	Select text and then press Ctrl+U or click the Underline icon on the toolbar
Center current line	Press Shift+F7
Right-align current line	Press Alt+F7
Indent current line	Press F7
Hanging indent current line	Press Ctrl+F7
Look at hidden codes	Press Alt+F3 or choose View➪Reveal Codes from the menu bar
Begin a new page	Press Ctrl+Enter
Set the margins	Press Ctrl+F8 or click and drag the dotted blue guidelines

IDG BOOKS WORLDWIDE™

Copyright © 1997 IDG Books Worldwide, Inc.
All rights reserved.
Cheat Sheet $2.95 value. Item 0189-5
For more information on IDG Books,
call 1-800-762-2974

®

COMPUTER BOOK SERIES FROM IDG

References for the Rest of Us! ®

Are you intimidated and confused by computers? Do you find that traditional manuals are overloaded with technical details you'll never use? Do your friends and family always call you to fix simple problems on their PCs? Then the *...For Dummies*® computer book series from IDG Books Worldwide is for you.

...For Dummies books are written for those frustrated computer users who know they aren't really dumb but find that PC hardware, software, and indeed the unique vocabulary of computing make them feel helpless. *...For Dummies* books use a lighthearted approach, a down-to-earth style, and even cartoons and humorous icons to diffuse computer novices' fears and build their confidence. Lighthearted but not lightweight, these books are a perfect survival guide for anyone forced to use a computer.

Already, millions of satisfied readers agree. They have made *...For Dummies* **books the #1 introductory level computer book series and have written asking for more. So, if you're looking for the most fun and easy way to learn about computers, look to** *...For Dummies* **books to give you a helping hand.**

™

IDG BOOKS
WORLDWIDE

5/97

Page 32 to save on disk

DUMMIES 101:®
WORDPERFECT® 8
FOR WINDOWS®

by Alison Barrows and
Margaret Levine Young

IDG Books Worldwide, Inc.
An International Data Group Company

Foster City, CA ✦ Chicago, IL ✦ Indianapolis, IN ✦ Southlake, TX

Dummies 101®: WordPerfect® 8 For Windows®

Published by
IDG Books Worldwide, Inc.
An International Data Group Company
919 E. Hillsdale Blvd.
Suite 400
Foster City, CA 94404
www.idg.books (IDG Books Worldwide Web site)
www.dummies.com (Dummies Press Web site)

Library of Congress Catalog Card No.: 97-72403

ISBN: 0-76450189-5

Printed in the United States of America

10 9 8 7 6 5 4 3 2 1

1M/SV/QX/ZX/IN

Distributed in the United States by IDG Books Worldwide, Inc.

Distributed by Macmillan Canada for Canada; by Transworld Publishers Limited in the United Kingdom; by IDG Norge Books for Norway; by IDG Sweden Books for Sweden; by Woodslane Pty. Ltd. for Australia; by Woodslane Enterprises Ltd. for New Zealand; by Longman Singapore Publishers Ltd. for Singapore, Malaysia, Thailand, and Indonesia; by Simron Pty. Ltd. for South Africa; by Toppan Company Ltd. for Japan; by Distribuidora Cuspide for Argentina; by Livraria Cultura for Brazil; by Ediciencia S.A. for Ecuador; by Addison-Wesley Publishing Company for Korea; by Ediciones ZETA S.C.R. Ltda. for Peru; by WS Computer Publishing Corporation, Inc., for the Philippines; by Unalis Corporation for Taiwan; by Contemporanea de Ediciones for Venezuela; by Computer Book & Magazine Store for Puerto Rico; by Express Computer Distributors for the Caribbean and West Indies. Authorized Sales Agent: Anthony Rudkin Associates for the Middle East and North Africa.

For general information on IDG Books Worldwide's books in the U.S., please call our Consumer Customer Service department at 800-762-2974. For reseller information, including discounts and premium sales, please call our Reseller Customer Service department at 800-434-3422.

For information on where to purchase IDG Books Worldwide's books outside the U.S., please contact our International Sales department at 415-655-3200 or fax 415-655-3295.

For information on foreign language translations, please contact our Foreign & Subsidiary Rights department at 415-655-3021 or fax 415-655-3281.

For sales inquiries and special prices for bulk quantities, please contact our Sales department at 415-655-3200 or write to the address above.

For information on using IDG Books Worldwide's books in the classroom or for ordering examination copies, please contact our Educational Sales department at 800-434-2086 or fax 817-251-8174.

For press review copies, author interviews, or other publicity information, please contact our Public Relations department at 415-655-3000 or fax 415-655-3299.

For authorization to photocopy items for corporate, personal, or educational use, please contact Copyright Clearance Center, 222 Rosewood Drive, Danvers, MA 01923, or fax 508-750-4470.

 is a trademark under exclusive license to IDG Books Worldwide, Inc., from International Data Group, Inc.

About the Authors

Alison Barrows: Alison has taken the long route to ...*For Dummies* writing, most recently thinking she would have a career in economics. A serious computer user since high school, she found herself irresistibly drawn to the software field (with help from friends who are ...*For Dummies* authors). During her continuing career in technical writing and training, she has designed and written software courses and taught hundreds of computer novices how to make computers work for them.

Since finding herself in a career as a writer, Alison has authored or coauthored six (and counting) books for IDG Books Worldwide including *Dummies 101: WordPerfect 7 for Windows 95, Excel 97 Secrets, Access 97 For Dummies Quick Reference,* and *Dummies 101: 1-2-3 97 for Windows.*

Alison and coauthor Margret Lavine Young met many years ago on Star Island and became friends despite the fact that only two showers were allowed during the weeklong conference. They have managed to stay friends through Alison's many relocations and have worked together a few times. This is their fourth book together.

Alison previously worked in technical support and training at The World Bank and at Information Resources, Inc. She has a Master's degree in Public Policy from the Kennedy School at Harvard University, and a Bachelor's degree in International Relations from Wellesley College. In addition to writing books, Alison teaches custom computer courses and writes technical documentation and training material. When she's ready to take a break from technical stuff, Alison sings with the New England Chorale, does yoga, plays Ultimate Frisbee, and dabbles in rock climbing. A special activity while working on this book was wedding planning — the wedding occurred just as the book was heading into production. She currently lives in Gardner, Massachusetts, with her husband.

Margaret Levine Young: Margy has used small computers since the 1970s. She graduated from UNIX on a PDP-11 to Apple DOS on an Apple II to MS-DOS and UNIX on a variety of machines. She has done all kinds of jobs, basically explaining that computers aren't as mysterious as they look. These jobs include managing the use of PCs at Columbia Pictures, teaching scientists and engineers what computers are good for, and writing and cowriting computer manuals and books. She coauthored *Understanding Javelin PLUS* (Sybex, 1986); *The Complete Guide to PC-File* (Center Books, 1991); *Access Insider* (Wiley, 1992); *UNIX for Dummies; MORE UNIX For Dummies; UNIX For Dummies Quick Reference; The Internet for Dummies;* and *Internet FAQs: Answers to the Most Frequently Asked Questions* (all from IDG Books Worldwide, Inc.).

Margy has a degree in Computer Science from Yale University and lives with her husband, two children, and numerous chickens in Cornwall, Vermont. In addition to writing books, she lectures and consults on using the Internet.

ABOUT IDG BOOKS WORLDWIDE

Welcome to the world of IDG Books Worldwide.

IDG Books Worldwide, Inc., is a subsidiary of International Data Group, the world's largest publisher of computer-related information and the leading global provider of information services on information technology. IDG was founded more than 25 years ago and now employs more than 8,500 people worldwide. IDG publishes more than 275 computer publications in over 75 countries (see listing below). More than 60 million people read one or more IDG publications each month.

Launched in 1990, IDG Books Worldwide is today the #1 publisher of best-selling computer books in the United States. We are proud to have received eight awards from the Computer Press Association in recognition of editorial excellence and three from *Computer Currents'* First Annual Readers' Choice Awards. Our best-selling *...For Dummies®* series has more than 30 million copies in print with translations in 30 languages. IDG Books Worldwide, through a joint venture with IDG's Hi-Tech Beijing, became the first U.S. publisher to publish a computer book in the People's Republic of China. In record time, IDG Books Worldwide has become the first choice for millions of readers around the world who want to learn how to better manage their businesses.

Our mission is simple: Every one of our books is designed to bring extra value and skill-building instructions to the reader. Our books are written by experts who understand and care about our readers. The knowledge base of our editorial staff comes from years of experience in publishing, education, and journalism — experience we use to produce books for the '90s. In short, we care about books, so we attract the best people. We devote special attention to details such as audience, interior design, use of icons, and illustrations. And because we use an efficient process of authoring, editing, and desktop publishing our books electronically, we can spend more time ensuring superior content and spend less time on the technicalities of making books.

You can count on our commitment to deliver high-quality books at competitive prices on topics you want to read about. At IDG Books Worldwide, we continue in the IDG tradition of delivering quality for more than 25 years. You'll find no better book on a subject than one from IDG Books Worldwide.

John Kilcullen
CEO
IDG Books Worldwide, Inc.

Steven Berkowitz
President and Publisher
IDG Books Worldwide, Inc.

*Eighth Annual
Computer Press
Awards ≥1992*

*Ninth Annual
Computer Press
Awards ≥1993*

*Tenth Annual
Computer Press
Awards ≥1994*

*Eleventh Annual
Computer Press
Awards ≥1995*

IDG Books Worldwide, Inc., is a subsidiary of International Data Group, the world's largest publisher of computer-related information and the leading global provider of information services on information technology. International Data Group publishes over 275 computer publications in over 75 countries. Sixty million people read one or more International Data Group publications each month. International Data Group's publications include: **ARGENTINA:** Buyer's Guide, Computerworld Argentina, PC World Argentina; **AUSTRALIA:** Australian Macworld, Australian PC World, Australian Reseller News, Computerworld, IT Casebook, Network World, Publish, Webmaster; **AUSTRIA:** Computerwelt Osterreich, Networks Austria, PC Tip Austria; **BANGLADESH:** PC World Bangladesh; **BELARUS:** PC World Belarus; **BELGIUM:** Data News, **BRAZIL:** Annuário de Informática, Computerworld, Connections, Macworld, PC Player, PC World, Publish, Reseller News, Supergamepower; **BULGARIA:** Computerworld Bulgaria, Network World Bulgaria, PC & MacWorld Bulgaria; **CANADA:** CIO Canada, Client/Server World, ComputerWorld Canada, InfoWorld Canada, NetworkWorld Canada, WebWorld; **CHILE:** Computerworld Chile, PC World Chile; **COLOMBIA:** Computerworld Colombia, PC World Colombia; **COSTA RICA:** PC World Centro America; **THE CZECH AND SLOVAK REPUBLICS:** Computerworld Czechoslovakia, Macworld Czech Republic, PC World Czechoslovakia; **DENMARK:** Communications World Danmark, Computerworld Danmark, Macworld Danmark, PC World Danmark, Techworld Danmark; **DOMINICAN REPUBLIC:** PC World Republica Dominicana; **ECUADOR:** PC World Ecuador; **EGYPT:** Computerworld Middle East, PC World Middle East; **EL SALVADOR:** PC World Centro America; **FINLAND:** MikroPC, Tietoverkko, Tietoviikko; **FRANCE:** Distributique, Hebdo, Info PC, Le Monde Informatique, Macworld, Reseaux & Telecoms, WebMaster France; **GERMANY:** Computer Partner, Computerwoche, Computerwoche Extra, Computerwoche FOCUS, Global Online, Macwelt, PC Welt; **GREECE:** Amiga Computing, GamePro Greece, Multimedia World; **GUATEMALA:** PC World Centro America; **HONDURAS:** PC World Centro America; **HONG KONG:** Computerworld Hong Kong, PC World Hong Kong, Publish in Asia; **HUNGARY:** ABCD CD-ROM, Computerworld Szamitastechnika, Internetto online Magazine, PC World Hungary, PC-X Magazin Hungary; **ICELAND:** Tolvuheimur PC World Island; **INDIA:** Information Communications World, Information Systems Computerworld, PC World India, Publish in Asia; **INDONESIA:** InfoKomputer PC World, Komputek Computerworld, Publish in Asia; **IRELAND:** ComputerScope, PC Live!; **ISRAEL:** Macworld Israel, People & Computers/Computerworld; **ITALY:** Computerworld Italia, Macworld Italia, Networking Italia, PC World Italia; **JAPAN:** DTP World, Macworld Japan, Nikkei Personal Computing, OS/2 World Japan, SunWorld Japan, Windows NT World, Windows World Japan; **KENYA:** PC World East African; **KOREA:** Hi-Tech Information, Macworld Korea, PC World Korea; **MACEDONIA:** PC World Macedonia; **MALAYSIA:** Computerworld Malaysia, PC World Malaysia, Publish in Asia; **MALTA:** PC World Malta; **MEXICO:** Computerworld Mexico, PC World Mexico; **MYANMAR:** PC World Myanmar; **NETHERLANDS:** Computer! Totaal, LAN Internetworking Magazine, LAN World Buyers Guide, Macworld Netherlands, Net, WebWereld; **NEW ZEALAND:** Absolute Beginners Guide and Plain & Simple Series, Computer Buyer, Computer Industry Directory, Computerworld New Zealand, MTB, Network World, PC World New Zealand; **NICARAGUA:** PC World Centro America; **NORWAY:** Computerworld Norge, CW Rapport, Datamagasinet, Financial Rapport, Kursguide Norge, Macworld Norge, Multimediaworld Norge, PC World Ekspress Norge, PC World Nettverk, PC World Norge, PC World ProduktGuide Norge; **PAKISTAN:** Computerworld Pakistan; **PANAMA:** PC World Panama; **PEOPLE'S REPUBLIC OF CHINA:** China Computer Users, China Computerworld, China InfoWorld, China Telecom World Weekly, Computer & Communication, Electronic Design China, Electronics Today, Electronics Weekly, Game Software, PC World China, Popular Computer Week, Software Weekly, Software World, Telecom World; **PERU:** Computerworld Peru, PC World Profesional Peru, PC World SoHo Peru; **PHILIPPINES:** Click!, Computerworld Philippines, PC World Philippines, Publish in Asia; **POLAND:** Computerworld Poland, Computerworld Special Report Poland, Cyber, Macworld Poland, Networld Poland, PC World Komputer; **PORTUGAL:** Cerebro/PC World, Computerworld/Correio Informático, Dealer World Portugal, Mac*In/PC*In Portugal, Multimedia World; **PUERTO RICO:** PC World Puerto Rico; **ROMANIA:** Computerworld Romania, PC World Romania, Telecom Romania; **RUSSIA:** Computerworld Russia, Mir PK, Publish, Seti; **SINGAPORE:** Computerworld Singapore, PC World Singapore, Publish in Asia; **SLOVENIA:** Monitor; **SOUTH AFRICA:** Computing SA, Network World SA, Software World SA; **SPAIN:** Communicaciones World España, Computerworld España, Dealer World España, Macworld España, PC World España; **SRI LANKA:** Infolink PC World; **SWEDEN:** CAP&Design, Computer Sweden, Corporate Computing Sweden, Internetworld Sweden, it.branschen, Macworld Sweden, MaxiData Sweden, MikroDatorn, Nätverk & Kommunikation, PC World Sweden, PCaktiv, Windows World Sweden; **SWITZERLAND:** Computerworld Schweiz, Macworld Schweiz, PCtip; **TAIWAN:** Computerworld Taiwan, Macworld Taiwan, NEW ViSiON/Publish, PC World Taiwan, Windows World Taiwan; **THAILAND:** Publish in Asia, Thai Computerworld; **TURKEY:** Computerworld Turkiye, Macworld Turkiye, Network World Turkiye, PC World Turkiye; **UKRAINE:** Computerworld Kiev, Multimedia World Ukraine, PC World Ukraine; **UNITED KINGDOM:** Acorn User UK, Amiga Action UK, Amiga Computing UK, Apple Talk UK, Computing, Macworld, Parents and Computers UK, PC Advisor, PC Home, PSX Pro, The WEB; **UNITED STATES:** Cable in the Classroom, CIO Magazine, Computerworld, DOS World, Federal Computer Week, GamePro Magazine, InfoWorld, I-Way, Macworld, Network World, PC Games, PC World, Publish, Video Event, THE WEB Magazine, and WebMaster; online webzines: JavaWorld, NetscapeWorld, and SunWorld Online; **URUGUAY:** InfoWorld Uruguay; **VENEZUELA:** Computerworld Venezuela, PC World Venezuela; and **VIETNAM:** PC World Vietnam. 3/24/97

Dedication

Alison and Margy dedicate this book to Star Island, which is where they first met many years ago and is still their spirits' home.

Alison also dedicates this book to Matt and to her mother, both of whom give her support above and beyond any possible call of duty.

Margy also dedicates this book to her family — Jordan, Meg, and Zac.

Authors' Acknowledgments

We'd like to thank Kathy Cox for doing a great job guiding this book through the many steps from manuscript to what you see in front of you. The supporting cast at IDG includes Jill Brummett, Joyce Pepple, Kevin Spencer, Stephanie Koutek, Mike Kelly, Sherry Gomoll and all the superb folks in Production and Proofreading. We'd also like to thank Allen Wyatt for his helpful technical review.

Alison thanks Matt (also known as "honey") for keeping the computers in such a condition that she could actually work on them. Matt also took on more than his fair share of the final wedding preparations so that this book could get finished.

Also jumping in because of the wedding was Jordan Young, who took over a considerable amount of the last-minute work so that the appropriate amount of attention could be paid to the wedding.

Thanks also go to TIAC and IECC, our Internet and e-mail providers.

Publisher's Acknowledgments

We're proud of this book; please send us your comments about it by using the IDG Books Worldwide Registration Card at the back of the book or by e-mailing us at feedback/dummies@idgbooks.com. Some of the people who helped bring this book to market include the following:

Acquisitions, Development, & Editorial

Project Editor: Kathleen M. Cox

Acquisitions Editor: Michael Kelly

Product Development Manager: Joyce Pepple

Copy Editor: Jill Brummett

Technical Reviewer: Allen Wyatt, Discovery Computing, Inc.

Editorial Manager: Mary C. Corder

Editorial Assistants: Donna Love

Production

Project Coordinator: Sherry Gomoll

Layout and Graphics: Cameron Booker, Lou Boudreau, Dominique DeFelice, Maridee Ennis, Jane Martin, Mark Owens

Proofreaders: Jon C. Weidlich, Christine Berman, Joel K. Draper, Rachel Garvey, Nancy Price

Indexer: Christine Spina

Special Help
Kevin Spencer, Associate Technical Editor; Access Technology, Inc; Stephanie Koutek, Proof Editor

---

General & Administrative

IDG Books Worldwide, Inc.: John Kilcullen, CEO; Steven Berkowitz, President and Publisher

IDG Books Technology Publishing: Brenda McLaughlin, Senior Vice President and Group Publisher

Dummies Technology Press and Dummies Editorial: Diane Graves Steele, Vice President and Associate Publisher; Judith A. Taylor, Product Marketing Manager; Kristin A. Cocks, Editorial Director; Mary Bednarek, Acquisitions and Product Development Director

Dummies Trade Press: Kathleen A. Welton, Vice President and Publisher

IDG Books Production for Dummies Press: Beth Jenkins, Production Director; Cindy L. Phipps, Manager of Project Coordination, Production Proofreading, and Indexing; Kathie S. Schutte, Supervisor of Page Layout; Shelley Lea, Supervisor of Graphics and Design; Debbie J. Gates, Production Systems Specialist; Robert Springer, Supervisor of Proofreading; Debbie Stailey, Special Projects Coordinator; Tony Augsburger, Supervisor of Reprints and Bluelines; Leslie Popplewell, Media Archive Coordinator

Dummies Packaging and Book Design: Patti Sandez, Packaging Specialist; Lance Kayser, Packaging Assistant; Kavish + Kavish, Cover Design

◆

The publisher would like to give special thanks to Patrick J. McGovern, without whom this book would not have been possible.

◆

Files at a Glance

Here's a listing of all the CD files and where in the book you can find more information about them. See Appendix B for installation instructions. Please go to the appropriate lesson or appendix for further instructions about the particular file.

Contents at a Glance

Table of Contents

Introduction

Welcome to *Dummies 101: WordPerfect 8 For Windows*, part of the tutorial Dummies 101 series from IDG Books Worldwide, Inc.

If you're new to computers and word processing, the best way to learn WordPerfect for Windows is to take a course — and that's just what this book is. This book isn't a standard reference. Instead, this book is a series of lessons that take you through each of the most important things you need to know, including running WordPerfect, making documents, printing things, saving files, and doing fancy formatting, from boldface and italics to tables and fonts. This tutorial takes the place of an actual class, with lessons, exercises, and even pop quizzes. You may want to work through the book from beginning to end, doing all the exercises, or you may prefer to pick out one or more lessons to learn a skill that you need to know.

This is the book for you if

▶ You've ever thought that computers might be useful if only you could figure them out.

▶ What you need to know now is how to use WordPerfect 8 to create fabulous looking documents.

▶ You want to take a class so that you can learn all the important features of WordPerfect, but you don't have the time to attend a structured, sit-down, teacher-walking-around-in-front class.

▶ You want to be proficient at all the basic tasks in WordPerfect — like editing, printing, and formatting — so that you don't have to beg your local expert to help you.

This book includes a CD-ROM that allows us to walk you through real life — except they're more fun — examples of how to use WordPerfect. We refuse to take WordPerfect, or for that matter, any software too seriously — life is just too short — and that's what makes this a *Dummies 101* book.

Who Are You?

This book is designed for the beginning or intermediate computer user who wants more than just technical talk about WordPerfect 8 for Windows 95. We have to make a few assumptions about you before we put one word into this book. This book assumes that

▶ You have a PC with DOS, Windows 95, and WordPerfect 8 for Windows 95 installed.

♦ You have some basic knowledge about how to use Windows 95 (some basics are covered later in this Introduction).

♦ WordPerfect is installed in the normal way and that you aren't trying to make it act like anything other than WordPerfect 8 for Windows 95.

Listen Up, Class!

Notes:

Even a book for beginners has a few prerequisites. We want you to know how this book is organized, and a few factoids that will make following along and following the directions a little easier.

One reason this book is fun to read is that it has character, like all *Dummies 101* books. Here's how the *Dummies 101: WordPerfect 8 For Windows* course works:

♦ The course contains 13 *units,* each starting with a general introduction of the topic or topics to be covered. After the introduction to the topic, the unit contains *lessons* that delve into particular topics — where the real learning takes place.

♦ Lessons contain hands-on *exercises* where you'll use the files on the CD to learn and practice your new skills.

♦ Topics that are a little more complicated or less widely used are covered in *Extra Credit* sidebars. These tidbits are less detailed than the regular text, but may give you the edge you need to make the next document look even better.

♦ When we tell you something especially important, you'll see a little note in the margin, summarizing the point we're making.

♦ Occasionally in the text, you'll see a paragraph labeled *Tip.* These paragraphs highlight shortcuts or caveats about the feature being discussed.

♦ At the end of each lesson is a Progress Check listing the skills you learned in the lesson.

♦ We try to remind you to pace yourself by using a *Recess* section to indicate a good place to stop and take a breather (you won't learn well when you're tired). When you reach a Recess section, we tell you how to wrap up what you're doing and how to get back into the swing of things when you're ready for more.

♦ At the end of each unit, there's a *quiz* to test your comprehension of the material — and to add some comic relief. You'll also find an exercise that lets you practice the skills you've learned in the unit. At the end of each part of the book, we've thrown in a test so that you can find out how many WordPerfect features you can still remember and which ones you'd like to review. (Psst — the test answers are in the Appendix; for the quizzes you're on your own.)

These are a few things you'll want to know before you start working through the book:

♦ When you have to press more than one key at the same time, we show the names of the keys connected with a plus sign, like this: Ctrl+C. Press and hold down the first key (Ctrl, in this example), press the second key (C), and then release them both.

♦ When we show commands you choose from the menu, the commands appear with little arrows between the parts of the commands, like this: File⇨Save. This means to choose the File menu and then to choose Save. Don't worry: We explain this all again more slowly in Unit 2, but we wanted to mention it here, in case you flip through the book and wonder what all the little arrows mean.

Before You Start

This section outlines some of the basic things you should already know about Windows 95. If you don't know some of this stuff, we highly recommend *Dummies 101: Windows 95*, for the tutorial approach, and *Windows 95 For Dummies*, for the more traditional approach, both by Andy Rathbone.

Before you start, make sure that you know:

♦ **How to use your mouse.** This includes recognizing the mouse pointer, clicking something, and right-clicking something.

♦ **How to start a program.** The Start button is the usual method, but double-clicking a desktop icon works also.

♦ **How to manage windows.** A program running in a window can have three looks: maximized, in a window, and minimized. You should know how to change the look of the window, and how to display a minimized window.

♦ **How to switch from one open program to another.** The taskbar does the job just fine.

♦ **Where to find some of the specialized keys on the keyboard.** You'll need to use the Alt, Ctrl, and Esc keys, and once in a while the function keys may come in handy. You'll also use the cursor control keys (the arrows and Home, End, PgUp, and so forth). Make sure that you also know how to use the Num Lock key to turn the number pad off and on.

♦ **How to use a menu.** In addition to menu choices, you may see triangles, ellipses, and check marks on WordPerfect menus. Triangles indicate a sub-menu, ellipses mean that the menu option displays a dialog box, and check marks indicate that an option is turned on.

♦ **How to manage files.** You should know something about how your hard disk is organized — into folders. Folders can contain other folders and files. You can manage files (move, copy, and delete them, for example) using My Computer or Windows Explorer.

♦ **How to close WordPerfect.** The Close button — the X in the upper-right corner — works well.

How This Book Is Organized

Notes:

The book is split into four parts:

Part I: Getting Comfortable with WordPerfect 8

Part I covers the basics that you need to know to create a simple document. You learn how to edit a document after you create it, how to store it on a diskette, and how to print.

Part II: Editing and Organizing Your Documents

In Part II, you learn more about how to be a savvy WordPerfect user — how to find phrases or documents, how to manage documents, how to spell check a document and use other intelligent tools, and how to move and copy text.

Part III: Adding Pizzazz

Part III covers all the fancy formatting tricks that you need to know to make your documents look professional. Fonts, spacing, margins, tabs, page numbers, headers, and footers — they're all here.

Part IV: Working with Advanced Features

Part IV covers some of the more advanced features that you're likely to use if you use WordPerfect in an office setting. You also learn about columns and tables and how to create form letters.

Icons Used in This Book

This icon tells you when you need to use a file that comes on the *Dummies 101* CD. The CD-ROM installs all the files on your hard drive for easy access.

Here's an item that you may need to know when you get to the quiz at the end of the unit, or to the test at the end of each part! Even if this information isn't on the test, we think it's important enough to help you become a WordPerfect pro.

extra credit

When we talk about a more advanced topic, it appears in a sidebar highlighted with this icon. Some exercises include an extra credit step to challenge you to try out a new feature or repeat a task without step-by-step instructions.

heads up

Heads up! Here's an important piece of information that you don't want to miss. The piece of information may be a warning, or it may be a tip. Whatever it is, keep your head up and eyes forward so that you don't miss it.

windows 95

All programs designed for Windows 95 have many features in common. This icon flags some of those features so you'll be ready to work other Windows 95-based programs.

Using the CD-ROM

The *Dummies 101* CD-ROM that comes with this book contains all the practice files you'll need to do the lessons and exercises in the book. By using the files on the CD, you won't have to do too much tedious typing when following the lessons in this book. We've done most of the boring typing for you. The files include letters with typos, reports that look boring, and flyers that need to be jazzed up.

Often, more than one version of a document is included on the CD-ROM so that you can do a single exercise in the book without having done the preceding exercise(s) that use the same file. Versions of the document that have some of the work already done have a number after them. If you do all the exercises and save your document after each, always use the document with no number in the file name. If you skip around, keep your eyes peeled for the version number in the file name, and open that file.

Note: The *Dummies 101* CD-ROM *does not* contain the WordPerfect for Windows program itself. You have to buy that from a regular old software store or get it from the computer department at your office and already have it installed on your computer. Our CD-ROM contains document files, not programs.

To install the files from the *Dummies 101* CD-ROM onto your hard disk, you need a CD-ROM drive and about 500K of free space on your hard disk. You also need to be running Windows 95. Directions for installing the CD-ROM files appear in Appendix B in the back of this book.

If you have problems with the installation process, you can call the IDG Books Worldwide, Inc., Customer Support number: 800-762-2974 (outside the U.S.: 317-596-5261).

If you prefer not to install the CD-ROM on your hard drive, you can still use the files on it to do the exercises. You just have to open them from the CD-ROM drive. You learn how in Unit 2, when you use the Open dialog box.

Remember, though, that you can't save a changed file back to the CD-ROM, but you can use the Save As dialog box to save it to your hard drive. Again, the details are in Unit 2.

After you complete the installation process, all the files you need for this book will be ready and waiting for you in the C:\MyFiles folder (the WordPerfect default document folder). You don't have to do anything with the files yet.

Note: The files are meant to accompany the book's lessons, so if you open a file to play with it, you may accidentally make changes to the file. Changes to a file may make the steps in an exercise that uses that file not make any sense. If you can't resist opening a file, just make sure not to save your changes. If you do save your changes, you can always reinstall the files from the CD-ROM.

Store the CD-ROM where it will be free from harm so that you can reinstall a file in case one that's installed on your computer gets messed up. The envelope in the back of the book is a good place to store the CD-ROM.

You can find detailed instructions on how to access the *Dummies 101* files in Unit 2, where you first need to open a file. The files are installed in the WordPerfect default directory, unless:

▶ You choose another folder during the installation process.

▶ On your computer, WordPerfect has a different default folder. The usual default folder is C:\MyFiles.

You can leave the files in a folder other than the default, but you have to learn how to find them when you need them. See Unit 2 for more information.

Send Us E-Mail

Please give us feedback about this book! If you can send e-mail, address messages to us at 101wp8@gurus.com. We'd love to hear how the course worked for you. If you want to know about other *Dummies 101* books, visit IDG's Web site at http:// www.idgbooks.com.

If you can't send e-mail, you can always send plain old paper mail to us using the reader response form in the back of the book. For your trouble, you'll get an attractive full-color catalog of other *Dummies 101* books. Collect them all!

Part I

Getting Comfortable with WordPerfect 8

In this part . . .

Learning a new word processor can be traumatic. "What? Give up my old Selectric? Replace my old word processor? No way!" After all, you spend many happy — or not so happy — hours typing away, creating lyrical prose, or crunching out boring reports. Whatever you use it for, your word processor has to become your friend. You know its ins and outs; even if your word processor is difficult to use, it's familiar.

WordPerfect is still a stranger, and not such a friendly looking stranger at that. What are all those little buttons on the screen for, anyway? And how can I use this thing just to type a simple letter?

Don't worry: This part of the book is just for you. In the first four units, you'll make friends with WordPerfect. You'll learn what to say to WordPerfect to get it to do your bidding. You'll learn what keys to press and mouse buttons to click. You'll learn basics about word processing that will stand you in good stead, no matter what word processor you use. In fact, by the end of the very first unit, you'll have written, saved, and printed a letter! By the end of Unit 4, you'll know all the basic skills you need to go on and learn about WordPerfect's more advanced features.

So get comfortable, limber up your typing fingers, and here we go with Unit 1.

Once Around the Block

Objectives for This Unit

✓ Creating a short document

✓ Printing your document

✓ Saving your document on your hard drive

✓ Exiting WordPerfect

Prerequisites

▸ Windows 95 is installed on your PC

▸ WordPerfect 8 is installed on your PC

▸ Your printer is hooked up and ready to print (optional)

▸ You're psyched to learn about WordPerfect 8

This unit is a preview of what WordPerfect can do for you. When you finish this unit, you'll know how to use WordPerfect to create, save, and print a document. The rest of the book is just icing on the cake!

So what is a document, anyway? Any time you type something in WordPerfect, you're working on a document. A *document* is the unit in which WordPerfect stores information. Each file that's created in WordPerfect and saved on your hard drive or on a floppy disk is a document. A document can be a letter, a report, a poem, a novel, or any other bunch of text you type.

What do you do with documents? Well, you save them on a hard drive or a disk so that you can work on them again later or send them electronically to other folks. You can also print them so you have copies to pass out to friends and coworkers.

windows 95

In the world as we've known it, a document has been something that consists mostly of words, so creating a document with a word processor makes perfect sense. Microsoft is playing with our minds, however, because in Windows 95, a *document* is any file that you create using software (more or less). That definition can include word processing files, spreadsheet files, graphics files, and so on. If you click the Start button on your Windows 95 desktop and then select Documents, you see a list of files you've worked with recently. That list can include WordPerfect files, graphics files, or other types of files. In this book, when we refer to documents we mean something that you (or we) create using WordPerfect, but we thought a definition was in order.

Now you're ready to fire up WordPerfect and start the first lesson. Although we give you a chance to take a break in the middle of this unit, we encourage you to complete the whole unit in one sitting. Other units have obvious points for a recess, and we always tell you how to get back to where you began the lesson in case you need to stop and continue later. This unit, however, is kind of special because it gives you a preview of what is to come and the confidence to continue through the book. This unit may even encourage you to use WordPerfect to write that novel you have in you!

Lesson 1-1

Starting WordPerfect and Typing a Letter

Before you can start the WordPerfect program, you must first turn on your computer, and you (or someone else) must have installed WordPerfect 8 on your hard drive. (**Note:** The CD with this book does not have WordPerfect on it.)

In this lesson, you learn how to start WordPerfect, type a letter, and correct mistakes. You don't need to learn how to use all the parts of the WordPerfect window to perform these steps. In fact, we use only two parts of the window, which you see in Figure 1-1:

> ▶ **The typing area:** The large, white space in the middle of the window
>
> ▶ **The toolbar:** The row of little pictures near the top of the window

Starting WordPerfect

Ready? Your computer should be on, and Windows 95 should be running. Use the following steps to start WordPerfect.

1 **Get psyched — and if your computer isn't on, turn it on.**

Think of how much easier WordPerfect is going to make your life! Pet your mouse, make it your friend, and give it a name (we have a friend who named his mouse Squeak). This is the beginning of an entertaining partnership between you, WordPerfect, and us.

2 **Open Corel WordPerfect 8.**

To start WordPerfect, click the Start button, move the highlight to Corel WordPerfect Suite 8, and then click on Corel WordPerfect 8.

The Start button is on one end of the Windows 95 taskbar — it probably appears in the bottom left corner of your desktop, although the taskbar, which contains the Start button, may be on any edge of the screen.

When you highlight a menu choice with an arrow next to it, like Corel WordPerfect Suite 8, you see a submenu that lists additional choices. If you don't see WordPerfect Suite 8 on the initial Start button menu, highlight Programs to find the Corel WordPerfect Suite 8 menu.

Margin notes:

toolbar: row of buttons you can click

Click the Start button, move to Corel WordPerfect Suite 8, and then click on Corel WordPerfect 8

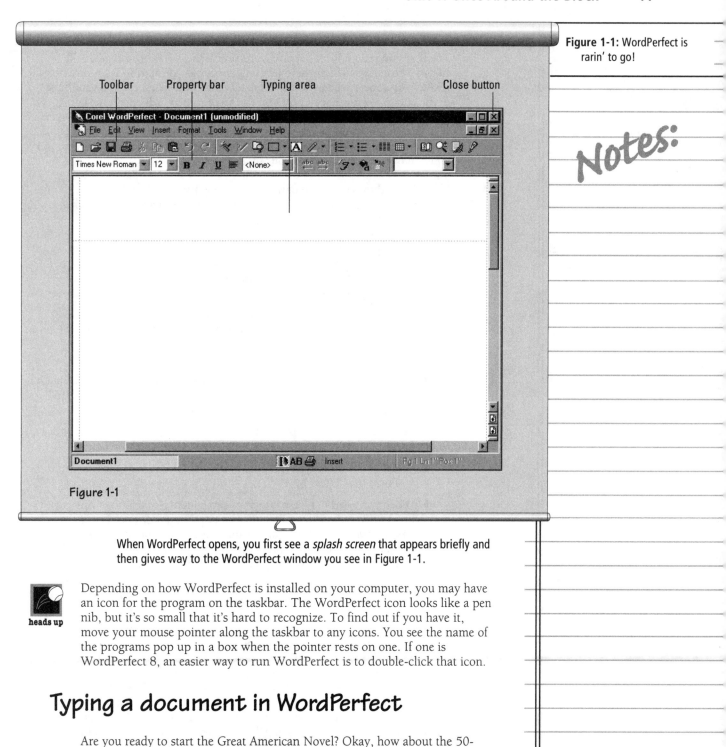

Figure 1-1: WordPerfect is rarin' to go!

Toolbar Property bar Typing area Close button

Figure 1-1

When WordPerfect opens, you first see a *splash screen* that appears briefly and then gives way to the WordPerfect window you see in Figure 1-1.

heads up

Depending on how WordPerfect is installed on your computer, you may have an icon for the program on the taskbar. The WordPerfect icon looks like a pen nib, but it's so small that it's hard to recognize. To find out if you have it, move your mouse pointer along the taskbar to any icons. You see the name of the programs pop up in a box when the pointer rests on one. If one is WordPerfect 8, an easier way to run WordPerfect is to double-click that icon.

Typing a document in WordPerfect

Are you ready to start the Great American Novel? Okay, how about the 50-page report you promised your boss? Good, because all you really need to do is start typing. In case you don't have that great opening line for your novel already in your head, we give you text to type, along with a few hints about how to use a word processor.

Notes:

Notes:

The first thing to know about any word processor is how to recognize the *cursor.* The cursor marks where text will appear as you start to type, or where text will disappear when you use the Backspace or Delete key. You can think of the cursor as your pencil point on the screen. In WordPerfect, the cursor is (usually) a flashing thick, vertical bar. It's like your pencil point on the screen. (Computer geeks sometimes call the cursor the *insertion point,* but we won't.) Don't confuse the *cursor* with the *mouse pointer,* which is usually an arrow, and which moves when you move your mouse.

If you learned to type on a typewriter, you may have habits that are not conducive to happy word processing. Remember the following hints when you're using a computer to process your words:

- When you start a new paragraph, don't use the spacebar to indent. Instead, use the Tab key if you want to indent the first line (or learn how to add an indent to the paragraph format in Unit 10). We talk about setting tabs in Unit 10, so for now just use whatever tabs are set.

- When you reach the end of a line, don't press the Enter key; just keep typing. WordPerfect takes care of putting the next word on the next line. This convenient feature is one of the niftiest things about word processing!

- When you want to start a new line that's a new paragraph or a new item in a list, *do* press the Enter key. The cursor moves to the beginning of the next line, where you can type your next word.

- To leave a blank line, press Enter twice. The cursor moves down two lines.

- When you need to type a capital letter, hold down the Shift key while you type that letter.

- When you need to type a bunch of capital letters, press the Caps Lock key and type the letters. Pressing the Caps Lock key once forces anything you type to appear in capital letters. When you finish typing capital letters, be sure to press the Caps Lock key again to release the lock so that everything else you type isn't in capitals.

  The Caps Lock on a computer keyboard works the same as it does on a typewriter, except that you always have to press the Shift key on the computer to use the special characters above the numbers. If you leave Caps Lock on by mistake and want to know how to fix your text without retyping it, see Lesson 8-3.

Enough talking; it's time to start typing. If you make mistakes, stay calm. You'll get the chance to correct mistakes later on in this lesson. A cool feature of WordPerfect 8 is that it underlines with a squiggly red line anything that it thinks is misspelled. Don't be surprised if the squiggly line falls under your name. For now, just let those squiggly red lines be — we'll get back to them later.

1 Type the letter you see in Figure 1-2. Start with your own name and address.

Position the pointer where you want your name to appear. You see the *shadow cursor,* which is a gray vertical bar with an arrow next to it. When the shadow

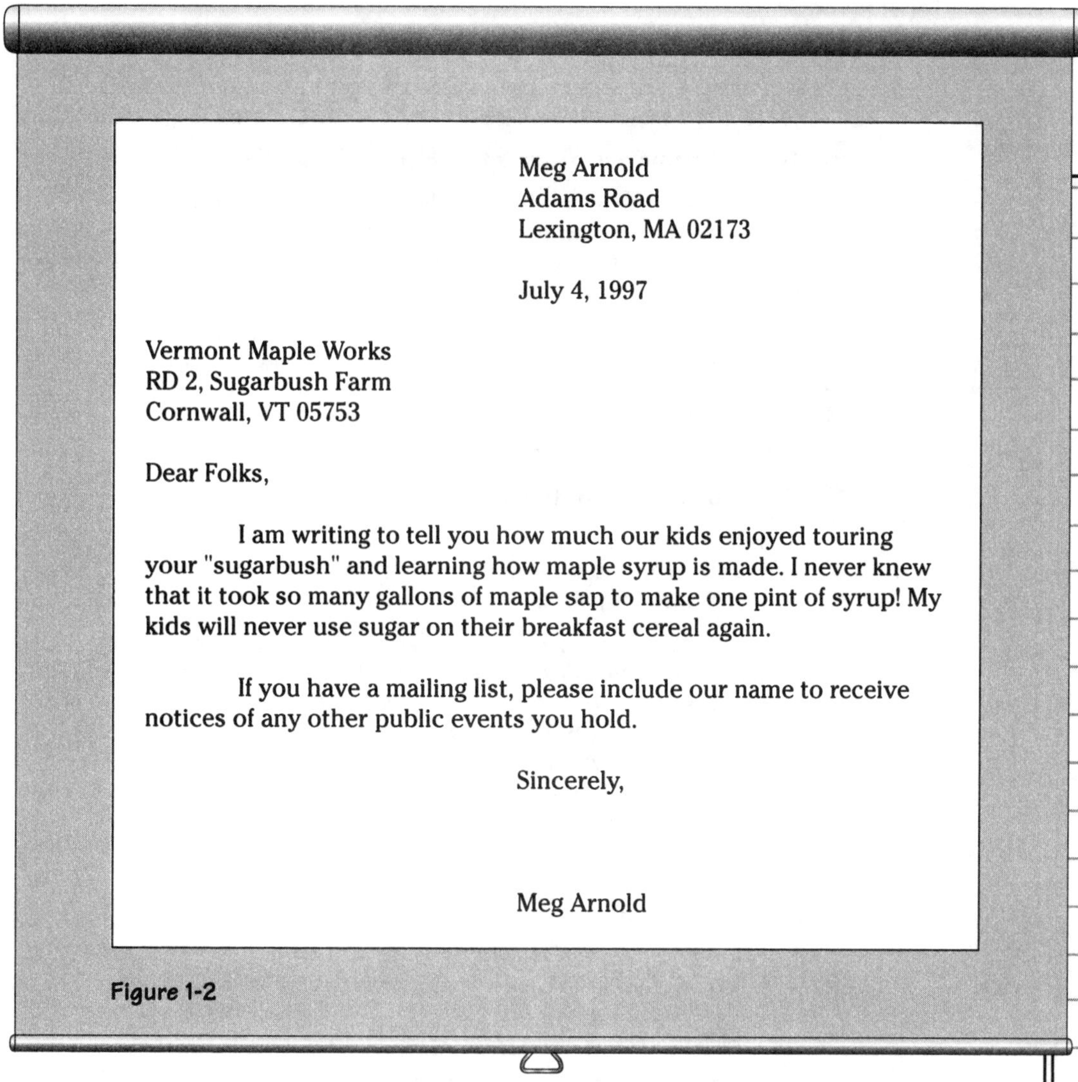

Meg Arnold
Adams Road
Lexington, MA 02173

July 4, 1997

Vermont Maple Works
RD 2, Sugarbush Farm
Cornwall, VT 05753

Dear Folks,

I am writing to tell you how much our kids enjoyed touring your "sugarbush" and learning how maple syrup is made. I never knew that it took so many gallons of maple sap to make one pint of syrup! My kids will never use sugar on their breakfast cereal again.

If you have a mailing list, please include our name to receive notices of any other public events you hold.

Sincerely,

Meg Arnold

Figure 1-2

Figure 1-2: Here's a letter you might send to the maple farm you recently visited.

Shadow cursor

cursor appears where you want to type, click the mouse button to move the cursor to that position. You can position the shadow cursor and click to begin each new line in the address.

Alternately, you can press the Tab key six times to get the name and address lines halfway across the page; then press Enter at the end of each of those lines (in this case, each line is a paragraph), and then press Tab another six times to begin the next line of the address. Repeat the steps for the third line of the address.

By the way, Enter may be called Return on your keyboard, or it may just be a hooked arrow. In this book, we always call it Enter. Don't worry: We cover setting tabs in more detail in Lesson 10-4. For now, just approximate the way the letter looks in the figure.

2 Type the date.

Position the shadow cursor so there is a blank line between the last line of the address and the position of the shadow cursor. Click the mouse button and type the date.

Notes:

If you prefer to stick with the keyboard, press Enter twice (once to finish the line you're on and once to leave a blank line) and then tab over again to type the date.

3 Type the name and address to which you're writing.

Press Enter twice to leave a blank line before the name and address of the addressee. Typing this address is even easier than typing your own address because it's *left justified,* or lined up against the left margin. When text is left justified (and most text is), you don't have to use tabs. You can just type and then press Enter at the end of each line.

Press Enter twice after the last line of the company's address to leave the extra line.

4 Type the salutation.

Dear Folks is also left justified.

5 Now type the text of the letter.

Remember to use Tab to indent the first line of each paragraph, rather than using a bunch of spaces. Let WordPerfect decide when to end a line. Don't press Enter unless you want to start a new paragraph.

If you need to, you can add additional characters (or words, or even paragraphs) to your letter by moving the cursor to the point in the letter where you need to make additions and typing. (When you don't press Enter at the end of a line, WordPerfect adjusts the spacing automatically when you need to add or delete something. If you had pressed Enter, that carriage return would remain next to the word you placed it after and cause the line to break at that point no matter where it fell in the paragraph.)

Remember to press Enter twice between paragraphs.

6 Type the closing.

You can position the shadow cursor where you want the "Sincerely" to appear. Line it up with the address and date at the top of the letter. Position the shadow cursor again and type your name so that three blank lines are between the closing and your name.

If you don't like using the mouse and the shadow cursor, press Enter twice to leave a blank line and to press Tab six times to indent the word *Sincerely.* Press Enter about four times to leave blank lines; then press Tab six times to indent your name.

That wasn't too bad, was it? Go back and read the letter again. Did you make any mistakes?

Correcting mistakse

In Unit 5, we describe many ways to correct mistakes and change your mind about what you've typed. The three easiest ways to correct a mistake are to

▶ Right-click on any word with red squiggly lines under it. A list of correctly spelled words appears — click on the word you meant to type to replace the misspelled word.

▶ Use the Backspace key to delete letters to the left of the cursor.

▶ Use the Delete key to delete letters to the right of the cursor.

Backspace deletes preceding character

Delete deletes following character

Before using the Backspace or Delete keys, you may need to move the cursor. You can do so by using the arrow keys on your keyboard or by positioning the mouse pointer and clicking to reposition the cursor. You can also type additional characters as needed — they will appear at the cursor.

extra credit

What's with the squiggly red lines anyway?

WordPerfect has a nifty feature called Spell-As-You-Go — and on-the-fly spelling is exactly what it does. When Spell-As-You-Go is turned on, your spelling is checked as you type. When WordPerfect thinks you've misspelled a word, it puts a squiggly red line under it. That line is a prompt for you to double-check the word before you print your document or hand a disk containing the document to your boss.

Of course, the WordPerfect dictionary doesn't contain every word that anyone ever used, so it will occasionally mark words that are spelled correctly. You can just ignore the mark because it won't appear on your printed document, or you can add the word to the dictionary by right-clicking on it and then choosing <u>A</u>dd.

☑ Progress Check

If you can do the following, you're ready to move on to the next lesson:

❑ Start WordPerfect.

❑ Type text into WordPerfect.

❑ Use Tab and Enter correctly.

❑ Correct mistakes using the Spell-As-You-Go feature.

❑ Delete incorrect characters by using the Backspace and Delete keys.

Printing a Document

Lesson 1-2

Printing your document is as simple as clicking a button, if your printer is set up correctly. We don't cover how to troubleshoot printer problems here. That topic is covered in Unit 4. If your printer is connected, turned on, and configured correctly, printing your document is extraordinarily easy.

This is your first chance to use a button on the toolbar (the toolbar is the row of buttons immediately under the menu, which is the row of words at the top of the WordPerfect window). To find out what a button on the toolbar does, hold the mouse pointer over the button, but don't click. A small box appears, listing the name of the button, what it does, and a keyboard shortcut you can use instead of clicking the button with your mouse.

Here's how to print your letter:

1 Click the Print button on the WordPerfect toolbar.

Unless someone has changed the way your toolbar looks, the Print button is the fourth button from the left. If you use your imagination, the button looks vaguely like a printer.

You see the Print dialog box, shown in Figure 1-3. You can also display the Print dialog box by pressing Ctrl+P or by choosing <u>F</u>ile⇨<u>P</u>rint from the menu.

Print button

Figure 1-3: To print your letter, click the Print button on the Print dialog box.

☑ Progress Check

If you can do the following, you're ready to move on to the next lesson:

❏ Identify the Print button.

❏ Print a document using the Print button.

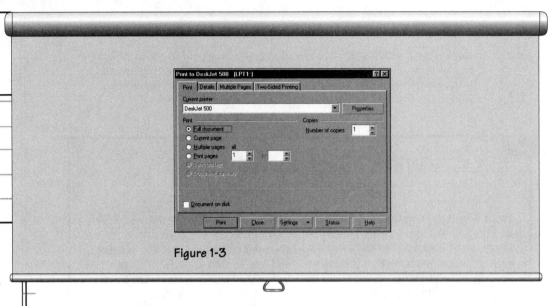

Figure 1-3

2 **Click the Print button.**

You see a box that says "Preparing document," and then the letter is printed.

That's it! Printing can be as simple as that. If you had trouble printing, you may want to go to Unit 4, where we cover the mechanics and pitfalls of printing in detail.

Lesson 1-3

Saving a Document and Closing WordPerfect

Right now the letter that you typed is in a document named *Document1* (see the name at the top of the WordPerfect window?). The document doesn't exist on the hard drive inside your computer or on a floppy disk in the disk drive — it just exists on the screen (really in the computer's RAM — random access memory — to be precise). So if you turn off your computer at this point or exit WordPerfect without saving the document, the document will evaporate into the ether, just like dew drying in the summer morning sun. (Hey, even we *Dummies 101* writers can wax poetic!) But to be a little more down to earth, if you ever want to see this document again, you'd better save it.

Don't panic: It's actually not so easy to lose a document. WordPerfect always asks you to confirm when it's trashing a file (unless you just switch off the computer or the power goes out, in which case WordPerfect can no longer do anything at all).

on the test

Each saved document has a name called a *filename,* which you give it the first time you save it. Windows 95 lets you name your files with up to 255 characters, including spaces and punctuation. Filenames usually have an *extension* at the end of them. An extension is a dot (.) followed by additional characters that tell Windows 95 what kind of file you've saved. Most programs add the extension for you. WordPerfect documents usually have the extension *WPD*.

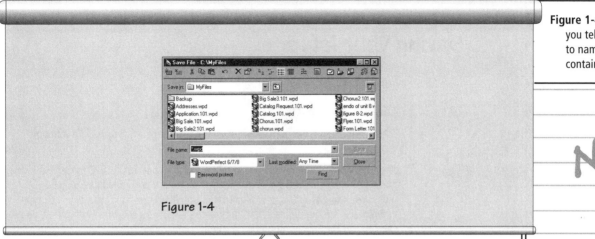

Figure 1-4

Notes:

Can you guess what that stands for? WordPerfect adds that extension for you every time you save a file, as long as your filename doesn't have a period in it.

on the CD

The sample files that come with the book all end with *101.WPD* to indicate that they came with this book, which is part of the *Dummies 101* series, and that they are WordPerfect documents.

The easiest way to save a document is to use the Save button on the toolbar, the third button from the left. Although it looks like a floppy disk, you usually use this button to save to a hard disk, but a picture of a hard disk wouldn't make such a cute button!

Save button

Naming a document

When you want to save a document, you have to think of a name for it. In Windows 95, that task is pretty easy. Just name it something that makes sense to you — but spend an extra second or so thinking whether the name you're about to give your document will still make sense to you later, when you're looking for your document.

When naming a document:

- You can include spaces and just about any character.

- WordPerfect adds the WPD extension for you if you don't specify an extension (it stands for *WordPerfect Document*, logically enough). We recommend that you name your file and let WordPerfect add the WPD extension. You'll have an easier time opening the document in all the funky ways that Windows 95 provides, which we cover in Unit 2.

- You can use capital letters, small letters, or a mixture of the two. Windows 95 doesn't pay attention to capitalization in filenames.

Hard drives have lots of space to store files (as opposed to floppy disks, which usually have less space to store files). For now, you can save to the WordPerfect *default directory*. WordPerfect automatically (by *default*) looks for document files in the default directory and saves them there, too. In Unit 2 we talk about saving files to different directories and disks (see Lesson 2-2) and changing the default directory (see Unit 2 extra credit).

Saving your letter

Try saving your letter:

1 Click the Save button.

The Save button is the third from the left on the toolbar. It looks like a floppy disk.

The Save As dialog box appears (see Figure 1-4). Look for *.WPD in the File name box near the bottom of the dialog box — it's probably highlighted in blue. When you type the new filename in the File name box, whatever you type will replace the highlighted text. In general, when you see text highlighted, you can replace the highlighted text by simply typing over it.

2 Type Mapleworks.

Mapleworks appears in the Name box. Because you're not typing a file extension, WordPerfect automatically gives the file the WPD-extension.

3 Press Enter or click the Save button.

WordPerfect saves the text you typed in Lesson 1-1 in a file called Mapleworks.WPD, in your default directory.

What if you already have a file named Mapleworks.WPD? If you do, WordPerfect asks if you want to replace it. Click the No button, enter a different filename (how about Dummies Letter?), and click OK.

As you may have guessed, we haven't covered everything about saving documents here. But now you know a simple way to save something you've written so that you can retrieve it later.

on the test

After you've given a document a name, saving it the second time is even easier: Just click the Save button. That's it; it's saved! WordPerfect saves the file with the same name it had the last time you saved it, and replaces the old version of the document with the new, updated version. Once you've saved the document, you have to choose File⇨Save As to see the Save As dialog box.

Closing WordPerfect

You should always exit both WordPerfect and Windows 95 before turning off your computer. You can think of it as putting your car in Park before turning off the ignition — getting started the next time will be easier.

As with many things in Windows 95 and WordPerfect, you have more than one way to exit a program. We'll tell you about all of them, and you can take your pick.

The following are easy ways to close WordPerfect:

- Click the X button in the upper-right corner of the WordPerfect window (refer to Figure 1-1 if you're not sure where it is).
- Choose File⇨Exit from the menu.
- Press Alt+F4.

click the X button in the top right of the window to close window

If you have made changes since you last saved your document, WordPerfect will ask you if you want to save those changes. Click Yes to save changes, No to discard changes, and Cancel to return to WordPerfect without closing the program.

If you are finished working and want to turn off your computer, you should exit Windows 95 first. Not that you *have* to turn your computer off after you are finished working — we leave ours on most of the time. We just turn the monitor (screen) and printer off to save power. But if you have your reasons for turning off the computer (such as an approaching lightning storm), click the Start button and choose Shut Down. Then check that Shut down the computer is selected and click Yes. Windows 95 will shut down any open programs. You may see the words It is now safe to turn off your computer, or your computer may simply turn off automatically. In either case, make sure you turn off your monitor, too.

Recess

Congratulations! You've reached a great place to stop and get a snack. But don't go away for too long just because you've reached the end of the unit. The quiz and exercise that follow will tell you how much progress you've made so far!

☑ Progress Check

If you can do the following, you're ready to move on to the next lesson:

❑ Use the Save button to save your document.

❑ Type a filename in the Save dialog box to name your document.

❑ Close WordPerfect.

Unit 1 Quiz

For each of the following questions, circle the letter of the correct answer or answers. Remember that we may have included more than one right answer for each question.

1. **An easy way to start WordPerfect is...**

   A. Click your heels and say three times, "WordPerfect is the best."

   B. Use the Start button to find Corel WordPerfect Suite 8 and the Corel WordPerfect 8 choice.

   C. Double-click the WordPerfect icon on the taskbar.

   D. Find the WordPerfect program file (WPWIN.EXE) in the Explorer and double-click it.

   E. Go to the refrigerator and take out a jar of pickles.

2. **A document is...**

   A. A file created by WordPerfect.

   B. Anything you type and save in WordPerfect.

   C. What you save when you click Save button on the toolbar.

   D. Something you get from a lawyer.

   E. Almost any file you create with a program in Windows 95.

3. **To create a document in WordPerfect, you must...**

   A. Open WordPerfect and then start typing.

   B. Open WordPerfect, set up margins and tabs, and change environment preferences before you can start typing.

   C. Open WordPerfect, click every single button on the toolbar, and see what happens.

   D. Hire a ghostwriter.

   E. Get out your parchment, quill pen, and ink, and start lettering.

4. **Which button is this?**

   A. Format my floppy.

   B. Save button.

   C. Insert program disk.

   D. Reset button.

   E. Label the floppy disk.

5. **Use this button when you want to...**

   A. Turn your computer into the newest, hottest computer on the market, all peripherals included (modem, printer, scanner, and so on).

   B. Turn your printer into a food processor.

   C. Print the document that is currently displayed on-screen.

   D. Display the Print dialog box.

   E. Exit WordPerfect.

6. **An easy way to close WordPerfect is to...**

   A. Click the Close button at the top right-hand corner of the window.

   B. Press Alt+F4.

   C. Choose File➪Exit from the menu.

   D. Wait until WordPerfect gets tired — then it will exit by itself.

   E. Turn the computer off. (**Hint:** This is a bad idea!)

Unit 1 Exercise

1. Open WordPerfect.

2. Type a short letter to a friend.

3. Save the letter, using a filename you'll remember later.

4. Print the letter.

5. Exit WordPerfect.

Creating, Opening, and Closing Your Documents

Prerequisites

▶ Running WordPerfect (Lesson 1-1)

▶ The urge to learn more about WordPerfect (no lesson number, just pure desire)

▶ You have installed the CD that comes with the book (see the Introduction for instructions)

▶ A 3½″ or 5¼″ floppy disk (that fits in a floppy drive on your computer)

Objectives for This Unit

✓ Telling WordPerfect what to do by using commands, dialog boxes, and toolbar buttons

✓ Understanding folder structure

✓ Opening documents you've already created

✓ Saving documents to different drives and folders

✓ Closing documents after you're finished with them

✓ Creating a new document

✓ Creating a new document based on one you already made

✓ Creating a new document based on a WordPerfect template

on the CD

▶ Mapleworks. WPD (you created it in Unit 1)

▶ Mapleworks2. 101.WPD

Typing a letter is all very well, but word processing is more than typing. This unit covers all the parts of the WordPerfect window and all the most common tasks you'll do with WordPerfect — creating a new document, closing one when you are finished with it, saving it, and working with different folders and disk drives.

Start by looking at all the parts of the WordPerfect window, which you see in Figure 2-1. Table 2-1 explains what all these little gizmos are called and what they do. You don't have to read the whole table right now, but you may want to skim through it. You can always refer to the table later to find out about each part of the WordPerfect window when you need to know about it.

Figure 2-1: The WordPerfect window has a menu bar at the top, loads of little buttons, and a great big white space where you can type.

Notes:

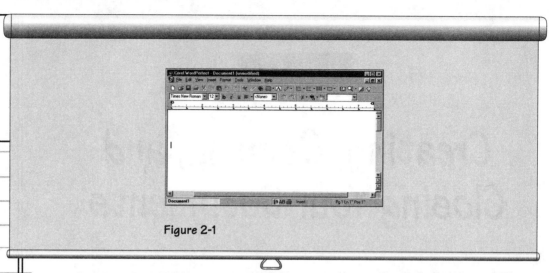

Figure 2-1

Table 2-1	Parts of the WordPerfect Window
Gizmo	*What You Can Do with It*
System menu button for WordPerfect	Double-click this button to close WordPerfect. Click it once to display a menu of things you can do with the WordPerfect window. The Restore, Minimize, and Maximize commands that appear on the menu control how the WordPerfect window appears. The Close command enables you to exit WordPerfect.
Title bar	This tells you that the window contains WordPerfect — big news — and displays the name of the document. It may also tell you that the document is *unmodified*, which means that neither you nor the 3-year-old who may be sitting in your lap has made changes to the document since you last saved it.
Menu bar	Click the words in the menu bar to choose the commands that you use to control WordPerfect.
System menu for the document	You use it to control how WordPerfect displays this document, not the whole program. You can have more than one document open in WordPerfect — we get to that in Unit 3.
Toolbar	Click these buttons for shortcuts to frequently used commands like Save and Print. You used these commands in Unit 1.
Property bar	Click the buttons on this bar to control how your text looks. The buttons help you change the font, size, and positioning of the text where the cursor is. We talk more about buttons on the Property bar when we discuss formatting your document in Unit 9.

Gizmo	What You Can Do with It
Typing area	This vast expanse of white, bounded by dotted margin lines, is just waiting for you to fill it with lucid prose or confusing, bureaucratic nonsense.
Horizontal scroll bar	You use this scroll bar for displaying parts of your document that may not fit in the window. If your document is too wide to be visible in the window, this scroll bar appears.
Vertical scroll bar	You use this scroll bar to see more of your document when it's too long to fit in the WordPerfect window, which can happen frequently.
Application Bar	Look at this bar for information about where you are in WordPerfect and what you're doing. You can click parts of it to change the information that you see.
Minimize button	You use this button to minimize the WordPerfect window to a button on the taskbar.
Maximize button	You use this button to maximize WordPerfect to take up the entire screen. When WordPerfect is already in full screen mode, this button turns into the Restore button.
Close button	You use this button to close WordPerfect.
Restore button	You use this to tell WordPerfect not to take up the whole screen, but to appear in a window.

click window to make it active

click Corel WordPerfect button on taskbar when WordPerfect is hidden

windows 95

You can have more than one application at a time open in Windows 95. To get back to WordPerfect after working in another application, click its button on the Windows 95 taskbar or click the WordPerfect window, if you can see it. The WordPerfect window then appears on top of the other windows that may be open on your screen, and it is the active window.

Understanding Dialog Boxes   Lesson 2-1

Many commands display dialog boxes, which are an important way to tell WordPerfect the details about the command. For example, after you tell WordPerfect that you want to open a document, it responds by saying, in effect, "Tell me more" — it displays the Open File dialog box so you can tell it which file to open. Often, WordPerfect asks you for more information than you want to consider, or even more than you know. But in most cases, you can tell WordPerfect just what you think is important, and it'll guess about the rest. You'll see this technique used in this book — sometimes we tell you to type something in one box and ignore the rest of the dialog box.

extra credit

Displaying and hiding bars

WordPerfect sure clutters up the screen with a lot of information, mainly in the form of bars — the menu bar, toolbar, Property bar, and Application Bar, to name a few. You may want to banish some of these bars so that you have more space on the screen for typing. Or, you may want to see the ruler bar so that you can tell how far your lines of text extend across the paper.

If you want to make bars appear or disappear, choose View⇨Toolbars from the menu. You see the Toolbars dialog box.

To remove a bar from the screen, click the box with the X in it to remove the X. Click OK to close the dialog box. If you want the bar back again, repeat the steps, this time clicking to put an X in the box.

To display the ruler, choose View⇨Ruler from the menu. When the ruler is displayed, this option on the menu has a check mark next to it. To make the ruler disappear, choose View⇨Ruler again to remove the check mark.

You already used a few different dialog boxes — you used the Save As and Print dialog boxes in the last unit. But you haven't used many of the gizmos and buttons that appear in dialog boxes. Table 2-2 describes each of the types of controls that appear on a dialog box, with instructions for using each one. Figure 2-2 shows the Font dialog box, which has a few different types of controls so that you can see what they look like. (The Font dialog box lets you control how text looks.)

Table 2-2	Ways to Use Dialog Boxes
Type of Dialog Thingy	*How to Use It*
Check box	If you want to turn a check box off or on, click the check box. A check mark appears or disappears from the box. Occasionally, you may see an 'x' instead of a check mark — both symbols do the same job. The Appearance part of the Font dialog box in Figure 2-2 contains check boxes.
List box	This box has a lot of options; you may need to use the scroll bar to see them all. Select the file or option you want. The Font Face option in the top left corner of the Font dialog box is an example of this type of setting.
Drop-down list	This is a box with a down arrow to its right. The selected option is displayed in the box. To choose another option, click the control to see the drop-down list and click the option you want. The Position option on the Font dialog box in Figure 2-2 is a drop-down list option.
Text box	This is a box that you type in. Click the box to put the cursor there and then type. (The File name box on the Open dialog box in Figure 2-3 is this type of option.) Don't press Enter after you've finished typing — WordPerfect will think that you're finished with the whole dialog box, as though you clicked the OK or Close button.

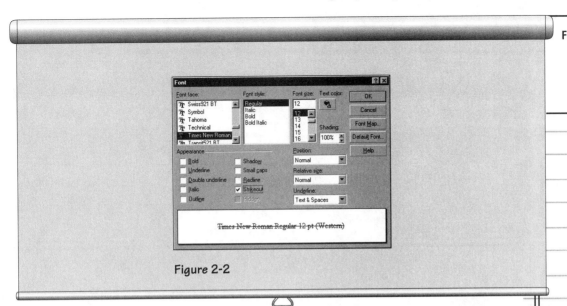

Figure 2-2

Notes:

Type of Dialog Thingy	How to Use It
Number box	This is like a text box, except it only contains numbers. You can change the number by highlighting it with the mouse (click, hold, and drag) and then typing the new number. You can also click the up or down arrow to the right of the number to make the number larger or smaller. (The Shading setting in the Font dialog box in Figure 2-2 works this way.)
Button	Click a button to perform an action. A button with an ellipsis opens another window, usually another dialog box. A button with a triangle displays a menu. Sometimes clicking a button displays a list you can choose from.
Icon	Occasionally, you see an icon in a dialog box. Double-click the icon to display the next dialog box. Choosing Edit⇨ Preferences brings up a dialog box of icons.
menu	Dialog boxes sometimes have menus across the top of them that work just like the regular WordPerfect menus. For example, the Open dialog box in Figure 2-3 has a menu.
Radio button	Radio buttons are usually in a list of choices, with a circle next to each choice. A circle with a dot in it indicates that the radio button is selected. Click the item you want selected or the circle next to it to move the dot to that item. Radio buttons are named after old-fashioned radio buttons, which can have only one button pressed at a time. When you press one button, the previously selected choice is no longer selected.

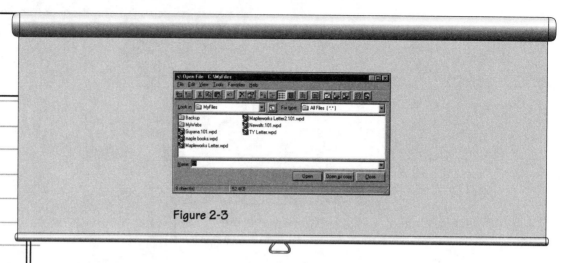

Figure 2-3

on the test

One warning about dialog boxes: When you press Enter in a dialog box, it's as if you clicked the highlighted button — usually OK or Close. The highlighted button has a darker border around it. Be careful not to press Enter accidentally when you type something into a text box, because the dialog box may suddenly close. If you need to move to another section of the dialog box, press Tab or use the mouse.

heads up

In almost every lesson in the rest of this book, you use WordPerfect dialog boxes, including dialog boxes that control fonts, colors, spacing, columns, and other fancy formatting. We describe how to use the settings in each of these dialog boxes, but our point in this lesson is that all dialog boxes work the same way. You display the dialog box, possibly change some settings in the dialog box, and after you are finished, you click a button, such as OK or Close — both of which save your changes. If you wish you hadn't started using the dialog box and don't want anything changed, you click Cancel or you press Esc.

Lesson 2-2

Opening, Saving, and Closing Documents

Notes:

Esc cancels a dialog box

Press Tab to move around a dialog box

a document is also called a file

a folder is sometimes called a directory

Before we go into the details of opening, saving, and closing documents, we want to talk about where documents are stored. You often store documents, also called *files*, on your computer's hard drive, but they can also be stored on a network drive or on a floppy disk.

Computer hard drives have plenty of space to hold lots of documents. So how does anyone ever find anything?

The answer is by using *folders,* also called *directories*, to divide the documents on your hard drive into groups. Folders help you store documents so that you can find them later.

Think of your hard drive as an infinitely divisible file cabinet. You decide how many drawers it has, how many categories each drawer has, and how many file folders (the paper kind) each category has. A drawer, category, or file folder is a *folder* on your hard drive (or one of your hard drives, if you're lucky enough to have more than one). You may even find that your computer contains your most organized filing system!

All kinds of documents — not just WordPerfect documents — are stored in folders. In addition to files, a folder can contain other folders. You can create hierarchies of subfolders within folders, which can make files easier to find.

Each hard drive (or floppy disk) contains a *root folder* — a file folder that contains everything else on the hard drive. Each drive, whether a floppy drive or a hard drive, is identifiable by a letter. The most common letter for your primary hard drive is *C*. Floppy drives are usually *A* and *B*. All the files and folders on the hard drive are in the root folder, or in folders that are in the root folder, or in folders in those folders — you get the idea.

Suppose that you store a document named Taxes.WPD in the Accounting folder, which is in the Business folder. You may have other files called Taxes.WPD, but not located in the Accounting folder that is in the Business folder. You can use a shorter way to identify this particular folder:

```
C:\Business\Accounting\
```

You can think of this long name, the folder's *pathname*, as the instructions for finding the folder. The *drive letter* is at the beginning of the pathname, followed by a colon and a backslash. Because folders can contain other folders, a pathname may include more than one folder name. Each folder name is followed by a backslash (note that a backslash is not the same symbol used to mean "divide by" — it is the other slash on your keyboard).

For directions on finding the file, you need the *fully qualified file name* which includes the path. For the file mentioned above, the fully qualified file name is:

```
C:\Business\Accounting\Taxes.WPD
```

Here's how you read C:\Business\Accounting\Taxes.WPD:

1 **Look on the C drive (your hard drive).**

2 **Starting in the root folder (C:\), open the Business folder.**

3 **Open the Accounting folder that is in the Business folder.**

4 **Find the Taxes.WPD file.**

If you're telling someone where to find a file, make sure that you communicate the whole pathname. But even the geekiest of us don't ask for a pathname. The exchange probably goes more like

"Where's that file again?"

"It's in business accounting on C."

You need to understand how your hard drive works in order to find files, however.

You can *navigate* folders in both the Open and the Save As dialog boxes. You use the same technique in each dialog box. Table 2-3 lists tasks that you may need to do and how to do each.

pathname takes you to a specific file

Table 2-3	Navigating Folders in the Open and Save As Dialog Boxes
When You Want To . . .	**Do This**
View the folders on a drive	Click the down-arrow at the Look in box, and choose the drive from the menu that appears
See the contents of a folder	Double-click the folder name
See the contents of the folder one level higher in the hierarchy	Click the Up One Level button
Identify your current folder	Look at the Look in box
Delete a file	Click the file to highlight it and then press Delete
See a list of recently used files	Click the down-arrow at the right of the File name box

The Open and Save As dialog boxes display part of the folder structure on your hard drive. To change the active folder and see other folder branches, click the Up One Level button to move upward through the directory. If you click this button enough times, you'll eventually land at the root directory. Double-click folder names to move down through the directory.

The same technique works when you want to save to a different drive — for example, to save something on a disk in the A drive. Simply click the Up One Level button until you see the list of drives, select the drive to which you want to save (in this case, the A drive), and then find the specific folder to which you want to save.

Up One Level button

Details button

extra credit

When did I make this file?

Click on the Details button in the Open dialog box to see details about each file in the current folder. WordPerfect displays the name, file size and type, and the date each file was last modified.

You can even sort your files according to when they were saved by clicking the column head above the dates that says Modified. Click the Name column head to sort your files back into alphabetical order, which may be less confusing the next time you are looking for a file.

Opening an existing document

Unless you don't like to save files, you will probably often need to open a document that you created and saved in another session. That's the reason floppy disks and hard drives were created — so you can fill them up with files that you may need again. You learned to save a document in Lesson 1-3. In this lesson, you learn how to retrieve a file that you or someone else has created, which could be useful if your code name is 007.

The most straightforward way to open a document is to use the Open button on the toolbar to display the Open dialog box.

You can also display the Open dialog box by

▶ Choosing File⇨Open from the menu.

▶ Pressing Ctrl+O.

After you display the Open dialog box, you may need to navigate folders on your hard drive or look at a different drive to find the file you want. Although the file you'll open in this exercise is in the *default folder* (the first place WordPerfect looks for files), you'll also get a chance to practice navigating folders.

Try opening the document you created in Unit 1:

1 Click the Open button to display the Open dialog box shown back in Figure 2-3.

2 Move your mouse pointer to the buttons at the top of the dialog box. Find the one that pops up a label that says List. Click it.

The files are probably displayed as small icons, which gets messy looking if you use long filenames. Clicking the List button displays the files in easy-to-navigate columns.

3 The current folder's name is in the Look in box. Write the name of the current folder in the margin (or circle it in the figure).

Although the name of the folder is important, you also need to know the *pathname* of the folder, which enables you to find it again.

extra credit

Depending on how Windows 95 is set up on your computer, you see the full pathname of the current folder on the title bar of the Open dialog box, or you may just see the folder name. To display the full path in the future, open My Computer or Windows Explorer, choose View⇨Options, and make sure the Display the full MS-DOS path in the title bar checkbox on the View tab is selected.

4 Click the down-arrow at the Look in box to display the drop-down list of disks and folders.

You see a list that includes all the drives you are connected to. Use the scroll bar, if one appears, to move through the list of drives and folders. Usually this list includes a hard drive (C:) and at least one floppy drive (usually A:, maybe B:). You may also have a CD-ROM drive, and possibly some network drives. You can view the contents of a drive by selecting the drive on this list.

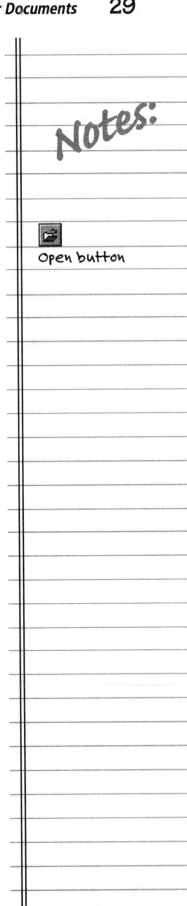

Notes:

Open button

the path of the
WordPerfect
default folder is
C:\MyFiles

the box in the
middle of the Open
dialog box is the
files box

Although this list does not include a full hierarchy of the folders on the current drive, you see the name of the current folder, MyFiles. If MyFiles had a *parent folder*, you would see the name of that folder, too. The full path for MyFiles is C:\MyFiles.

5 **Click the MyFiles folder in the drop-down list to make the list disappear.**

Because you were already viewing the contents of the MyFiles folder, the contents of the Files box (the box in the middle of the dialog box) doesn't change.

In general, when you want to view the contents of a different drive, you use the Look in box. When you want to view the contents of a different folder on the current drive, you may find it easier to use the Up One Level button to move up the folder structure and double-click a folder name to move down the folder.

6 **Click the Up One Level button to see the contents of the folder that is one level up the hierarchy.**

In this example, you see the contents of the root directory, C:, in the Files box. Notice that the Look in box displays the name of the current folder as C:.

7 **Now find the MyFiles folder in the Files box and then double-click the folder.**

You may need to use the scroll bar to find the folder. When you double-click a folder, that folder becomes the current folder and files stored in that folder are displayed in the Files box.

8 **Find the document called Mapleworks.WPD that you created in Unit 1 and click it once to select it.**

You may have to use the scroll bar at the bottom of the Files box to see the Mapleworks.WPD document. You may have saved the file you created in Unit 1 with a different name — if so, find that file and select it.

If you didn't create Mapleworks.WPD, or you have deleted it by mistake, don't panic. We have cheated on your behalf and included the letter to the maple syrup farm as a document called Mapleworks2.101.WPD. We're always thinking of you!

9 **Click the Open button at the bottom of the Open dialog box.**

WordPerfect opens the file. You can also double-click the file to open it.

You've just had a taste of navigating folders and drives. Remember these navigating rules:

- To view the contents of a different drive, use the Look in box.
- Use the Up One Level button to move up the folder hierarchy.
- Double-click a folder name to move down the hierarchy.

If you want to see the folder structure in the Open dialog box, click the Tree View button on the Open dialog box toolbar. The folder structure appears on the left side of the Files box. The files and folders in the current folder appear on the right side. To make the folder structure disappear, click the folder structure button.

Other ways to open a document

There are many ways to open a document—the Open dialog box gives you the most options for opening a document on any drive, in any folder. You may find that you can use these other methods of opening documents:

- Recently used documents appear at the bottom of the File menu. Click File on the menu and click the file name to open it.

- Click the Windows 95 Start button, go to Documents, and see if your document appears in the list of documents. If it does appear, select it. WordPerfect starts and opens that document.

- Locate the document using Explorer or My Computer and then double-click the file. If the file has the extension .WPD, Windows 95 knows that the file is a WordPerfect document, starts WordPerfect, and opens the file.

Dealing with documents from other word processors

You can use the Open File dialog box to open a document that was created with a different word processor. If you pick a document that isn't a WordPerfect document, an additional dialog box appears with WordPerfect's best guess about the type of the file that you're trying to open (each kind of software creates a particular type of file). If the type is correct, just press Enter. If WordPerfect chose the wrong type, choose the correct software type.

When you save the document, WordPerfect displays a dialog box that enables you to save the file as a WordPerfect file, or in its original file type. If you'll be giving the document back to whomever gave it to you and that person has another word processor, save it in the other file type (and suggest that he or she step up to WordPerfect!). If you'll use it with WordPerfect, save it as a WordPerfect file. If you need to convert a document from WordPerfect format to another format, use the As type option in the Save As dialog box (File⇨Save As).

Saving a document to any disk or folder

What if you just wrote a fantastic report and your boss wants to edit it and make a few little changes? What if you want to make a backup copy of the report on a floppy disk so you have a duplicate copy, in case disaster strikes?

It's a good idea to make backup copies of your documents. If you don't have a more reliable scheme for backing up all the documents on your hard drive, consider saving your documents to floppy disk on a regular basis. Better safe

make backup copies of important documents

than sorry! Imagine what a drag rewriting that long report would be. The Save As dialog box works the same way the Open dialog box does: You use the Up One Level button and <u>L</u>ook in box to navigate through folders and drives. (A caveat: Floppy disks are not a totally reliable medium, but if you keep them clean, away from anything magnetic, and at a fairly constant temperature, they work fairly well.)

on the CD

You can use the <u>File</u>⇨Save <u>A</u>s command to save a document to a floppy disk. You should have the Mapleworks.WPD or Mapleworks2.WPD document on your screen. Save the file to a floppy disk that you don't need for anything important by following these steps:

1 Put the floppy disk into the disk drive.

Although this lesson doesn't delete anything from the floppy disk, you should use a pre-formatted floppy disk that you don't need for anything else — just in case.

2 Choose <u>File</u>⇨Save <u>A</u>s from the WordPerfect menu bar.

The Save As dialog box appears.

3 Click the little down-arrow button at the right end of the <u>S</u>ave in box to display the drop-down list.

WordPerfect displays a list of your disk drives and folders.

The Open dialog box has a similar setting, called <u>L</u>ook in, where you can tell WordPerfect where to find the file you want to open.

4 Click the letter of the drive that contains your floppy disk.

You may have to use the Up arrow to see the drive that you want. The floppy disk drive whirs, and WordPerfect displays a list of files on that disk in the selected folder.

If WordPerfect has a problem reading the disk, it displays an error message. First, try the other drive (if you picked A, try B, and vice versa). If that doesn't work, the floppy disk may be no good, not formatted, incompatibly formatted, or a Macintosh floppy disk in disguise. Try another pre-formatted floppy disk.

5 Click in the File <u>n</u>ame box so its contents are highlighted. Type the document name that you want to use.

The box already contains the name that the document had on the hard drive. If you want to use the same name for the document when you save it to the floppy disk, skip this step.

For this example, type **Thanks**.

6 Click OK.

WordPerfect saves the document to the floppy disk and names it Thanks.WPD. The document is still on your hard drive, as you last saved it under its original name.

If you are keeping two copies of a document, you may want save it twice without making any changes to it — once to the hard drive and once on the floppy disk. Each time you save it, use the Save As dialog box to make sure you're saving it to the correct place.

an error message may mean the wrong drive was selected

extra credit

You can copy a document to a floppy disk without opening it. First save the file; then display the Open or Save as dialog box. Right-click the file, choose Se<u>n</u>d to from the menu, and then pick the floppy disk drive to which you want to copy the file. Away it goes!

You can even copy multiple files to a floppy disk this way. Select more than one file by holding down Ctrl as you click additional files. Then right-click with the mouse pointer pointing at one of the selected files.

extra credit

Managing your documents with folders

Here are some recommendations for saving documents in folders:

- Create a set of folders that makes sense to you. Once a folder contains about 20 documents, you may want to organize your documents in subfolders or new folders.

- Use subfolders, but don't overuse them. A project — for example, this book — could have a root folder named WP101 with subfolders such as Chapters, Figures, and Disk Documents. A subfolder for each chapter could be cumbersome.

- You may use folders to file documents by date. For example, older documents may clutter up folders where new ones exist. You may want to move the older documents to a subfolder called Old, or keep files by quarter or half year. For example, you can keep your old

estimates from the first quarter of 1997 in a folder named C:\Business\Estimates\1Q97.

- Clean out folders and closets regularly. Get rid of what you don't need because it will get in the way of the search for what you do need. Consider copying files to floppy disks or tapes if you're reluctant to delete them altogether.

- Make a folder named Temporary to put temporary files in. Temporary files are ones that you don't plan to keep for long. From time to time, look through the files in the Temporary folder and delete the ones that you no longer want.

If you don't know how to move, rename, or delete files, you may want to check out *Windows 95 For Dummies* from IDG Books Worldwide, Inc., by Andy Rathbone, to learn more about managing files.

Notes:

Notes:

extra credit

Changing the default folder

When WordPerfect is installed, it creates a folder for your documents, usually named C:\MyFiles. This is the *default folder* for documents. Each time you start WordPerfect, it assumes that the documents that you're working with are in that folder. The list of documents that you see in the Open dialog box is in the default folder. When you save a document without changing the folder, WordPerfect saves it in the default folder.

If you usually use a different folder, changing the WordPerfect default folder saves you clicks each time you save or open a document. Follow these steps to change the default folder:

1. **From the menu bar, choose Tools⇨Settings.**

   You see the Settings dialog box, with lots of cute icons (see Figure 2-4).

2. **Double-click the Files icon.**

   The Files Settings dialog box appears, as shown in Figure 2-5. If your Files Settings dialog box doesn't look like Figure 2-5, click the Document tab in the upper-left corner of the dialog box so that you see the document-related settings.

   The Default document folder is the second option on the dialog box. It is usually set to C:\MyFiles. Now you can change it to the folder in which you will store most of your documents.

3. **To change your default folder, click the small file folder button to the right of the Default document folder box.**

   WordPerfect displays the Select Default Document Folder dialog

box, where you view your folder structure and choose a folder. You can also type the path of the new default folder into the Default document folder box.

4. **Select the folder that you want as the default folder.**

   Click the Up One Level button to move one folder above the current folder, and then double-click a folder name to move down to it. When you find the folder you want to use as your default folder, click the folder name so that it appears in the Look in box.

5. **Click the Select button.**

   You see the Files Settings dialog box again. The Default document folder box now has the name of the folder that you selected.

6. **Click OK.**

   The Files Settings dialog box closes, and the Settings dialog box appears.

7. **Click Close.**

Now, when you run WordPerfect, it assumes that you want to work on documents in the new default folder rather than the old one. Remember that, unless you specified a different folder when you installed the documents that came with this book, those documents are still stored in C:\MyFiles. If you continue with the exercises in this book, either change the default folder back to what it was or change the current folder to C:\MyFiles each time you need one of those documents.

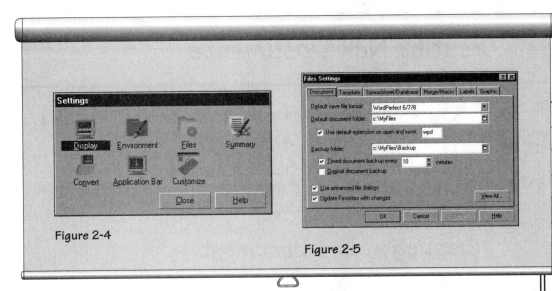

Figure 2-4

Figure 2-5

Figure 2-4: The Settings dialog box.
Figure 2-5: The Files Settings dialog box.

Closing a document without closing WordPerfect

If you do any amount of word processing, you probably finish with one document but still have other word processing tasks to do, so you don't want to close WordPerfect. You can close a document without closing WordPerfect in these ways:

File→Close closes current document Ctrl+F4 or the document Close button closes document, too

- ◆ Choose File⇨Close from the menu bar.
- ◆ Click the Close button (the X button).
- ◆ Press Ctrl+F4.

on the CD

If you didn't take a break before continuing to this lesson, you still have the letter to the Vermont Maple Works on your screen. If you did take a break, open the Mapleworks.WPD or Mapleworks2.101.WPD document now. Close the document now by using one of the previously listed methods.

☑ **Progress Check**

If you can do the following, you're ready to move on to the next lesson:

❑ Open a document.

❑ View the contents of another folder or drive.

❑ Save a document to a floppy disk.

❑ Close a document without closing WordPerfect.

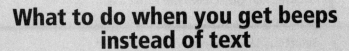
extra credit

What to do when you get beeps instead of text

Occasionally, you'll try in your humble way to type a letter, and all you'll get from uncooperative WordPerfect are beeps. A pull-down menu may also appear. What's going on?

The problem is that you accidentally pressed Alt, which tells WordPerfect that you want to choose a command from the menu bar. WordPerfect is trying to do its

best to execute a command. This problem isn't a bug, it's a feature. Alt enables you to continue using WordPerfect even if your mouse dies.

If you get beeps when you want to type, press Esc a few times. WordPerfect is now happy to accept your Pulitzer-Prize-quality prose.

Lesson 2-3   Creating New Documents

You have two straightforward ways to create a new document:

▶ Click a button to display a blank document window.

▶ Use an old document and edit it to make a new one.

You may also find the WordPerfect *templates* useful. *Templates* are formatted documents that you can open and fill with your own details.

Creating a blank document

The easiest way to create a new document is to click the New Blank Document button. A new, blank document window appears.

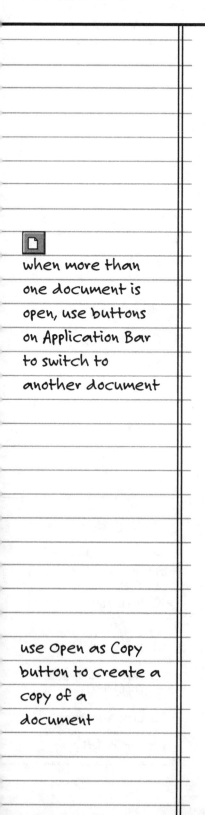

on the test

Notice that each open document has a button on the Application Bar, the last line of the WordPerfect window. Click these buttons on the Application Bar to switch from one document to another.

Creating a new document from an old one

You may want to use an existing document as the basis for a new document, but still use the original document. For example, if you're a big fan of farms, you may want to send a letter similar to Mapleworks.WPD to another farm. You can tell WordPerfect that you want to open a document as a copy, which means you can edit the document, but you must save it using a different document name. So you end up with two documents on disk: your original document with its original name and your new document with a new name.

To edit an existing document and save it with a new name, opening the document as *read only* is best. This way you cannot save the new document with the original document's name. Follow these steps to learn how to open a document as read only:

1 Choose File⇨Open from the menu bar.

You see the Open File dialog box, as shown back in Figure 2-3.

on the CD

2 Select the Mapleworks document.

If you didn't do Unit 1, click Mapleworks2.101.WPD instead.

3 Click the Open as copy button in the dialog box.

This button is in the lower-right part of the dialog box.

WordPerfect opens the document. In the title bar of the WordPerfect window, the words (Read Only) tell you that you can't save this document with its original name. You have to rename it.

use Open as Copy button to create a copy of a document

4 Edit the document to match Figure 2-6.

Change the name and address of the farm and edit the first paragraph of the letter.

5 **From the menu, choose File⇨Save As.**

WordPerfect displays the Save As dialog box, as shown in Figure 2-7.

6 **In the File name box, type the document's new name.**

When the dialog box appears, the cursor is in the File name box, so what you type appears there. To give the file a new name, type **Busy Bees**. This new filename replaces the filename that originally appeared. You don't have to add the filename extension .WPD because WordPerfect adds it for you.

7 **Click Save to close the Save As dialog box and save the document with the new name, Toy Letter to Gardner.WPD.**

Creating a file with a template

WordPerfect comes with many templates, from fax cover sheets to gift tags. A *template* is a document shell to which you can add text. Six categories of templates are available: business, education, legal, personal, publish, and Web. Here's how to open and use a template:

1 **Choose File⇨New from the menu.**

The New dialog box appears, as shown in Figure 2-8. You see the Create New tab of the New dialog box with two options. The drop-down list option is set to [Corel WordPerfect 8]. This setting determines the type of templates that are shown in the list box below it. In the figure, all WordPerfect templates are shown in the list box.

2 **Change the contents of the drop-down list box to see a specific template category.**

The lower box contains the name of templates in the selected category. Select a template to see a short description of it at the bottom of the dialog box.

3 **To open a template, select its name and click the Create button.**

As WordPerfect creates the new document you may be asked to enter information. When the document is complete, the WordPerfect window looks like Figure 2-9. On the right is the document template, where you add to it or print it. On the left is the Perfect Expert, where you can click a button to do common actions. You click button with the question mark to get more information about the template.

4 **Add text to your template by clicking in the document and typing.**

Just like any other document you can delete and add text in a template.

5 **Customize your template by using the buttons on the left — click a button to display a dialog box or a list.**

The dialog boxes you see are the same dialog boxes you'll learn to use in this book, but the Perfect Expert gives you a way to access them without having to remember menu commands. In general, work through the buttons from top to bottom.

You can save your document using the method you've already learned (clicking the Save button), or you can use the Perfect Expert Save or Finish button.

Notes:

F3 is shortcut for
File→Save As

Figure 2-6: Why type a letter from scratch if you can recycle an existing letter?

Figure 2-7: The Save As dialog box enables you to give a new document a name.

Figure 2-8: You can choose a template, or create a regular old blank document by using the New dialog box.

Figure 2-9: When you use a WordPerfect document template, you see the document on the right and the template control panel on the left.

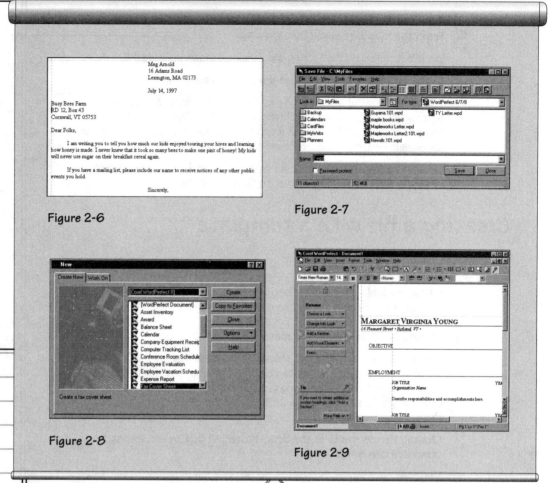

Figure 2-6

Figure 2-7

Figure 2-8

Figure 2-9

Perfect Expert
button

☑ **Progress Check**

If you can do the following, you're ready to move on to the quiz:

❑ Create a new document.

❑ Open a document as read only and use it to create a similar document.

❑ Open a WordPerfect template and create a document.

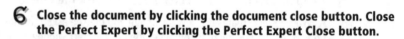

6 **Close the document by clicking the document close button. Close the Perfect Expert by clicking the Perfect Expert Close button.**

You can also make the Perfect Expert disappear by clicking the Perfect Expert button on the toolbar. Any time you want to display the Perfect Expert again, just click the Perfect Expert button.

Recess

Good work! in this Unit you have learned about the WordPerfect screen and about dialog boxes. You've used the menu, toolbar buttons and shortcut keystrokes to do common word processing tasks. Take a break to recover, but come back soon to take the quiz.

Unit 2 Quiz

For each of the following questions, circle the letter of the correct answer or answers. Remember, we may give you more than one right answer for each question.

1. **The row of little buttons just below the menu bar is called...**

    A. The toolbar.

    B. The Application Bar.

    C. The scroll bar.

    D. The sand bar.

    E. Joe's Bar and Grill.

2. **A folder is...**

    A. Where you look to find phone numbers.

    B. An object created using origami, the Japanese art of folding paper.

    C. Something that contains files and other folders.

    D. The contortionist at the circus.

    E. A place on your hard drive to store files.

3. **You want to create a new report much like the one you wrote last month. What do you do?**

    A. Open the old one, make the edits, and save it with the same name.

    B. Open the old one as read only, make the edits, and save it with a new name.

    C. Click the New Blank Document button to create a blank document and type the whole report.

    D. Make a photocopy of the old report, and then use whiteout and a typewriter to make the changes to create this month's report.

    E. Forget the report! Isn't it time for happy hour at the place with the delicious clams and casino?

4. **You can find the following on a dialog box:**

    A. Radio buttons.

    B. VCR remote controls.

    C. Text boxes.

    D. Gift boxes.

    E. Drop-down list boxes.

5. **You display the Open dialog box when you...**

   A. Press Ctrl+O.

   B. Press Alt, F, O.

   C. Click the Open button.

   D. Choose File⇨Open from the WordPerfect menu.

   E. Double-click a WordPerfect file in My Computer or Windows Explorer.

6. **To view the contents of another folder on the current drive you...**

   A. Click the Up One Level button.

   B. Double-click a folder name in the files box.

   C. Display the Look in drop-down list and choose another folder on the same drive.

   D. Display the folder structure by clicking the Tree View button and click a folder name.

   E. Type a folder name into the File name box.

Unit 2 Exercise

on the CD

1. Open Mapleworks.WPD or Mapleworks2.101.WPD as a copy.

2. Save the file with the name Hated Your Farm.WPD.

3. Rewrite the letter to say that the farm visit was lousy.

4. Save the document, still with the name Hated Your Farm.WPD.

Cool Word Processing Moves

Prerequisites
- Opening an existing document (Lesson 2-2)

on the CD
- Maple Books.101 .WPD
- Invitation.101 .WPD
- Invitation2.101 .WPD
- Confirmation.101 .WPD

Objectives for This Unit

✓ Getting around your documents

✓ Using Enter and Ctrl+Enter to end paragraphs and pages

✓ Splitting and combining paragraphs

✓ Inserting characters versus overwriting what you've typed

✓ Undoing mistakes and redoing things that weren't mistakes

✓ Displaying a ruler across the top of the typing area

✓ Displaying the WordPerfect online help screens

Unlike your old electric typewriter, WordPerfect has a clue about what you're writing. No, it can't understand the words, but it knows what a sentence is, what a paragraph is, and when you're getting close to the bottom of the page. As much as possible, you want to let WordPerfect handle the things that it knows how to do, like figuring out how much text fits across each line and how many lines fill up a page. Later, in Lesson 11-2, when you find out how to number pages automatically, the same principle will apply: Let WordPerfect handle putting page numbers on each page because it will be able to do so more consistently than you can.

This unit introduces you to a number of topics that can turn you into a savvy word processor — unembarrassed when an old computer pro (or a young one, as the computer pros so often tend to be) looks over your shoulder. We tell you how to set up your WordPerfect window so it contains the things that you actually want to see, how to type documents so they're easy to edit later, and how to get around in longer documents.

| Lesson 3-1 | # Getting Around Your Documents |

If this lesson were a class, it would be a geography class. We tell you how to get from one place in your document to another using three methods (you may have noticed that WordPerfect never gives you only one way to do something).

on the test

Before you start moving, figuring out where you are is a good idea (after all, when you're lost, you need to know where you're starting from, or you can't use a map). One way to figure out where you are is to check out the Application Bar (the bottom line of the WordPerfect window). The last box of the Application Bar tells you where you are in your document. It tells what page the cursor is on (Pg x), how far the cursor is from the top of the page, including the top margin (Lnx"), and how far the cursor is from the left side of the page, including the left margin (Pos $x.xx$ "). For example, when the cursor is at the very beginning of a document, the Application Bar reads Pg 1 (because it's the first page), Ln 1" (because the top margin is 1", the cursor is 1" from the top of the page), and Pos 1" (because the left margin is also 1", the cursor is 1" from the left edge of the page).

Using the mouse to move the cursor

use mouse or arrow keys to move around document

If you're going somewhere you can see, you have two easy ways to move your cursor there:

- ◆ Use the mouse to move the pointer there and then click once to move the cursor to that spot.
- ◆ Use the arrow keys on your keyboard.

Using the mouse may be the best way to go. WordPerfect has a nifty feature that makes it easy. When you move the mouse pointer, WordPerfect attaches a shadow cursor (the vertical bar that tells you where you are in the document) so that you can see exactly where you will be after you click the mouse button.

Using keys to move the cursor

The arrow keys can move you anywhere in your document, but if your document is long, this method can take forever. Following are a few things you should know about moving around in a larger document:

- ◆ Your document may extend farther than you can see. Think of it as a scroll, extending up and down off your screen.

◆ The cursor has to stay on text. It can't hang out in margins.

◆ The mouse pointer, however, can go anywhere on the screen.

◆ Your cursor will do its darndest to move where you ask it to move. If you press the right-arrow when you're at the end of a line, the cursor moves to the next character, which is at the beginning of the next line. If your cursor is on the last line in the window and you press the down-arrow, WordPerfect moves the text up a little to show you the next line.

on the test

Table 3-1 shows some keys that you can use for moving around in your documents.

Table 3-1	Cursor Control Keys
Keystroke(s)	**Where It Gets You**
Arrow key	One line or character in the direction indicated
Ctrl+up-arrow	To the beginning of the current paragraph or, if you are at the beginning of the paragraph, to the beginning of the previous paragraph
Ctrl+down-arrow	To the beginning of the next paragraph
Ctrl+left- or right-arrow	Left or right one word
Home	To the beginning of the line
End	To the end of the line
PgUp (Page Up) or PgDn (Page Down)	To the top or bottom of the screen, or up or down one screen
Ctrl+Home	To the beginning of the document
Ctrl+End	To the end of the document

extra credit

When arrows are numbers

You may have noticed that you have two sets of arrows on your keyboard (not all keyboards do, but most do). This design is in the interest of repetition, which has made great strides in the computer world with the introduction of Windows.

The cursor control keys on the far right of your keyboard make up the *numeric keypad* and have both arrows and numbers on them. These keys can be used as numbers when you are in *Num Lock mode*, or arrows when you're not. To switch to or from Num Lock mode, press the aptly named Num Lock key. Most keyboards have a Num Lock light, too. If the Num Lock light is on, you're in Num Lock mode, and the numeric keypad types numbers. When the light is off, the keys move the cursor.

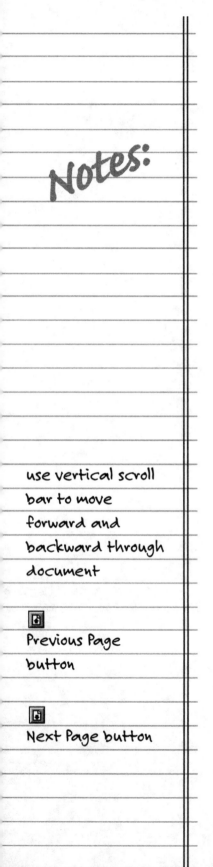

Using scroll bars to see different parts of a document

The gray stripe along the right edge of the WordPerfect window is called the *vertical scroll bar*, as shown in Figure 3-1. If WordPerfect can't show you the whole width of your document, the *horizontal scroll bar* appears along the bottom of the window, just above the Application Bar. Check Figure 3-1 if you're having any trouble identifying the scroll bars. Both scroll bars work the same way, but we talk mostly about the vertical scroll bar because documents are much more commonly long than wide.

windows 95

Most Windows-based programs use scroll bars to help you find your way around something that is too big to fit on your screen. Scroll bars don't move the cursor, but they change what part of the document WordPerfect displays in the WordPerfect window. This can be tricky, because you may expect the cursor to be in the part of the document you're looking at.

Each scroll bar has three parts: arrows on the end, a gray area between the arrows, and the scroll box somewhere in the gray area. The WordPerfect vertical scroll bar has an extra part: two buttons below the down-arrow that allow you to move up and down, page by page, instead of one screen at a time.

The *scroll box* tells you approximately what part of the document you are viewing. If the box is at the top, you're looking at the top of your document, and if it's about a quarter of the way down, you're looking at a section of the document about three-quarters of the way from the end.

heads up

The scroll bar does *not* tell you where your cursor is, which may be a tad confusing. If your cursor is at the beginning of a document, you can use the scroll bar to view the end of the document, but your cursor is still sitting at the beginning of the document. If you type something, what you type appears at the spot where the cursor is. If the cursor is off the top or bottom of the screen, WordPerfect hurriedly displays the part of the document where the cursor is, so you can see what you're typing. A quick click of the mouse before you start typing puts the cursor in the text that you're viewing.

You can use a scroll bar in three ways to display different parts of a document:

* **Move the display one line at a time.** Click the arrows at the ends of the scroll bar.

* **Move the display one screen at a time.** Click between the arrow and the scroll box. If you click between the top of the scroll bar and the scroll box, you move up. If you click between the scroll box and the bottom of the scroll bar, you move down.

* **Move the scroll box to reflect the part of the document you want to see.** That is, click the scroll box, hold down the mouse button, and drag it along the scroll bar. Your view of the document changes to match the new position of the scroll box when you let go of the mouse button.

At the bottom of the vertical scroll bar are two buttons that look like pieces of paper with arrows on them. The first button takes you to the top of the previous page; the second button takes you to the top of the next page.

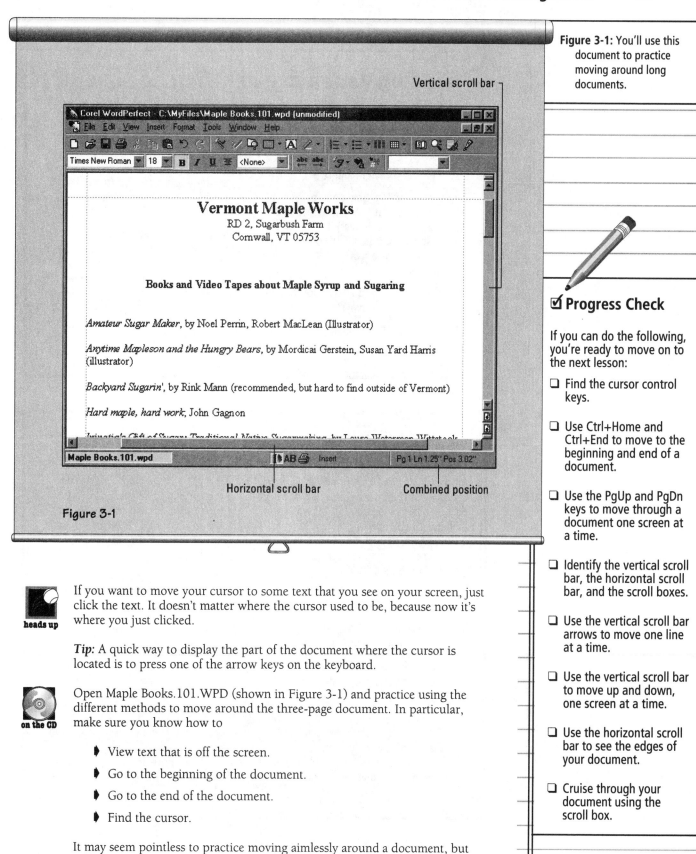

Vertical scroll bar ⌐

Vermont Maple Works
RD 2, Sugarbush Farm
Cornwall, VT 05753

Books and Video Tapes about Maple Syrup and Sugaring

Amateur Sugar Maker, by Noel Perrin, Robert MacLean (Illustrator)

Anytime Mapleson and the Hungry Bears, by Mordicai Gerstein, Susan Yard Harris (illustrator)

Backyard Sugarin', by Rink Mann (recommended, but hard to find outside of Vermont)

Hard maple, hard work, John Gagnon

Horizontal scroll bar   Combined position

Figure 3-1

Figure 3-1: You'll use this document to practice moving around long documents.

☑ Progress Check

If you can do the following, you're ready to move on to the next lesson:

❑ Find the cursor control keys.

❑ Use Ctrl+Home and Ctrl+End to move to the beginning and end of a document.

❑ Use the PgUp and PgDn keys to move through a document one screen at a time.

❑ Identify the vertical scroll bar, the horizontal scroll bar, and the scroll boxes.

❑ Use the vertical scroll bar arrows to move one line at a time.

❑ Use the vertical scroll bar to move up and down, one screen at a time.

❑ Use the horizontal scroll bar to see the edges of your document.

❑ Cruise through your document using the scroll box.

heads up

If you want to move your cursor to some text that you see on your screen, just click the text. It doesn't matter where the cursor used to be, because now it's where you just clicked.

Tip: A quick way to display the part of the document where the cursor is located is to press one of the arrow keys on the keyboard.

on the CD

Open Maple Books.101.WPD (shown in Figure 3-1) and practice using the different methods to move around the three-page document. In particular, make sure you know how to

♦ View text that is off the screen.

♦ Go to the beginning of the document.

♦ Go to the end of the document.

♦ Find the cursor.

It may seem pointless to practice moving aimlessly around a document, but memorizing a few keystrokes turns out to be time well spent in the long run.

Ctrl+G for Go To
dialog box

Last Position in Go
To dialog box
returns cursor to
previous location

Finding your place in a long document

You already know about moving around in the document by using the mouse and the keyboard. When documents get long, WordPerfect has a powerful way for you to find your way around: the Go To dialog box, which is shown in Figure 3-2.

The Go To dialog box enables you to specify places that you want to be (the Bahamas is not on the list). It also allows you to specify the position you were at last, the top or bottom of the current page, or a particular page.

You can display the Go To dialog box in any of the following ways:

▶ Choose Edit➪Go To.

▶ Press Ctrl+G.

▶ Put your mouse on a scroll bar, click with the *right* mouse button, and then select Go To off the QuickMenu that appears.

▶ Click the combined position section of the Application Bar (the far right of the bottom line, the part that says something like *Pg 1 Ln 1 " Pos 1 "*).

The Last Position setting in the Go To dialog box is a quick way to get your cursor back to where it was before you moved it. The Go To dialog box is also useful for moving to a specific page in a long document. Just enter a page number in the Page number box and click OK.

Finding where you left off

WordPerfect has a nifty feature that bookmarks where your cursor was when you last saved the document. That way you can pick up right where you left off when you next open it. The special bookmark is called a QuickMark, but you don't have to know anything about bookmarks to use it. Here's how to turn on the QuickMark feature.

1. **From the menu, choose Tools➪Bookmark.**

   You see the Bookmark dialog box, as shown in Figure 3-3.

2. **Click the Set QuickMark on file save check box to display a check mark.**

   This step sets a bookmark, called a QuickMark, each time you save a file. There can only be one QuickMark at a time, so when you create a new one the old one is lost.

3. **This step is optional: If you want to return to where the cursor was the next time you open the document, click the Go to QuickMark on file open check box to display a check mark.**

   You can find your QuickMark by using the Go To dialog box if you don't complete Step 3.

4. **Click Close to close the Bookmark dialog box.**

   Once you turn the QuickMark feature on, WordPerfect creates a QuickMark in every document you save.

   If feature is turned off, display the Go To dialog box and choose the Bookmark radio button to find your QuickMark. Make sure that the Bookmark drop-down list option shows QuickMark, and then click OK.

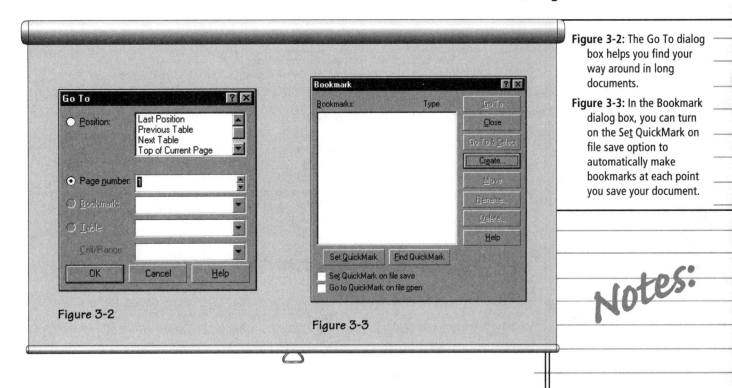

Figure 3-2

Figure 3-3

Figure 3-2: The Go To dialog
box helps you find your
way around in long
documents.

Figure 3-3: In the Bookmark
dialog box, you can turn
on the Se̱t QuickMark on
file save option to
automatically make
bookmarks at each point
you save your document.

Notes:

Starting New Paragraphs and New Pages

Lesson 3-2

In Unit 1, you did a little typing to create a document. Now we give you some how-tos and a warning about typing when you're using WordPerfect (or any other word processor, for that matter).

When you press Enter, you tell WordPerfect that you want to start a new paragraph. It types an invisible carriage return character into your document. Here's the warning: Don't make the mistake of using too many Enters and spaces, instead of Tabs. Not only will this mark you as a word processing beginner, but it will also make your documents considerably more difficult to edit. Make your life a little easier and learn to use Enter as we describe in this lesson.

Word processors do a wonderful thing called *word wrap,* which means that when you reach the end of a line, WordPerfect automatically puts the next word on the next line. Why is this feature useful? Well, it means you don't have to press Enter at the end of each line, and when you change margins or the size of the letters, WordPerfect moves the words around but keeps them in order, so that they still perfectly fill out the lines! If you press Enter at the end of every line, you have to delete the carriage returns (which are what are put in your document when you press Enter) when you change the margins or font size to have full lines. Rule number one is: Only press Enter at the end of a paragraph.

press Enter for new
¶ and new lines in a
list only

press Ctrl+Enter
for new page

Notes:

You may also be tempted to press Enter until you're at the top of a new page. If you change the format of your document, the number of lines you inserted may no longer be the correct number of lines needed to finish the page. Rule number two is: Use Ctrl+Enter to start a new page. You can also choose Insert➪New Page from the menu.

WordPerfect is smart enough to automatically start a new page after you've typed too much text for one page. The only time you need to use Ctrl+Enter is when you want to force WordPerfect to start a new page, For example, to start the bibliography at the end of a term paper, or add a page with a list of funny quotes that you want to enclose with a letter, you can use Ctrl+Enter. Otherwise, just keep typing and let WordPerfect decide where each new page starts.

Splitting a paragraph

on the CD

For this exercise, add a new paragraph to the invitation that the Vermont Maple Works sent to you. Open the document Invitation.101.WPD, which you see in Figure 3-4. Lesson 2-2 describes how to open an existing document.

1 **Move the cursor to the beginning of the second sentence, which says "Sugaring is a traditional. . . ."**

Begin a new paragraph at this point. Use your mouse or the arrow keys to move the cursor.

2 **Press Enter twice, to create separation between the two paragraphs**.

If you press Enter once, you tell WordPerfect to start the new paragraph on a new line. If you press it again, WordPerfect leaves an empty line between your new paragraph and the existing second paragraph of the letter.

Always start new paragraphs with the Enter key. In Lesson 10-1, we talk about how to get WordPerfect to automatically add space between paragraphs.

Adding a new paragraph

You can add a new paragraph using a similar technique. Try adding a paragraph after the third paragraph:

1 **Move the cursor to the end of the third paragraph.**

This is the paragraph that ends with ". . . sap down into syrup."

2 **Press Enter twice.**

The first moves the cursor to the second line, the second leaves a blank line, which is the style used in this document.

3 **Type a new paragraph that reiterates the invitation.**

We used a one sentence paragraph: "We welcome visiting groups — we like the change of pace!" You may want to write your own paragraph.

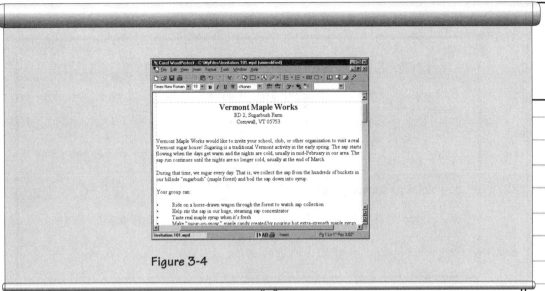

Figure 3-4: Invitation.101 .WPD contains the invitation that you receive in response to your letter in Unit 1.

Figure 3-4

Combining two paragraphs

Deciding where to break a paragraph can be hard. Your fourth-grade English teacher probably had a rule of thumb — at least, ours did, but we can't remember it. Anyway, if you decide that your paragraphs are too short and choppy, you can remove the space between two paragraphs, combining them. Here's how:

1 Move your cursor to the end of the first of the two paragraphs that you want to combine.

In the Invitation.101.WPD letter, combine the second and third paragraphs of the letter: Move the cursor to the end of the second paragraph.

After your cursor is on the last line of the first paragraph, you can use the End key to get to the end of the line.

2 Press Delete.

This action deletes the carriage return (Enter) at the end of the paragraph. If no blank line appears between the two paragraphs, the beginning of the second paragraph leaps up to continue where the first paragraph leaves off, and you're finished.

3 If the second paragraph still starts on a new line, press Delete again.

After you have deleted all the carriage returns between the end of the first paragraph and the beginning of the second, the second will start on the same line as the end of the first one.

If the second paragraph started with a tab character to indent its first line, press Delete again to delete the tab.

4 You may need to insert a space between the end of the last sentence in the first paragraph and the beginning of the first sentence in the second paragraph.

5 Click the Save button to save your work.

Notes:

Ctrl+Enter starts
new page

☑ **Progress Check**

If you can do the following,
you're ready to move on to
the next lesson:

❑ Start a new paragraph by
using Enter.

❑ Combine two paragraphs
by deleting the carriage
returns that separate
them.

❑ Split a paragraph in two.

❑ Start a new page by
using Ctrl+Enter.

---

extra credit

Gizmos at the ends of your paragraphs

You know that carriage returns are littered all over your document, telling WordPerfect where your paragraphs end. But how can you tell *exactly* where they are?

WordPerfect is happy to show them to you. Choose View⇨Show ¶ from the menu bar. Poof! Your document is suddenly filled with strange characters! When you choose this command, WordPerfect displays arrows, which point to the right, wherever you pressed Tab. It displays paragraph signs wherever you pressed Enter, and dots in place of your spaces (they float a little above the line, so they don't look like periods). Don't worry: None of these strange symbols appear when you print the document. They do, however, give you inside information about how your document is formatted.

To make these symbols disappear, choose View⇨Show ¶ again.

Starting a new page

on the CD

If the Invitation.101.WPD document isn't already on screen, open it following the steps in Lesson 2-1. Now put the list of uses for maple syrup that appears at the bottom of the Invitation.101.WPD letter on a separate page.

1 **Put your cursor where you want the new page to begin.**

Start the new page near the end of the letter, with your cursor at the beginning of the line that says "Vermont Maple Works: Great Uses for Maple Syrup."

To get to the end of the document, press Ctrl+End, Page Down, or use the scroll bar.

2 **Press Ctrl+Enter to start a new page.**

WordPerfect inserts a page break, which looks like a large gap between the end of one page and the beginning of the next. You see it almost as it will be printed, including the rest of the empty page, and the gray bar that indicates the end of one page and the beginning of the next (the bar does not print). You can see how your page should look in Figure 3-5. If you are in Draft view, described in Lesson 4-1, you see a double line across the whole WordPerfect window.

3 **Save your changes.**

Recess

If you would like to take a break now (maybe all the moving and reorganizing has given you ideas about how your furniture should be arranged), use Alt+F4 to exit WordPerfect. When you're ready to learn more about WordPerfect, double-click the WordPerfect icon to start the program, or use your favorite method.

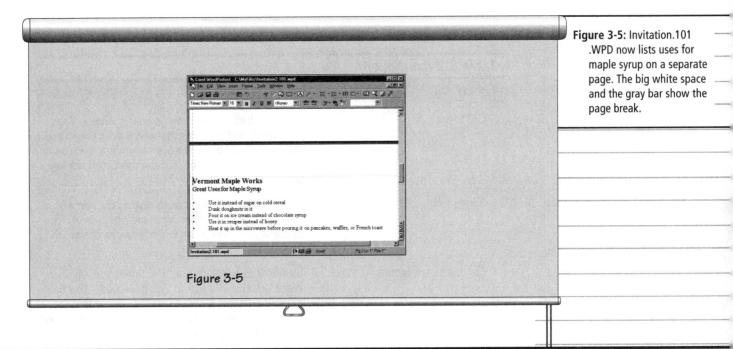

Figure 3-5

Figure 3-5: Invitation.101 .WPD now lists uses for maple syrup on a separate page. The big white space and the gray bar show the page break.

Insert versus Typeover Mode

Lesson 3-3

WordPerfect has two typing modes: *Insert* and *Typeover*. The way to tell the difference is to look at the Application Bar, so we'll take a short detour by the Application Bar.

Introducing the Application Bar

The Application Bar tells you a lot of cool things, and it doesn't just sit there, either. You can actually click on the Application Bar to make things happen. For example, in the next section you learn that you can click the General Status indicator in the Application Bar to change the typing mode from Insert to Typeover. To find out more about any part of the Application Bar, put the mouse pointer on it, and a little box pops up with information. You can also read Table 3-2 to find out about the Application Bar.

Table 3-2	What's That Stuff on the Application Bar?
Stuff	**What the Stuff Means**
Document buttons	A button appears for each document you have open in WordPerfect. Click a document button to display that document.
Shadow Cursor icon	When pushed in the shadow cursor appears; otherwise, the shadow cursor does not appear. You click the icon to turn the setting off or on.

(continued)

Notes:

Table 3-2 *(continued)*

Stuff	What the Stuff Means
CAPS icon	When pushed in, Caps Lock is on. Otherwise, Caps Lock is off, which means that you type in lowercase unless you hold down the Shift key. Click the icon to turn Caps Lock off or on. (Or use the Caps Lock key on your keyboard.)
Printer icon	Put the pointer on the icon to display the name of the printer that WordPerfect thinks you have. Click to display the dialog box where you can change the printer.
General Status button	Usually Insert or Typeover, which tells you whether WordPerfect is in Insert or Typeover mode. This box displays different types of statuses, depending on what you're doing. Click to change status from Insert to Typeover, or vice versa.
Combined Position button	Looks like Pg *x* Ln *x.xx*'' Pos *x*'. Tells you the position of the cursor, including the page you're on, the line *(Ln)* measured in inches from the top of the printed page, and the position *(Pos)* from the left edge of the printed page, also measured in inches. Click to display the Go To dialog box.

Changing typing mode

on the test

We prefer Insert mode — most people do. Typeover mode is startling, because each character you type replaces the character to the right of the cursor. You can delete (type right over) a sentence or two before you notice what's going on in Typeover mode. Insert mode, which is usually the default typing mode in WordPerfect, inserts the text where the cursor is and then pushes the text that follows to the right.

You can tell what mode you're in when you look at the Application Bar — the last line of the WordPerfect window. Table 3-2 describes the Application Bar elements. The second to last setting on the Application Bar is the General Status Indicator setting, which usually reads either *Insert* or *Typeover*. To change the setting, press the Insert key. This setting is what computer nerds call a *toggle setting:* The Insert key changes the setting to the other setting. You can also click the General Status Indicator box on the Application Bar, that reads either *Insert* or *Typeover,* to switch to the other setting.

on the CD

To practice using these two typing modes, open the Invitation.101.WPD document if it's not already on your screen. If you didn't do Lesson 3-1, open Invitation2.101.WPD. See Lesson 2-1 if you forgot how to open an existing file.

Insert key switches between Insert and Typeover modes

1 Press the Insert key until the General Status Indicator setting says *Typeover*.

Remember, the Insert/Typeover setting is a toggle setting. If it already says *Typeover,* you press Insert twice to change the setting to *Insert* and then back to *Typeover.* If you're in Insert mode, press the Insert key once to change the mode to Typeover. You can also click the part of the Application Bar that says *Insert.*

2 Put your cursor on the first letter of *Taste* in the third bullet point of the document.

You're going to add another bullet point to the list.

3 Type Help filter and bottle the fresh maple syrup.

Notice that as you type each letter, it replaces a letter from the sentence that follows. Also notice that letters don't replace carriage returns — after you run out of letters to type over, WordPerfect acts like it would in Insert mode — letters in the next paragraph are not overwritten.

Tip: Incidentally, if you type very carefully, or wait until after the next exercise to fix errors in this sentence, the next exercise goes more smoothly.

4 Press the Insert key until the General Status Indicator setting of the Application Bar says *Insert* again.

5 Click the Save button to save your document.

You always want to save "early and often," because you never know when the power is going to burp. Having a recently saved copy of your document increases peace of mind.

Typeover mode is occasionally useful — it may be what you use. Remember, however, that if WordPerfect replaces existing text as you type, and you don't want it to, press the Insert key.

Now don't change a thing before you go on to the next lesson, where you retrieve that sentence you just deleted.

☑ Progress Check

If you can do the following, you're ready to move on to the next lesson:

❑ Change the typing mode from Insert to Typeover, and then back to Insert.

❑ Think of a situation in which Typeover mode would be useful.

Undeleting and Undoing   Lesson 3-4

Possibly the best excuse for not using a word processor (and one used by Winona Ryder's character in the movie *How to Make an American Quilt* on why, in the '90s, she won't write her thesis using a computer) is that they lose things. Unfortunately, we have more than one way to lose text, but the most popular way is to delete it ourselves, either by mistake or by Freudian slip. WordPerfect has two features that allow you to undo mistakes and get rid of excuses for not using a computer: Undelete and Undo. They work slightly differently, so pay attention.

We'll start with an explanation of the Undelete feature. WordPerfect remembers the last three chunks of stuff you deleted. Anything beyond that goes to where things go when they are truly lost (we think it's Newark, NJ). *Chunks of stuff* is defined as

▶ A single character, if that is all that you deleted

▶ Contiguous characters, deleted when you repeatedly press the Delete or Backspace key, without doing anything else in between each press

▶ A block of text replaced when you type over it in Typeover mode

▶ A block of text deleted all at once

You'll probably need the Undelete feature sometime; such as if you delete a crucial paragraph, page, or table and would do anything to get it back. Well, don't go to extremes because all you need to do is press Ctrl+Shift+Z,

on the test

An added feature of Undelete is that the text is restored to *where the cursor is*, not necessarily to where the text was originally. This ability to specify where the restored text should be put in the document can be useful, but it can also be confusing. Just remember to put your cursor where the previously deleted text goes, before you use the Undelete feature.

The Undo feature is useful when you want to undo the last thing you did. Maybe you moved text that you wished you hadn't or formatted text until it was really ugly. Maybe you accidentally deleted something. Maybe you have no idea what you did, and you'd rather not try to untangle the results. The Undo command is ready and waiting for you, to fix what might otherwise be unfixable. Undo also undeletes text, but it places the text where it was located in the document, not where the cursor is. Undo remembers your last 300 actions — but we hope you never mess up a document that badly! To Undo something:

▶ Choose Edit⇨Undo from the menu bar.

▶ Click the Undo button.

▶ Press Ctrl+Z.

Tip: Undelete's advantage over Undo is that, even if you've done many things since you last deleted something, Undelete simply restores the last thing you deleted, without undoing other types of edits you may have done in the meantime (like adding text or formatting). When you use Undo, however, your actions are undone in reverse order. So if you deleted some text, typed some new text, and changed margins, you have to click the Undo button at least three times to restore your deleted text; and the Undo feature will first undo your margin changes and delete the text you added before it finally restores the text that you want back.

Undo's twin is *Redo*, the button next to it that points in the other direction. Redo undoes what Undo just did. Redo something by doing one of the following:

▶ Choosing Edit⇨Redo from the menu bar

▶ Clicking the Redo button

▶ Pressing Ctrl+Shift+R

Notes:

press Ctrl+Shift+Z
to undelete

The Undo button

The Redo button

Undeleting text

You can easily begin typing, adding a sentence or a couple of words, and suddenly realize that you're in Typeover mode instead of Insert mode. Fortunately, you can retrieve the text you typed over. You use the Undelete button.

You should have Invitation.101.WPD or Invitation2.101.WPD open already — you used it for the last exercise when you typed over one of the bullet points.

If you've exited WordPerfect since the last lesson, or if the exercise isn't working for you, open Invitation.101.WPD or Invitation2.101.WPD, change to Typeover mode, and type something somewhere in the text.

1 Place the cursor immediately before the "M" in "Make" in the last bullet point.

You're going to get back that sentence that you deleted in the last exercise when you typed over it.

2 To retrieve the text that you deleted, press Ctrl+Shift+Z.

Two things happen: the Undelete dialog box appears, and the last thing you deleted is highlighted where the cursor is.

The Undelete dialog box allows you to <u>R</u>estore the text that was deleted, look at the <u>P</u>revious text that was deleted, the <u>N</u>ext text that was deleted, or completely cancel the undelete action.

With luck, your screen now looks something like Figure 3-6. If it doesn't, keep reading.

3 If you don't see the sentence you typed over, click the <u>P</u>revious button.

The last three chunks of text you deleted are saved. When you click the <u>P</u>revious or <u>N</u>ext button, you cycle through what you deleted. Click <u>P</u>revious until you see the sentence that you want to retrieve.

If you deleted more than three times, and you can't get the sentence back, read the introduction to this exercise and try again.

4 Click <u>R</u>estore to get back the text that you want.

The restored text is inserted where the cursor is.

5 Press Enter to add a carriage return between the two items.

6 To put a bullet before the last line in the list, put your cursor somewhere in the line "Make sugar on snow . . .", and then click the Bullets button.

The line is formatted as a bullet point.

The Undelete command is the perfect solution to accidentally deleted text.

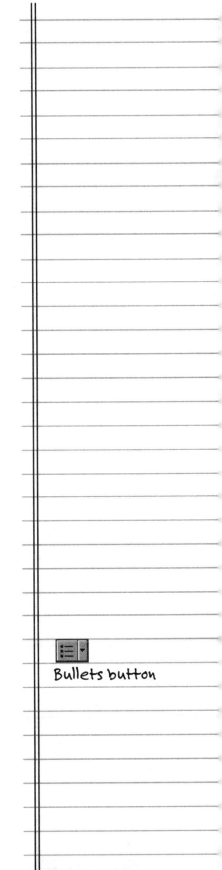

Bullets button

Figure 3-6: WordPerfect asks what you want to undelete.

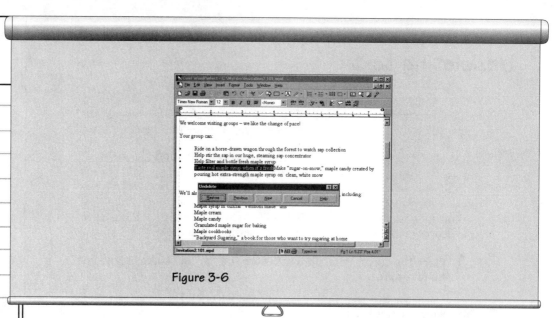

Figure 3-6

Notes:

☑ **Progress Check**

If you can do the following, you're ready to move on to the next lesson:

❑ Undelete a chunk of text.

❑ Undo the last thing (or the last few things) you did.

Undoing a formatting mistake

If you make a change to your document, and then wish you hadn't, you can usually tell WordPerfect to undo the change. Undo by clicking the Undo button or pressing Ctrl+Z. Redo, the button to the right of the Undo button, allows you to reinstate the last action that you undid.

1 **In the Invitation.101.WPD or Invitation2.101.WPD document, move your cursor anywhere in the first paragraph.**

2 **Press Shift+F7, as if by mistake.**

You don't know yet what the Shift+F7 command does (it centers the text after the cursor). With your cursor in the middle of a paragraph, it makes a strange mess. Yikes!

3 **Click the Undo button on the toolbar or press Ctrl+Z.**

Whew! Your paragraph looks normal again. If you actually want the text centered, you can click the Redo button now.

4 **Save and close the document.**

Lesson 3-5   Getting Help

You may have realized that you have a lot to remember, and you may already have questions about WordPerfect. Therefore, we've decided to introduce WordPerfect Help to you here. The more intrepid of you may use Help to take off and learn about arcane features that aren't even covered in this book. Even if that possibility doesn't appeal to you, the Help system is a good place to go when you've forgotten how to do something or you want a little more information about a command.

Using Help screens

We don't give you a guided tour of the Help system — that could take the whole book! Instead, we give you a sneak preview, and show you how much Help can do for you. To start the Help system, press F1, or choose Help from the menu. (We prefer F1 — using the menu forces you to decide what kind of help you want, and at this point you may not know.)

You can also get help about menu commands by pressing F1 when you're in the middle of giving a command. A Help screen with information about the highlighted command appears. This is called *context sensitive* help.

If you press F1 to get help when you aren't in the middle of a menu command, you see something like the window in Figure 3-7 — the active tab of the window may be different.

WordPerfect Help appears in its own window on your screen. In fact, it's a separate program. Two kinds of Help windows exist: One is the Help Topics window that you see in Figures 3-7, 3-8, and 3-9 that helps you find the kind of help that you need. The other is the Help window with a yellow background that *has* the help that you need. We start with the Help Topics window.

The Help Topics window has three buttons and four tabs. The buttons are Display, Print, and Cancel. Display opens help on the selected item, Print sends the help on the selected item to your printer without displaying it, and Cancel closes the WordPerfect Help.

The tabs help you find what you need in different ways:

▶ **Contents:** Displays the expandable table of contents that you see in Figure 3-7. Double-click an item with a book next to it to expand the outline to display more topics. Double-click a topic with a question mark to display a help screen about that topic.

▶ **Index:** Displays an alphabetical index of help topics you see in Figure 3-8. To find help on a particular topic, type the first few letters of the topic in the top box — the index entry will shift to show you items starting with those letters. You can then select one and click Display to see the Help window on that topic.

▶ **Find:** Gives you a powerful full text search option. Before you can use Find to search, you have to create the database that Find searches. Just follow the directions in the window. If you're not sure what to do, pick the recommended option. After the database is built, use it in the same way you use the Index.

▶ **Ask the Perfect Expert:** Enables you to pose a question in English. The Perfect Expert then appears with a list of help topics that may answer your question. Select a topic and click the Display button to see the Help screen.

F1 is the Help key

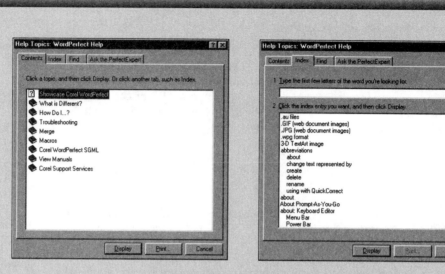

Figure 3-7: This window is what you usually see when you press F1 to get help. You click the tabs at the top to get different kinds of help.

Figure 3-8: The WordPerfect Help Index allows you to look for help on a particular topic.

Figure 3-9: The Ask the Perfect Expert tab in the Help Topics dialog box allows you to ask questions in English.

Figure 3-7   Figure 3-8

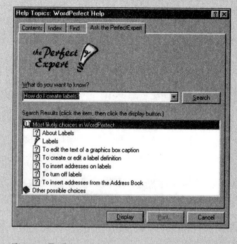

Figure 3-9

The Help screens, the ones that contain the actual help, also have features you should know about. Each Help screen has three buttons:

- **Help Topics:** Takes you back to the Help Topics window.

- **Back:** Takes you to the previous Help screen.

- **Options:** Allows you to keep the Help window always on top, annotate, copy, and print the Help screen, and create bookmarks in the Help system.

Help screens also have *links* that you can click to see another Help screen on a related topic. You also often see a small representation of a bookshelf on a help screen with Related Topics next to it, an open book that links to a definition, or a box that leads to step-by-step instructions. When the mouse pointer gets near any link, it changes to a hand. Click on the link and it takes you to another Help screen.

Tip: The How Do I topic on the Contents tab gives you easy access to step-by-step instructions on commonly needed WordPerfect features. Use it liberally.

Tip: One last thing that may be of help: When you get to a window that tells you how to do something, you may want to keep the window on top of the WordPerfect window, so that you can see it as you follow the steps. To do this, click the Options button, choose Keep Help on Top, and then choose On Top. After you're finished with the Help window, click the Close button.

Getting guidance from the Perfect Expert

WordPerfect has a super nifty feature called the Perfect Expert. The Perfect Expert helps you do things with WordPerfect you may not know how to do using menus, toolbar buttons, and dialog boxes. You began to learn about the Perfect Expert in Lesson 2-3 in the exercise on using a template to create a new document.

To start the Perfect Expert, click the Perfect Expert button on the toolbar. You see the WordPerfect screen in Figure 3-10. The Perfect Expert control panel appears on the left side of the window, and the ordinary typing area appears to the right.

Get guidance on any of the topics in the control panel when you click that button. To return to the original panel, click the Home button.

You can use Perfect Expert to create an outline, format a document, check spelling, add graphic elements, and perform other tasks. The Perfect Expert leads you through creating a document without having to know where to find the correct menu command.

You can turn the Perfect Expert off at any time by clicking the Perfect Expert button.

Recess

If you're ready to take a break, choose File⇨Exit to exit WordPerfect, but come back soon to take the Unit 3 Quiz.

Perfect Expert button

☑ **Progress Check**

If you can do the following, you're ready to move on to the unit quiz:

❑ Get help about a WordPerfect feature you used.

❑ Get help about a WordPerfect feature you haven't used.

❑ Use Perfect Expert to perform a task in WordPerfect that you would not otherwise know how to do.

Figure 3-10: When you click the Perfect Expert button, you see the gray Perfect Expert control panel (notice that the Perfect Expert button looks pushed in).

Notes:

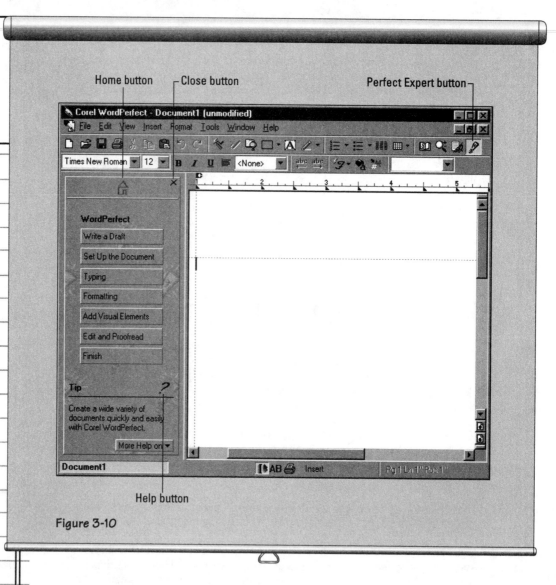

Home button — Close button   Perfect Expert button ⌐

Help button

Figure 3-10

Unit 3 Quiz

For each of the following questions, circle the letter of the correct answer or answers. Remember, we may have included more than one right answer for each question.

1. **The best way to start a new paragraph is to...**

   A. Click the button with the paragraph sign.

   B. Press Enter.

   C. Type `code=start new paragraph`.

   D. Talk to WordPerfect. Tell it gently that you would like to start a new paragraph now.

   E. Press the spacebar until the cursor is at the beginning of the next line.

2. **The best way to start a new page is to...**

   A. Press Enter until WordPerfect gets to the next page.

   B. Type until the page is filled and WordPerfect starts a new page for you.

   C. Type gibberish to fill up the current page. "Jabberwocky" from *Alice in Wonderland* is a good example of this technique.

   D. Press Ctrl+Enter to insert a page break.

   E. Choose Insert⇨New Page from the menu bar.

3. **When you need help with WordPerfect...**

   A. Press the F1 key.

   B. Shout a lot. Maybe your coworker will hear you and come to tell you how to do whatever it is.

   C. Use the index of this book to find what you need.

   D. Buy *WordPerfect 8 For Windows For Dummies,* from IDG Books Worldwide, to get help on topics that aren't covered in this book.

   E. Click the Perfect Expert button to see if you can find a button for the task you need to do.

4. **If you want to combine two paragraphs...**

   A. Print the document, and then with tape and scissors put the two paragraphs together.

   B. Delete the carriage return(s) between the two paragraphs.

   C. Move your cursor to the end of the first paragraph, retype the text in the second paragraph, and delete the second version of the text that you just retyped.

   D. Use the move feature to move the text.

   E. Type `code=join paragraphs`.

5. **A scroll bar is...**

   A. Something of great historical significance found near the Dead Sea.

   B. An odd feature unique to WordPerfect.

   C. The gray bar on the right (and sometimes the bottom) of the WordPerfect window.

   D. Where a scroll goes when it's thirsty.

   E. A tool of document navigation.

6. **Pressing the Home key...**

   A. Has the same effect as clicking the heels of your ruby slippers.

   B. Starts that automatic map thing that some cars have nowadays.

   C. Takes you to the beginning of the line where your cursor is.

   D. Takes you to the top of the document.

   E. Displays the Taskbar.

Unit 3 Exercise

on the CD

1. Open Confirmation.101.WPD, a file you installed from the CD.

2. Split the large paragraph into two paragraphs before the fifth sentence that starts "We hope . . ."

3. Put the order list on a separate page.

4. Save the document.

Printing Your Document

Objectives for This Unit

✓ Using print preview to see how a document looks

✓ Printing pages of a document

✓ Printing extra copies

✓ Canceling a print job

✓ Printing an envelope

✓ Faxing directly from WordPerfect (optional, and only if you have a fax modem and fax software)

Printing is usually the ultimate goal of word processing. Few people buy WordPerfect just to see the words on a screen. Usually the computer, the word processing software, and the printer all substitute for, and improve on, a typewriter.

In Unit 1, you learned how to print a document by using the Print button on the toolbar. In this unit, you'll learn even more about printing, and we'll show you how to use the Print dialog box to make refinements to the printing process.

First things first: Before you print, make sure that your printer is turned on and is online. *On* means that the printer is getting power from the socket in the wall. *Online* means that the printer is ready to receive information from your computer. You should see both a power switch and an online button (or at least a light) on your printer. Make sure that a cable leads from your computer to the printer. If you're in a networked office, finding the cable may just be too difficult, so identify whom to bribe in case of network problems.

When you're sure that your printer is on and online, make sure that it is loaded with printer ink (in the form of toner or a cartridge or whatever your printer needs) and paper.

heads up

This may be the most important prerequisite to printing: When Windows 95 was installed on your computer, your printer should have been identified so that Windows knows what kind of printer you have and where it is each time you give the print command from any application. Windows shares that information with WordPerfect. If Windows, and therefore WordPerfect, does not know about your printer, you will have difficulty printing. In the first lesson of this unit, we tell you how to check that Windows knows what kind of printer you have.

You may very possibly be one of the lucky ones, however. All you may need to do is tell WordPerfect to spit out that paper!

Lesson 4-1

Seeing How Your Printed Document Will Look

The document on the WordPerfect screen looks pretty close to what the document will look like on paper, but you may want to see how the whole page looks (even if you can't read it) rather than just the part that fits readably on the screen. That way you can check how close your margins are to the edges of the page, where headings fall on the page, and the general flow of text. WordPerfect provides features that let you preview your document before you print it.

You use two tools to see your document on screen the way it will look on paper: the View menu and the Zoom button.

View menu controls the document's on-screen look

If you click View on the menu bar, the View pull-down menu appears. You see that WordPerfect has four ways of looking at your document: Draft, Page, Two Page, and Web Page. For now we'll discuss just the first three options:

- Draft view is imitation WYSIWYG (What You See Is What You Get — pronounced *whizziwig*). Most of the document looks more or less the way it will look on paper, but certain parts of the printed page — such as headers, footers, and watermarks — do not appear on your screen. Each page break is displayed as a line that extends across the typing area — a forced page break, made when you press Ctrl+Enter, appears as a double line; a natural page break that occurs after you've typed too much to fit on one page appears as a single line.

- Page view, as shown in Figure 4-1, is full WYSIWYG. This may be the view that you are using, except that you probably don't have it zoomed out like we do for the figure. You see everything that will be printed on the page, including headers and footers. Page breaks display as they would on paper: white space to the end of the page, followed by a break and the top margin of the next page.

- Two Page view, as shown in Figure 4-2, is just what it sounds like. You see two pages displayed side by side as they will look printed (that is, in page view rather than draft view). You can't read the words on the pages, unless you used a very large font, but you can get an overall look at your page layout.

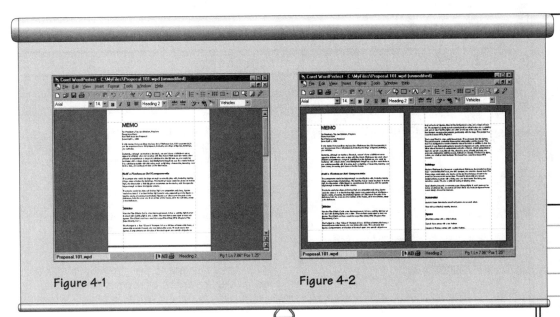

Figure 4-1

Figure 4-2

Figure 4-1: Page view with Full Page zoom shows your entire page so you can get a general idea of your page layout.

Figure 4-2: Two Page view enables you to see facing pages of your document, but you can't read normal sized text unless you have a magnifying glass.

heads up

We generally prefer to use <u>P</u>age view. If we need to know how each whole page will look on paper, we briefly zoom to check it out (don't worry — we'll show you how to zoom soon). Page view is the default view — you have to use the <u>V</u>iew menu to see draft view — so why not stick with it? If you prefer to get as much text on your screen as you can, without all that white space for top and bottom margins, you will probably prefer <u>D</u>raft view. The choice doesn't require a big philosophical debate; which view you choose is simply a matter of personal preference.

Although what you see in the WordPerfect window when you're using Page view is what you get, remember that the squiggly lines marking misspelled words or questionable grammar are not printed.

Zooming to see the Full Page

The Zoom button controls the size of the document in the WordPerfect window. Click the zoom button to change the size of the document and choose a zoom level from the drop-down list. Changing the zoom only affects the size of the letters on the screen — zooming has no effect on the way the document appears on paper.

Normally, you look at your document in either 100 percent zoom, which is approximately the size it will print, or in Page Width zoom, which sizes the text so that the document and margins appear in the WordPerfect window. To see a whole page, you want to zoom to Full Page, reasonably enough. See Table 4-1 for the rundown on zoom choices.

Zoom button

Table 4-1	Zoom Choices
Choice on Zoom Button Drop-Down List	*What It Does*
Various percentages	Zooms the document to the given percentage: 100 percent displays text at approximately the size it appears on paper; smaller percentages display the text in a smaller size, and larger percentages enlarge the text on-screen
Margin Width	Displays the document so that the body of the page, excluding the margins, fits across the window
Page Width	Displays the document so that the width of the page, including margins, fits across the window; displays text in a smaller size than Margin Width
Full Page	Displays a full page in the WordPerfect window
Other	Displays the Zoom dialog box, where you can select any of the above choices or type your own zoom level

on the CD

We'll start by zooming a document to Full Page, just to get an idea of how it will look on paper:

1   Open Proposal.101.WPD on the CD.

Use the Open button on the toolbar to open Proposal.101.WPD. It's a document from a toy designer proposing a new toy set.

2   Make sure you're in Page view — choose <u>V</u>iew⇨<u>P</u>age from the menu.

If you're not in Page view, you won't see the document as it will look on paper.

3   Click the Zoom button.

You see a drop-down list of options. You can zoom to a given percentage or to one of the special options: Margin Width, Page Width, or Full Page.

4   Click Full Page on the Zoom button drop-down list to see a print preview of the document.

WordPerfect zooms the document so that one page fits in the on-screen window. The percentage zoom depends on how big the WordPerfect window is.

5   To see the next page, press Page Down twice.

The first Page Down moves the cursor to the bottom of the first page. When you press Page Down the second time, WordPerfect displays the second page of the letter.

6   To return to the zoom you're used to, Page Width, click the Zoom button again and choose Page Width from the drop-down list.

WordPerfect zooms in to give you a view where you can actually read the text.

☑ **Progress Check**

If you can do the following, you're ready to move on to the next lesson:

❑ Use the Zoom feature to change the size of your document on-screen.

❑ View two pages at a time.

❑ Display your document so that you can read the text.

open button

The easiest way to preview how a document will look when it's printed is to click the Zoom button on the toolbar and choose Full Page from the drop-down list.

Previewing a printed document using Two Page view

Another way to preview the layout of your document before you print it is to use Two Page view.

on the CD

1 **If Proposal.101.WPD isn't already open, open it now.**

2 **Choose View⇨Two Page from the menu bar.**

The typing area changes to display two sheets of paper, side by side, with your text on them in itty-bitty letters that you can't possibly read.

To move around in Two Page view, use the regular cursor control keys. PgUp and PgDn move you through the pages. You can even type in this view, but you might not want to risk typing when you can't read what you write.

3 **When you're ready to go back to doing real work, choose View⇨Page or View⇨Draft from the menu.**

Now you can comfortably see and write text.

on the test

Another way to see what your document will look like on paper is to select View⇨Two Page from the menu.

View→Two Page shows two pages at a time

Printing Just What You Want   Lesson 4-2

Most of the time, you'll probably want to print your whole document. You learned back in Lesson 1-4 that printing your whole document is easy. Just click the Print button on the toolbar to display the Print dialog box, then click the Print button on the dialog box to print the document.

At times, however, you may not want to print the whole document. Perhaps you only want to print certain pages or certain blocks of text. This may happen when you notice a typo on the fifth page of your ten-page essay, or when you want to print section 100 of your 207-section welfare reform proposal. Whatever the occasion, learn how to print just what you need and save some trees.

To print a portion of a document, use the options on the Print dialog box. The Print radio buttons on the Print tab allow you to choose how much of your document you want to print. We refer to the Print radio buttons frequently during the rest of this unit. Have a look at Figure 4-3 now, so that you know what we're referring to.

Print the whole document by displaying the Print dialog box and clicking its Print button

The Details tab of the Print dialog box contains another useful setting: the Print in reverse order check box. Some printers spit out the pages so that they have to be collated to be in the right order. Selecting Print in reverse setting (putting a check mark in the check box) takes care of that inconvenience for you.

extra credit

We can't guarantee this little trick will work (it's undocumented), but if you press Ctrl+Shift+P, your document should go straight to the printer — you do not pass go, you do not collect $200, and you do not have to mess with the Print dialog box!

Printing one page

on the CD

Printing the page that the cursor is on is easy. In this exercise, you change one word on the second page of Proposal.101.WPD and print just that page. If Proposal.101.WPD isn't already open, open it now.

1   On the second page of Proposal.101.WPD, change *horn* to *whistle*.

Find the reference to the **horn** in the tower of the firehouse in the sections on Buildings, and then change the word to **whistle**.

Because you made a change on the second page of the document, you know that the cursor is on that page. Now you're ready to print just the current page.

heads up

Before you print the current page, make sure that the cursor is actually on the page that you want to print. Just because the page is on your screen doesn't mean that your cursor is on that page. If you're not sure where your cursor is, click once with the mouse on the page that you want to print.

2   Press Ctrl+P or click the Print button.

You see the Print dialog box.

3   Change the Print setting from *Full Document* to *Current Page*.

Click the Current Page radio button.

4   Click Print.

WordPerfect tells you that the document is being prepared for printing, and then the specified page is printed.

The Current Page option in the Print dialog box lets you print just the page where your cursor is.

Printing selected pages

on the CD

You can use the Page range settings to print specific pages of a document. Follow these steps to print pages 1 and 2 of Proposal.101.WPD:

1   Display the Print dialog box.

Choose File⇔Print or press Ctrl+P.

Margin notes (left):

Click Print button, press Ctrl+P, F5, or choose File→Print for Print dialog box

Current Page in Print option prints just the page the cursor is on

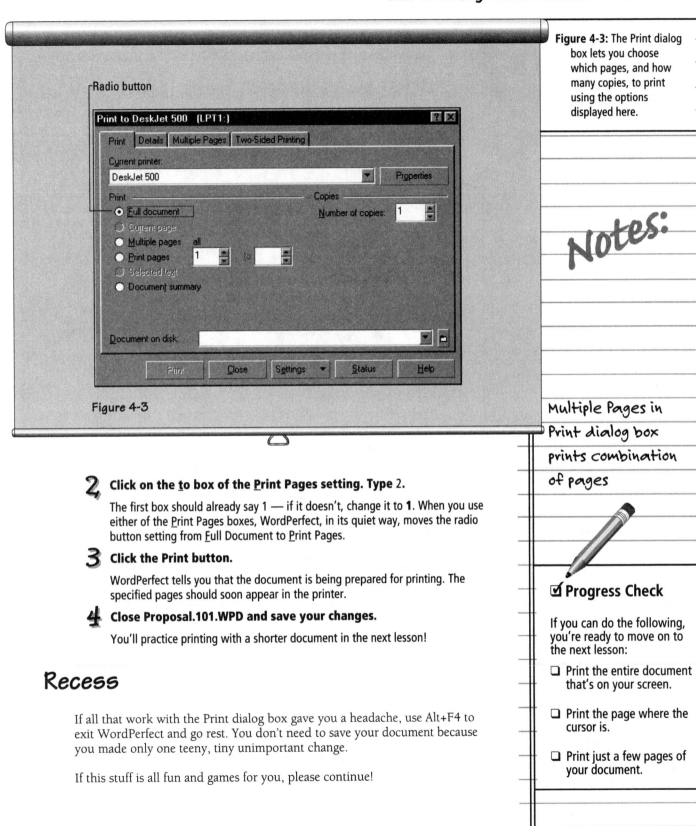

Radio button

Print to DeskJet 500   [LPT1:]   ? X

Print | Details | Multiple Pages | Two-Sided Printing |

Current printer:
DeskJet 500   ▼   Properties

Print ──────────────────────────────   Copies ──────────
○ Full document   Number of copies: 1 ▲▼
○ Current page
○ Multiple pages   all
○ Print pages   1 ▲▼   to: ▲▼
○ Selected text
○ Document summary

Document on disk: ▼ 🗎

Print   Close   Settings ▼   Status   Help

Figure 4-3

Figure 4-3: The Print dialog box lets you choose which pages, and how many copies, to print using the options displayed here.

Notes:

Multiple Pages in Print dialog box prints combination of pages

2 **Click on the to box of the Print Pages setting. Type 2.**

The first box should already say 1 — if it doesn't, change it to **1**. When you use either of the Print Pages boxes, WordPerfect, in its quiet way, moves the radio button setting from Full Document to Print Pages.

3 **Click the Print button.**

WordPerfect tells you that the document is being prepared for printing. The specified pages should soon appear in the printer.

4 **Close Proposal.101.WPD and save your changes.**

You'll practice printing with a shorter document in the next lesson!

Recess

If all that work with the Print dialog box gave you a headache, use Alt+F4 to exit WordPerfect and go rest. You don't need to save your document because you made only one teeny, tiny unimportant change.

If this stuff is all fun and games for you, please continue!

☑ **Progress Check**

If you can do the following, you're ready to move on to the next lesson:

❑ Print the entire document that's on your screen.

❑ Print the page where the cursor is.

❑ Print just a few pages of your document.

Other ways to save trees (print only what you want)

You can print multiple pages even if they're not contiguous. Click the Multiple Pages tab of the Print dialog box to see the Page(s)/label(s) option. The other settings of this dialog box are for truly long documents. Input the pages you want in the Page(s)/label(s) setting, using the rules that follow, and then click the Print button to actually print the pages you specified.

Here are ways you can specify which pages you want to print:

- Specify one page number (for example, **3**) to print that page.

- Specify more than one page number, separated by commas or spaces (for example, **3,5** or **3 5**), to print those pages but not the pages in between (WordPerfect prints pages 3 and 5 but not page 4).

- Specify a range (for example, **3-5**) to print all the pages in that range.

- Specify a page to start, followed by a dash (for example, **3-**), to start printing on that page and continue printing to the end of the document.

- Type a dash followed by a page to end (for example, **-5**), to print from the beginning of the document through the end of that page.

- Use a combination of the above (for example, **1, 3-5** to print pages 1, 3, 4, and 5). The pages must be specified in ascending numeric order.

You can also print a chunk of text by selecting it (you'll learn lots about selecting text in Unit 5) and then displaying the Print dialog box. WordPerfect then assumes that you want to print just the selection — in fact, if you want to print the whole document, you need to make sure to change the Print setting. The Selection choice only appears when text is selected, so don't be surprised if you haven't seen it yet.

Lesson 4-3   Printing More Than One Copy

If you want more than one copy of your document and you'd rather print them than wander down the hall to the photocopier, you can tell WordPerfect to print copies.

All you need to do to print multiple copies is play with the Print dialog box again!

1 **Open Mapleworks.WPD, the letter you created in Unit 1.**

If you didn't do Unit 1, open Mapleworks2.101.WPD instead.

2 **Display the Print dialog box.**

Press Ctrl+P or F5.

Number of copies in Print dialog box prints duplicate copies

3 **Change the Number of copies from 1 to 2.**

The easiest way is to click the up-arrow next to the number. If you're printing an obscene number of copies — maybe 15 — you may not want to click the up arrow 14 times; in that case, click and drag the mouse over the number, and then type the new number in its place.

4 **Click Print.**

Away goes the printer — a piece of cake!

The Number of copies option in the Print dialog box enables you to tell WordPerfect to print more than one copy of your document. You can also use this option with the Print Selection setting to print more than one copy of the current page or multiple pages.

☑ **Progress Check**

If you can do the following, you're ready to move on to the next lesson:

❑ Print more than one copy of whatever you want to print.

❑ Plant a tree to make up for all the paper you'll be using now that you can print lots of copies of your WordPerfect documents.

Canceling a Print Job

Lesson 4-4

Canceling a print job is relatively simple if your computer is hooked up directly to a printer, but probably not so easy if you print through a network. If you regularly use a networked printer, you should talk to your network administrator (who, in our cases, are our sweeties) to find out how to cancel a print job. If you don't have a network, read on for the gory details.

When you command a document to be printed, WordPerfect formats the document and sends it off to the printer. You can only stop the document from being printed for as long as it is in WordPerfect's court. After it goes to the printer, you may still be able to stop it, but not by using WordPerfect — so stopping is beyond the scope of this book.

heads up

You may think that the best way to cancel a print job is to turn off the printer. Unfortunately, this approach usually doesn't work and just complicates matters. Your computer and Windows notice when you turn off the printer and complain about it until you turn it back on. Try the steps in this lesson instead!

If you want to try this procedure, use Proposal.101.WPD. It's long, giving you a little extra time to try to stop it. Also, read the steps through before you begin printing. WordPerfect and printers are so quick these days that WordPerfect could have finished sending the document to the printer before you get far enough in the steps to stop it!

☑ Progress Check

If you can do the following, you're ready to move on to the next lesson:

❑ Change your mind about printing a document.

❑ Cancel printing a document by using the Print Status and History window.

After you've sent a print job to a local printer (one attached directly to your computer, not through a network), you can cancel it in the following way:

1 Press Ctrl+P or click the Print button.

You see the Print dialog box.

2 Click the Status button.

You see the Print Status and History dialog box. It gives you a lot of information about your current and past print jobs that you'll probably never need to know.

The current print job appears at the top of the list. If the Status column says something other than Complete, you're in luck.

3 To stop the print job, choose Document⇨Cancel Printing from the menu at the top of the window.

The status of the first print job on the list changes to Canceled. The printer may print some of the document anyway (whatever was sent to the printer before you canceled the job), but you should have succeeded in canceling some of the print job.

4 To close the Print Status and History window, click the Close button (the X button).

The Print Status and History window is not really a dialog box — it's more like a separate program that comes with WordPerfect. If you like, you can leave it open so that you can switch to it easily to check on the status of your print jobs.

Don't waste paper if you realize that you don't want to print your document after all — you can stop a print job by using the Status button on the Print dialog box and then choosing Document⇨Cancel Printing.

Lesson 4-5

Printing an Envelope

Not all printers can print envelopes, but if yours does, you may want to learn to use the envelope-printing feature. This feature sure beats going back to the typewriter to create a presentable envelope.

Many printers require you to feed envelopes individually. Each time you want to print an envelope, you feed your printer a size 10 envelope, assuming that it's hungry. The first step in printing an envelope is to figure out how to feed envelopes into your printer. Your printer may have a little diagram that shows you how to feed in an envelope. If yours doesn't, you may have to resort to reading the manual.

WordPerfect tries to make printing addresses on envelopes easy. Usually WordPerfect can even find the address on a letter and automatically print it on the envelope.

Creating an envelope for a letter

on the CD

The following steps are the easiest way to print an address onto an envelope, using your printer and the letter you wrote in Unit 1 to the Vermont Maple Works. Before starting this exercise, open either Mapleworks.WPD (if you created it in Unit 1) or Mapleworks2.101.WPD.

1 Choose Format⇨Envelope from the menu bar.

You see the Envelope dialog box, which appears in Figure 4-4. The mailing address appears in the Mailing addresses To box at the top right of the dialog box and on the preview envelope at the bottom left of the dialog box (WordPerfect makes it easy, doesn't it?).

If WordPerfect doesn't find the address, you can exit the dialog box, select the address, and display the Envelope dialog box again. The address will be there this time.

2 Click in the Return addresses box and type your return name and address there.

You can press Enter to start each new line of the address, despite our warnings about pressing Enter in a dialog box.

After you've put your name and address (the return address) in once, you won't have to do it again. WordPerfect remembers the information (still enabling you, of course, to put in a different name and address if you want to).

3 Click Print Envelope.

Now you need to feed an envelope to your printer. Depending on what kind of printer you have, you may see a message on-screen asking you to insert an envelope, or your printer may wait for you to insert an envelope before printing. (Another possibility is that your printer can't print envelopes — get a new printer!)

The Format⇨Envelope command lets you tell WordPerfect what you want on your envelope. WordPerfect takes over from there, printing the addresses in the correct places on the envelope.

Recess

If you don't have a fax modem, you can skip the next lesson and go right to the Unit 4 Quiz. If you want to take a break, exit WordPerfect first by pressing Alt+F4 or choosing File⇨Exit from the menu bar.

☑ **Progress Check**

If you can do the following, you're ready to move on to the next lesson:

❏ Print an envelope.

❏ Think of someone to write a letter to, just so you can practice printing envelopes. If you'd like to tell us what you think of this book, write to: Alison Barrows and Margy Levine Young, c/o IDG Books Worldwide 919 E. Hillsdale Blvd., Suite 400 Foster City, CA 94404 (USA).

Faxing Using a Fax Modem

Lesson 4-6

Faxing is printing a document to a fax modem, which prints your document on a piece of paper in someone else's office (unless the person at the other end also has a fax modem, in which case he or she may simply look at it on-screen).

Notes:

☑ Progress Check

If you can do the following, you're ready to move on to the next lesson:

❑ Know whether you have a fax modem installed.

❑ Print your document to someone else's fax machine rather than your printer.

❑ Switch your print settings back to those of your regular printer.

The key is to have fax modem software installed that works as a Windows printer driver. If you do have a fax modem printer driver, it appears as a printer option. To send a fax, you simply specify the fax modem software as the printer and print normally (so in this lesson you're also learning how to change the printer to which WordPerfect prints). When you give the command to print to the fax modem software, the fax modem software appears on-screen to ask you to specify the fax phone number and other cover sheet information.

If you don't have both a fax modem and fax software that works as a Windows printer driver, the instructions in this lesson won't work. Skip right to the Unit 4 Quiz.

To fax a document, follow these steps:

1 Display the Print dialog box.

Do you have a favorite method yet? How about Ctrl+P?

You see the Print dialog box with the three tabs at the top.

2 Notice what appears in the Current printer text drop-down list box.

Make a mental or written note (you can even write it in the margin) of what is selected right now, so that you can put the settings back this same way when you're finished faxing.

3 Click the Current printer box to see the printer options that are available.

Now you can tell WordPerfect *which* printer you want to use. Instead of choosing a real printer, you'll choose the printer driver software that sends your text as a fax.

WordPerfect displays a list of the printers that your copy of Windows knows. Somewhere in that list should be your fax modem software, if it's been installed correctly. For example, if you use WinFax PRO fax software, you might see WINFAX on COM2, which means that the document will be faxed using the WinFax PRO printer driver and a fax modem connected to the COM2 port of your computer.

If you don't see an entry for your fax software, it was not installed correctly. Refer to the manual for your fax software or get some help!

4 Pick your fax modem software from the list.

When you click the fax modem printer driver, it appears in the Current printer box.

5 Click the Print button.

Your fax modem software takes over and asks you to supply the phone number and name of the person to whom you're sending the fax. Type that information and then click Send Fax or OK, whichever your fax software requires. Fax modem packages work differently. You may need to look at your fax modem documentation for more specifics.

6 After the fax has been sent, display the Print dialog box again.

Use the same method you used in Step 1. You need to select your regular printer again. Otherwise, your next print request will be faxed, too.

7 Click the Current printer option and choose the same settings that were in place before you chose your fax modem.

Refer to the mental or written note you made in Step 2.

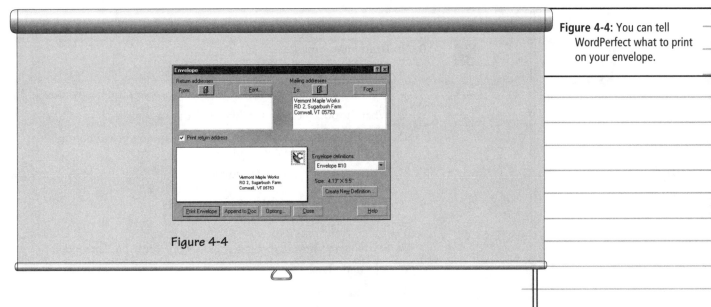

Figure 4-4

Figure 4-4: You can tell
WordPerfect what to print
on your envelope.

8 **Click Close to close the Print dialog box without printing anything.**

Isn't technology amazing? Your WordPerfect document went zinging across
the phone wires in the form of a fax, only to get printed at the far end in
someone else's office. Happy faxing!

Unit 4 Quiz

For each of the following questions, circle the letter of the correct answer or
answers. Remember that we may include more than one right answer for each
question!

1. **What does this button do?**

    A. Turns your printer into a typewriter — for when you need to do
       envelopes.

    B. Same thing as Ctrl+P.

    C. Same thing as F5.

    D. Same thing as File⇨Print.

    E. Prints the current document without displaying the Print dialog box.

2. **The best way to see a preview of a whole page when it's printed is
   to...**

    A. Print it.

    B. Use View⇨Two Page.

    C. Use the Zoom button on the toolbar to zoom to Full Page.

    D. Hold a thin sheet of paper up to the screen.

    E. Fax it to someone and have that person tell you how it looks.

Notes:

3. **In Draft view, you see...**

   A. What the document would have looked like if you had typed it.

   B. What the document would have looked like if you had handwritten it.

   C. What the document looked like before it was finished.

   D. Just the text of the body of the document — no top and bottom margins, headers, footers, and so on.

   E. Whatever your spouse lets you see.

4. **To fax a letter from WordPerfect you need...**

   A. A fax modem.

   B. Fax modem software that is set up to work with your fax modem.

   C. A second phone line.

   D. A fax machine.

   E. A printer.

5. **The best way to address an envelope is to...**

   A. Print the to and from addresses on separate sheets of paper, cut them out, and paste them onto an envelope.

   B. Get a good pen and write the address neatly.

   C. Hire a calligrapher.

   D. Use the Format⇨Envelope command.

   E. Faxing is really much easier. Besides, you won't need a stamp!

Unit 4 Exercise

1. Close the document you are working on, so that you see a blank document in WordPerfect.

2. Type a letter to thank someone you know for doing something nice for you. If no one you know has done anything nice for you recently, write *us* a letter c/o IDG Books telling us what you think of this book! IDG's address is at the end of Lesson 4-5.

3. Save the document so that your valuable opinion isn't lost, using the name THANKYOU.WPD.

4. View the document in Page view to make sure it looks right.

5. Print two copies of the letter, one for you and one to send.

6. Print an envelope using your own return address.

7. Mail the letter. (Don't forget the stamp!)

Part I Review

Unit 1 Summary

- To start WordPerfect for Windows, click on the Start button, choose Corel WordPerfect Suite 8, and then click on Corel WordPerfect 8.

- To type text in a document, move the pointer to the point where you want the text to appear, click, and start typing.

- Don't press Enter at the end of each line, only at the ends of paragraphs.

- Use the Backspace key to delete the character immediately before the cursor, or the Delete (or Del) key to delete the character immediately after the cursor.

- To save a file, click on the Save button on the toolbar. (Or press Ctrl+S or choose File⇨Save from the menu bar.)

- To print a file, click on the Print button on the Toolbar and then click Print when you see the Print dialog box. (You can also display the Print dialog box by pressing Ctrl+P or choosing File⇨Print from the menu bar.)

- Exit from WordPerfect by clicking on the Close button in the top right corner of the window — the button with an X in it. Or you can click on the System menu box and choose Close (or press Alt+F4 or choose File⇨Exit from the menu bar).

Unit 2 Summary

- To open an existing document, choose File⇨Open from the menu bar, click on the Open button on the toolbar, or press Ctrl+O.

- To close a document, choose File⇨Close from the menu bar, click on the document close button, or press Ctrl+F4. If you made changes to the document and didn't save them, WordPerfect asks if you want to do so.

- To create a new document based on an existing one (why start from scratch?), choose File⇨Open from the menu bar and then choose the Open as copy button on the dialog box. Make changes to the document and save the document giving it a new name.

- To open a document that is stored on a diskette, choose File⇨Open from the menu bar; then change the Look in setting on the Open dialog box to show files on the diskette drive.

- Create a new document by clicking the New Blank Document button on the toolbar.

- Create a document from a template by choosing File⇨New from the menu, selecting the template you want to use, and clicking Create.

Unit 3 Summary

- Use the mouse pointer or the cursor movement keys to move the cursor.

- To start a new paragraph, press Enter.

- To start a new page, press Ctrl+Enter.

- To replace text with new text, switch to Typeover mode by pressing the Insert key. Press Insert again to switch back to Insert mode.

- Click the Undo button to undo what you just did.

- Press Ctrl+Shift+Z to undelete the last chunk of text you deleted.

- To see online help, press F1.

- Click the Perfect Expert button to display the Perfect Expert which provides help on creating your document.

Part I Review

Unit 4 Summary

▶ To see how your document will look when printed, use the Zoom button to zoom to Full Page or choose View⇨Two Page to see two facing pages.

▶ To print your document, click on the Print button on the toolbar, or press Ctrl+P, or choose File⇨Print from the menu bar. When you see the Print dialog box, click on the Print button.

▶ To print only one page, move the cursor to that page, click on the Print button on the toolbar to display the Print dialog box, choose Current Page, and click on Print.

▶ To print a range of pages, click on the Print button on the toolbar to display the Print dialog box, click the Print pages tab, type the range of page numbers, and click on Print.

▶ To print more than one copy of a document, click on the Print button on the toolbar to display the Print dialog box, change the Number of copies setting, and click on Print.

▶ If you decide that you want to stop a document from printing, click on the Print button on the toolbar to display the Print dialog box and click on the Status button. Select the print job to be deleted and press Del.

▶ If your printer can print on envelopes, choose Format⇨Envelope from the menu bar and click on Print Envelope to print an envelope with the address listed in the letter that you're working on.

▶ To fax a document using a fax modem or change the printer WordPerfect prints to, click the Print button on the toolbar to display the Print dialog box and change the Current printer to your fax modem software. Then click the Print button.

Part I Test

The questions on this test cover all of the material presented in Part 1, Units 1-4.

True   False

T   F   1. You can save a file without giving it a name.

T   F   2. As soon as WordPerfect is open, you can start typing a document.

T   F   3. WordPerfect gives you an electric shock if you type something that is not perfect.

T   F   4. To choose a command from a menu, click on the command or press the Alt key and then press the underlined letter of the command.

T   F   5. WordPerfect is an excellent tool for writing postcards.

T   F   6. A dialog box is the balloon in a comic strip that contains what the character is saying or thinking.

T   F   7. Press the F1 key to get help anytime.

T   F   8. You can use the View⇨Zoom command to access WordPerfect's flight simulator feature.

T   F   9. You can move around your document by telekinesis.

T   F   10. To start a new paragraph, press Enter.

Part I Test

Multiple Choice

For each of the following questions, circle the correct answer or answers. Remember, there may be more than one right answer for each question!

11. **Is turning off the computer without exiting from WordPerfect a good idea?**

    A. No.

    B. Yes.

    C. Sure, if you don't mind losing the document that you're working on.

    D. It's fine if you don't mind a confused computer.

    E. This is a good way to discharge negative feelings about WordPerfect.

12. **Which of the following do not appear in the WordPerfect window?**

    A. The strip joint.

    B. The Candy Bar.

    C. The Milk Bar.

    D. The menu bar.

    E. The Toolbox.

13. **Snoopy's sparrow friend is named:**

    A. Tweety.

    B. Woodstock.

    C. Burlington.

    D. Toto.

    E. Chirpie.

14. **How do you save a document?**

    A. Press Ctrl+S.

    B. Choose File⇨Save from the menu bar.

    C. Click on the Save button on the toolbar.

    D. Press Esc a lot.

    E. Throw it a life preserver.

15. **What happens when you press the Del key?**

    A. The calories in the cookies that you are eating disappear (similar to crumbling the cookie before eating it).

    B. The character to the left of the cursor disappears.

    C. The character to the right of the cursor disappears.

    D. The entire document disappears.

    E. The computer disappears.

16. **How do you run WordPerfect?**

    A. Ask it politely.

    B. Choose it from the Corel WordPerfect Suite 8 part of the Start menu.

    C. Double-click on the filename Wpwin.EXE in Windows Explorer.

    D. Select the WordPerfect icon on the taskbar.

    E. Reinstall WordPerfect from the CD-ROM.

17. **What happens when you press Ctrl+End?**

    A. The end of the world.

    B. WordPerfect automatically adds a closing to your letter.

    C. The cursor moves to the end of the line.

    D. The cursor moves to the end of paragraph.

    E. The cursor moves to the end of the document.

18 **What's the name of the TV game show where the host gives you the answer and you have to give the question?**

    A. Wheel of Fortune.

    B. Good Morning America.

    C. Star Trek.

    D. Jeopardy!

    E. What's My Line?

Part I Test

Matching

19. **Match each of the following buttons with what it does when you click on it:**

A. 1. Closes WordPerfect (when you double-click on it)

B. 2. Displays the Open File dialog box

C. 3. Saves the document on the disk

D. 4. Shrinks the WordPerfect window to a little tiny icon

E. 5. Displays the Print dialog box

20. **Match the following keys with what they do:**

A. Home 1. Cancels a dialog box or the last menu command that you chose

B. Del (Delete) 2. Deletes the character to the left of the cursor

C. Esc 3. Deletes the character to the right of the cursor

D. Backspace 4. Switches between Insert and Typeover modes

E. Ins (Insert) 5. Moves the cursor to the beginning of the line

Part I Lab Assignment

This is the first of several lab assignments that appear at the end of each part of the book. These lab problems are designed to allow you to apply the skills you learned while studying the lessons in realistic situations. (Well, almost realistic, anyway. Your real-life word-processing chores probably won't be as fun as these.)

These lab assignments aren't quite as directed as the exercises that appear in the lessons. For example, you aren't told exactly which keys to press and which buttons to click. Instead, you're given more general tasks to complete — such as "save the document with the name Hire Designer.WPD" — and you are left to your own devices to figure out how best to accomplish the task. In case you're not sure how to accomplish a task, look back at the Part I Review to see where the task is described.

In this lab assignment, you, the Manager of Product Testing of the Vermont Maple Works, will write a letter to a product designer telling him that he is hired.

Step 1: Type the letter

Create a new document that is formatted as a letter. Type the address of the Vermont Maple Works (you can use your own address) at the top of the letter. Then type the date and the name and address of the person you are hiring. For the text of the letter, you can use the text shown in the figure here or make up your own letter. Make it friendly and enthusiastic.

Part I Lab Assignment

```
                              Henry Thoreau
                              Vermont Maple Works
                              RD 2, Sugarbush Farm
                              Cornwall, VT 05753

                              April 1, 1997

Mr. Harold Houdini
1 Way Out
Appleton, Wisconsin 87654

Dear Harry,

As per our discussion earlier today, I am thrilled to be
able to offer you a position as a product designer for
our new line of maple products, starting immediately. We
have an exciting new line planned, and your background as
a cotton candy artist indicates that you will be a
valuable member of the design team. We look forward to
your knowledge and flair making Vermont Maple Works
products even more fun and exciting than they already
are.

The salary is as we discussed last week at your
interview. If you have any questions, call our personnel
director, Peter Pratfall. Please report to work on April
16, at 8 am. Attached is a list of meetings you will need
to attend on your first day, to acquaint you with Vermont
Maple Works, and the company with you.

We look forward to you joining our happy community!

                              Sincerely,



                              Henry
                              Vermont Maple Works
```

At the end of the letter, close with your own name. Save the letter using the filename Hire Designer.WPD.

Part I Lab Assignment

Step 2: Edit and format the letter

Append a list of interviews that the new employee will have to attend on his first day at work, as shown in the following figure. Insert a page break so that this list appears on page two.

```
Please attend the following meetings on April 16th.

8:30 am        Peter Pratfall, Director of Personnel
10:00          Rosie Spinner, V.P. of Product Planning
11:00          Matt Ronn, Product Liability Manager


The first planning meeting will be at 3:00 p.m. -- ask
Rosie where it will be held.
At 5:00 p.m. there will be a party in the staff lounge to
welcome you to the company.
```

Join or separate paragraphs as you think necessary. Feel free to edit the text, too.

Step 3: Print the letter

Print one copy of the letter.

Step 4: Close WordPerfect

Save the document again and exit WordPerfect.

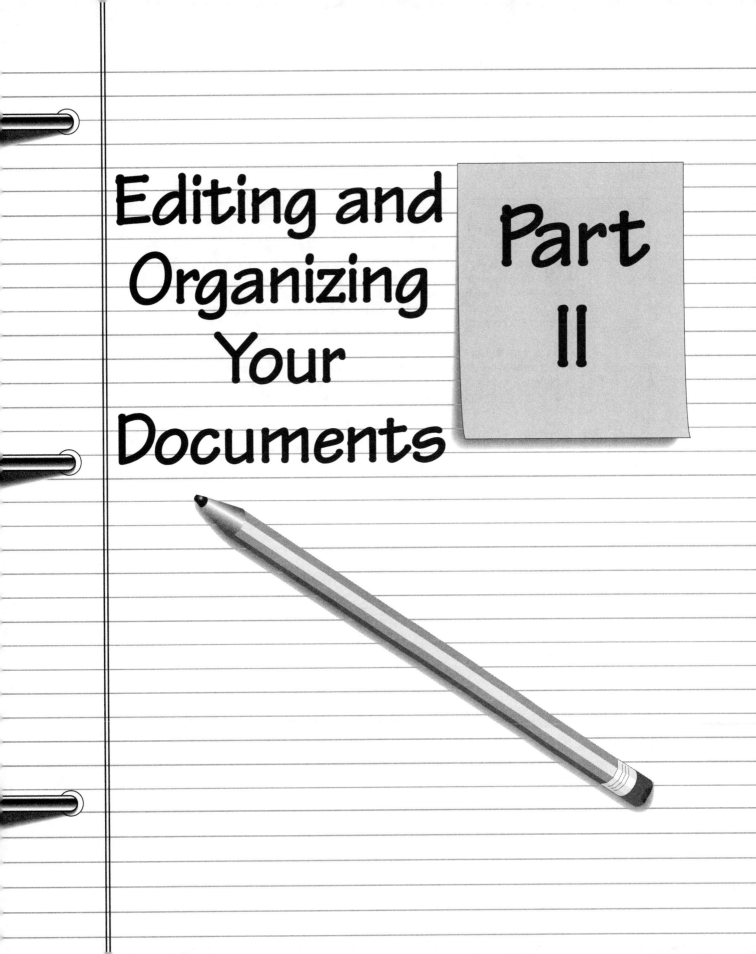

In this part . . .

No one gets everything right the first time — at least, no one *we* know does. This part of the book concentrates on editing: getting rid of text you regret having written, moving things around to make more sense, searching for stuff that you're sure you must have written, and making sure that all your spelling and grammar are correct.

Luckily, WordPerfect makes editing a breeze. The lessons in this part of the book teach you how use the WordPerfect cut-and-paste features to move text, as well as its find-and-replace features to fix errors throughout a document. You'll also learn how to check your spelling, word choice, and even your grammar. Try doing *that* with your old typewriter!

Selecting, Moving, Copying, and Deleting Text

Objectives for This Unit

✓ Selecting text to work with in your document

✓ Copying text

✓ Moving text

✓ Getting rid of text completely

Prerequisites

◗ Opening a document (Lesson 2-2)

◗ Moving around your document using keys (Lesson 2-4)

on the CD

◗ Tour Reservation .101.WPD

◗ Favorite .101.WPD

What's the point in using a word processor if you're not going to stir the words around a bit, or even slice and dice them? When you peruse the first draft of an important letter, you frequently see things that can get moved around. That introductory paragraph, for example, might go better at the end of the letter as a wrap-up.

In this unit, you learn how to select text for slicing and dicing. Then you learn things that you can do with selected text, including moving it to another location in your document, deleting it completely, and making copies of it. You even learn how to move the text to another program completely — for example, to an electronic mail program so that you can include some of your gorgeously crafted prose in an e-mail message.

Lesson 5-1

Selecting and Deleting Text

on the test

Before you can work with a chunk of text, you have to tell WordPerfect which text you want to work with. You mark the text you're working with by *selecting* it.

You can select text at least three ways:

- ◗ Hold down the mouse button while you move the pointer from the beginning to the end of the text.

- ◗ Hold down the Shift key while you use the cursor movement keys, otherwise known as *arrow keys,* to move from the beginning to the end of the text. See Table 5-1 for more information.

- ◗ Double-, triple-, and — believe it or not — quadruple-click to select a word, sentence, or paragraph. See Table 5-2 for more details.

WordPerfect displays the selected text in reverse video, which is a fancy computer geek phrase that means you see white letters on a black background.

to select text, hold down Shift while moving cursor

Table 5-1	Ways to Select Text with the Keyboard
To Select This Much Text . . .	**Press This**
Character to the right of the cursor	Shift+→
Character to the left of the cursor	Shift+←
From the cursor to the beginning of the next word	Shift+Ctrl+→
From the cursor to the beginning of the current word	Shift+Ctrl+←
From the cursor to the same position all the way on the next line	Shift+↓
From the cursor to the same position up one line	Shift+↑
From the cursor to the end of the line	Shift+End
From the cursor to the beginning of the line	Shift+Home
From the cursor to the beginning of the next paragraph	Shift+Ctrl+↓
From the cursor to the beginning of the current paragraph	Shift+Ctrl+↑
From the cursor to the end of the document	Shift+Ctrl+End
From the cursor to the beginning of the document	Shift+Ctrl+Home
From the cursor to the bottom of the screen	Shift+PgDn
From the cursor to the top of the screen	Shift+PgUp

Table 5-2	How to Select Text with the Mouse
When You Want to Select This . . .	**Do This**
Word	Double-click with the mouse pointer anywhere on the word.
Multiple words	Double-click the first or last word. Hold down the mouse button on the second click and move to the other end of the selection. The text is selected word by word, rather than character by character.
Sentence	Triple-click the sentence or click once in the margin to the left of the sentence.
Multiple sentences	Select a sentence, using one of the methods in this table. Hold down the mouse button on the last click and move the pointer to the other end of the selection.
Paragraph	Quadruple-click the paragraph or double-click to the left of the paragraph.
Multiple paragraphs	Select a paragraph, using one of the methods in this table. Hold down the mouse button on the last click and move the pointer to the other end of the selection.
From the cursor to the mouse pointer	Shift+click.

After you've selected text, you can press keys, click buttons, or choose commands from menus to do something to the text. You can do lots of things with selected text. Moving, copying, and deleting the text is just the start. In later units, you find out how to make selected text bold or italicized, change its size, check its spelling, or even change its capitalization. Feeling confident about selecting text is important because most of the whiz-bang word processing features require that you know how to select text. Fortunately, selecting text is not difficult.

The easiest thing to do with a bunch of text is to delete it, plain and simple. So why not start there? While we're at it, we'll explore several ways of selecting text.

To give you something to delete, open Tour Reservation.101.WPD, as shown in Figure 5-1, supplied with this book. Tour Reservation.101.WPD is a letter from a school to the Vermont Maple Works, reserving tickets for a school trip.

Blowing text away

This exercise gives you practice selecting and deleting text. You get the chance to select a word, sentence, and phrase. As you're doing the exercise, you might want to refer back to Tables 5-1 and 5-2 to experiment with different ways of selecting text.

Notes:

to deselect text,
just move cursor
using arrows

Figure 5-1: Tour Reservation.101.WPD contains a letter from a school, arranging a trip to the Maple Works. In this figure, one sentence is selected.

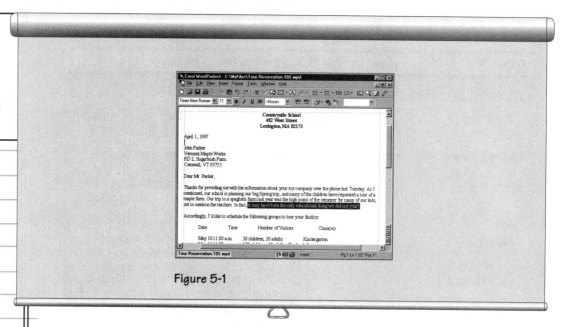

Figure 5-1

heads up

to select text, hold mouse button down while dragging mouse pointer across text

to deselect text, click anywhere in text

Delete key deletes selected text

Currently, the letter making the reservation is a little too candid. It needs to be cleaned up!

1 Select the last sentence of the first paragraph of the letter.

This sentence reads, "In fact, it may have been the only educational thing we did!" Remember to refer to Tables 5-1 and 5-2 for details.

The easiest way to select text is to triple-click the sentence or click once in the left margin next to the sentence. If neither of those mousy methods appeals to you, you may want to try use the arrow keys while holding down the Shift key.

Clicking in the margin may not always work — WordPerfect selects the sentence that is at the beginning of the line. If the sentence that you want to select is short, and does not begin a line (as in Figure 5-1), you'll have to use another method to select it.

Whatever way you choose, the entire last sentence of the paragraph should be selected, as it is in Figure 5-1, and should appear in white letters on a black background.

If you need to deselect the text (maybe because you started in the wrong place), move the cursor without holding down the Shift key.

2 Press the Delete (or Del) key.

The sentence goes up in smoke. Just kidding. Deleting text is not a fire hazard.

Now try to select and delete a phrase. The last sentence in the first paragraph — that is, the *new* last sentence, now that you've deleted the original last sentence — doesn't sound right.

3 Move your mouse pointer to the last sentence of the first paragraph, and place it just before the comma.

Right now the last sentence reads, *Our trip to a spaghetti farm last year was the high point of the semester for many of our kids, not to mention the teachers.*

Put the mouse pointer just before the comma that separates the last phrase from the rest of the sentence.

4 Hold down the mouse button and move the mouse pointer to the end of the sentence, just before the period. Release the mouse button after you've selected the phrase to delete.

As you move the mouse, WordPerfect selects the text, starting with where the mouse pointer was when you pressed the mouse button. Select the phrase, *not to mention the teachers.* Be sure to include the comma at the beginning of the phrase, but not the period at the end. The idea is to not delete the period, because you still need it at the end of the sentence.

If you miss and want to try again, just start over. If you already deleted the phrase and want to retrieve it, click the Undo button, or undelete it by pressing Ctrl+Shift+Z. If you've selected text and want to deselect it, click the mouse pointer once anywhere in your text.

5 Press Delete.

Shazam! The phrase disappears, and the period moves over to end the sentence.

If you deleted the period by mistake or didn't delete the comma, just use Backspace and Delete to clean up your sentence and then retype the period.

6 Move to the end of the letter so that you can see the last paragraph.

Press the Page Down button or use the scroll bar.

You decide that the word *Phooey* detracts from the businesslike tone of the letter.

7 Double-click the word *Phooey.*

WordPerfect selects just the word, not the exclamation point after it.

8 Press Delete to delete the word.

WordPerfect deletes the word and the space before it, which it figures you don't want anymore. That extra exclamation point is still there, however.

9 Press Delete again to delete the extra exclamation point.

Looks good. On second thought, perhaps the whole sentence in parentheses should be deleted.

10 Click in the margin next to the sentence in parentheses.

You have to click next to the second line of the paragraph. If you click in the left margin next to the first line of the paragraph, WordPerfect selects the first sentence. You can also triple-click the sentence to select it.

11 Press Delete to delete the sentence.

Kablooey! The sentence is gone.

Tip: When you select multiple lines of text with the mouse, you can move the pointer in a straight line from the first character that you want to select to the last. You don't have to select the text line by line.

Notes:

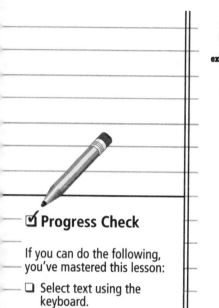

☑ **Progress Check**

If you can do the following, you've mastered this lesson:

❑ Select text using the keyboard.

❑ Select text using the mouse.

❑ Delete selected text.

❑ Retrieve accidentally deleted text.

WordPerfect mouse tricks

WordPerfect makes using the mouse to select complete words easy — it assumes that you want whole words, and jumps the selection to include each full word. Usually this feature is useful — when you want just part of a word, you can select just that. If, however, you find it annoying, you can turn the feature off:

1. **Choose Tools⇔Settings.**

2. **Double-click the Environment icon in the Settings dialog box.**

3. **On the General tab of the Environment Settings dialog box, click the check box next to Select whole words instead of characters so that it is deselected.**

4. **Click the OK button to return to the Settings dialog box, and then click the Close button to return to the document.**

This action turns off the word selecting feature permanently (or until you turn it on again).

Oops! Getting deleted text back

What if you delete something by accident? Not a problem, as long as you notice it quickly. Press Ctrl+Shift+Z, which is the keyboard shortcut. The deleted text reappears — it may not appear exactly where you deleted it from, though — it reappears where the cursor is. Click Restore to undelete the text. You may need to give the command again to get back more deleted text, if you deleted it in two steps. Undelete works even when you've done other things with your document after you mistakenly deleted text.

If deleting text was the last thing you did, you can use Edit⇔Undo, or just click the Undo button, to get it back.

Always remember to save your document often, especially before you make drastic changes.

Lesson 5-2 — Copying Text

One useful thing that you can do is copy the selected text to the *Windows Clipboard*. The Windows Clipboard is a usually invisible parking space for information. (You may be able to look at the Windows Clipboard; choose Programs⇔Accessories⇔Clipboard Viewer from the Windows 95 Start menu. However, the option has to be installed with Windows 95.) After you copy or move information to the Clipboard, you can copy it from the Clipboard back into your document or into any other Windows-based application.

Using QuickMenus

WordPerfect has a set of menus that you have not yet used. They're called *QuickMenus,* and they appear when you click the right mouse button. Which QuickMenu appears depends on where the mouse pointer is and what you're doing. QuickMenus offer yet another way to choose commands.

If you click the right mouse button when the mouse pointer is in the typing area, you see a QuickMenu that is relevant to formatting characters. If you click the right mouse button when the mouse pointer is in the left margin, you get a QuickMenu that allows you to select various portions of text, using the cursor as the reference point, not the mouse pointer. Figure 5-2 shows the Select Text QuickMenu.

Other QuickMenus appear when you click other parts of the screen. Clicking with the right mouse button on the status bar, scroll bars, Application Bar, or toolbar displays different QuickMenus with options that are related to that part of WordPerfect. We tell you when a QuickMenu is available for you to choose a command.

Table 5-3 tells you what you can do with text using the Windows Clipboard. Before using any of the buttons, menu commands, or keyboard shortcuts, you have to select the text you want to work with.

Table 5-3	Using the Windows Clipboard	
Use This button	**Or Press This**	**To Do This**
✂	Ctrl+X or Edit⇨Cut	**Cut:** You can move text from your document to the Windows Clipboard, which is called *cutting.* When you cut text, it is deleted from your document.
📋	Ctrl +C or Edit⇨Copy	**Copy:** You can also copy text from your document to the Windows Clipboard. This action, quite reasonably, is called *copying.* Copied text exists in both your document and the Windows Clipboard.

The text on the Windows Clipboard stays there until you cut or copy different text to the Windows Clipboard. After you cut or copy something new to the Windows Clipboard, the previous contents of the Windows Clipboard vanish.

heads up

You can paste the text from the Windows Clipboard into your document more than once. In fact, you can paste it as many times as you want. This feature is a convenient way to make a bunch of copies of some text; just copy it to the Windows Clipboard and then paste it a bunch of times.

heads up

And remember, if you want to undo the cut, copy, or paste you just did, press Ctrl+Z to undo it.

heads up

Figure 5-2: The Select text Quick Menu.

Notes:

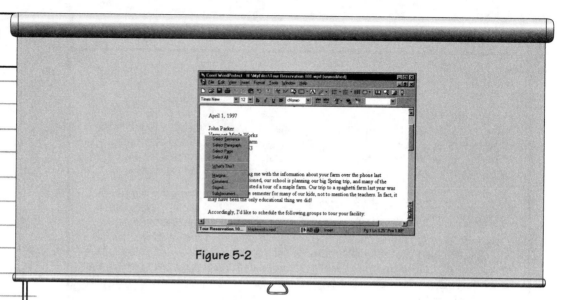

Figure 5-2

heads up

You can cut or copy information from one document onto the Clipboard and then paste it into another document — just use the buttons on the Application Bar to switch to another open program. You can even copy from one application to another — switch to another application by using the buttons on the Windows 95 taskbar.

windows 95

The Windows Clipboard works for almost all Windows-based programs. Almost all programs use the same commands and keystrokes (Ctrl+X, Ctrl+C, and Ctrl+V) for cutting and pasting.

The Clipboard holds only one chunk of information, although the chunk can be fairly huge. Remember that after you cut or copy other text, the new text replaces whatever was in the Clipboard.

Copying a selection

WordPerfect makes copying text easy. All you need to do is select the text that you want to copy, use Ctrl+C or the Copy button to store the text on the Windows Clipboard for later use, move the cursor to the position where the text should be copied, and use Ctrl+V or the Paste button to insert the text there. You can also find the Copy and Paste commands in the Edit menu.

on the CD

If you haven't already opened the Tour Reservation.101.WPD document, open it now. Reading the letter, you notice that on May 12, a total of 142 children are going to the Vermont Maple Works. You decide to send some of those kids the next day, so you need to add an extra line to the letter and change some of the numbers. Follow these steps:

1 **Select the line that starts *May 12.***

Use your favorite method. The easiest method may be to click once in the margin to the left of the line.

The entire line is highlighted.

More ways to select text and extend a selection

You may think that you know plenty of ways to select text, and you do. But whether you like it or not, WordPerfect has even more ways to select text — and they are:

▶ **Selecting text with menus:** To get the QuickMenu you see in Figure 5-2, click the right mouse button when the pointer is in the left margin. This menu allows you to select the Sentence, Paragraph, Page or All (the whole document) where your cursor is.

You can use the regular menu to get the same choices — it just takes longer. Choose Edit⇨Select and choose Sentence, Paragraph, Page, or All. The hotkeys aren't very consistent — who uses the underlined letters anyway?

▶ **Using F8:** WordPerfect has a Select mode that you can turn on. When Select mode is on, you can select text with the keyboard, without

using the Shift key. For example, press the End key to select the text from the cursor to the end of the line. Press the F8 key to turn Select mode on and off.

If you have made a selection only to discover that you really should have selected more, never fear. WordPerfect has a relatively simple method to extend a selection, or rather several methods (Higher Being forbid that WordPerfect have only one way to do something).

If you need to extend a selection, try one of the following:

▶ Press Shift and click the point to which you would like the selection extended.

▶ Press Shift and use the arrow keys or other selection keyboard key combinations.

☑ Progress Check

If you can do the following, you've mastered this lesson:

❏ Copy text to the Windows Clipboard.

❏ Cut text from a document to the Windows Clipboard.

❏ Paste copies of text from the Windows Clipboard into your document.

---

2 **To copy the selection to the Windows Clipboard, press Ctrl+C or click the Copy button.**

The selection is copied to the Clipboard without anything noticeable happening to your letter.

3 **Press End to move to the cursor to the end of the line; then press Enter to add a new line.**

This is where you want to add a copy of the line.

4 **To copy the selection, press Ctrl+V or click the Paste button.**

WordPerfect inserts a copy of the line from the Clipboard to the line where the cursor is. Your cursor is at the end of the text you just pasted into the document.

5 **Edit the line, changing the date to the 13th, the number of kids to 70, and the number of adults to 4.**

To be consistent, change the information for the 12th so that the number of kids is 72 and the number of adults is 4.

6 **Save the document.**

Click the Save button on the toolbar.

Recess

If it's time to feed the chickens, save your document and exit WordPerfect. Choose File⇨Exit from the menu bar or press Alt+F4. Your chickens would probably love the crust of that danish you didn't finish!

When you're ready to come back and finish the unit, open WordPerfect and open Tour Reservation.101.WPD.

Lesson 5-3

Moving Text

WordPerfect has two ways to move text. You may have already figured out the first way: You can use the cut and paste features of WordPerfect. The other way to move text is to select it and drag it.

Cutting and pasting

on the CD

You may still have Tour Reservation.101.WPD open. If not, open it now.

Move the paragraph that starts *We will pay for the tours* earlier in the letter, using the WordPerfect cut and paste feature:

1 Select the paragraph you want to move.

Use your favorite method to select the paragraph:

- Position the cursor at the beginning of the paragraph. Hold down the Shift key as you use the arrow keys to get to the end of the paragraph. Remember, you can use the down-arrow key to move to the end of the paragraph. You don't have to press the right-arrow key forever.

- Click and drag the mouse from one corner of the paragraph to the opposite one.

- Quadruple-click anywhere in the paragraph.

- Double-click in the left margin.

- Right-click in the left margin next to the paragraph and choose Select Paragraph from the QuickMenu.

2 Cut the paragraph.

Press Ctrl+X, choose Edit⇨Cut from the menu or click the Cut button.

heads up

The paragraph disappears, but don't worry: It's on the Windows Clipboard, and you can get it back easily as long as you don't cut or copy anything else.

3 Move your cursor to where the paragraph is to be inserted.

In this case, move your cursor to the beginning of the paragraph that starts *Accordingly, I'd like to schedule the following groups to tour your facility.*

4 **Insert the paragraph by pressing Ctrl+V, choosing Edit⇨Paste from the menu, or clicking the Paste button.**

The paragraph is pulled from the Clipboard and inserted where the cursor is.

5 **If you didn't select the carriage returns at the end of the paragraph you moved, insert or delete carriage returns as needed.**

If no carriage return appears between the paragraph that you just moved and the next paragraph *(Accordingly . . .)*, move your cursor there and press Enter twice.

If you see extra blank lines where the paragraph that you moved used to be, move your cursor there and delete the lines.

on the test

One way to move text is to select it, cut it from its current position, and paste it to the new position.

Congratulations! By learning to use the cut, paste, and copy features of WordPerfect, you have learned skills that will be useful throughout Windows.

Dragging and dropping

You can move text without ever putting it on the Clipboard — as easily as selecting it, dragging it to a new location, and dropping it there. Even normal people (and not just compugeeks) call this technique drag-and-drop. Sometimes using drag-and-drop can be more trouble than it's worth unless you can see both the initial position of the text that you're moving, and where you want to move it, on the screen without scrolling.

To try dragging, move two sentences to a different part of the letter:

1 **Scroll the screen so that you can see both the paragraph that begins *We will pay for the tickets in advance* and the one that begins *We plan to arrive by bus.***

Again, this technique is difficult to use unless you see the text you're moving and where you want to move it on the screen at the same time.

2 **Select the sentences *We plan to bring bag lunches — let me know if this is a problem. Buying lunch in a cafeteria tends to be far too confusing (and too expensive) for this large a group!***

These sentences are at the end of the paragraph that starts *We plan to arrive by bus.* Use your favorite method to select the sentences.

3 **Click the selected text and hold down the mouse button.**

The mouse pointer changes when the mouse is moved. A little box is now added to the pointer to indicate that the selected text is being moved as the mouse pointer moves. If the little box doesn't appear immediately, give it a second.

4 **Continue to hold down the mouse button and move the mouse pointer where you want to put the text.**

In this case, move the mouse pointer to the end of the paragraph that begins *We will pay for the tours in advance.*

Notes:

drag selected
text to new
location

☑ **Progress Check**

If you can do the following, you've mastered this lesson:

❏ Cut and paste text to move it to a new position.

❏ Use drag-and-drop to move selected text to a new position.

As you move the mouse pointer, the insertion point moves too, indicating where the text will go when you let go of the mouse button.

5 **Let go of the mouse button.**

The text moves to the new position. Notice that it stays selected, so if it didn't land in exactly the right place, you can drag it to a new position.

6 **Click the mouse in the text, and then add the missing space before the first of the two sentences you just moved.**

7 **Press Ctrl+S to save your document.**

on the test

The intuitive way to move text is to select the text and then drag it to its new position.

heads up

A caveat: You can move the selected text to a point that is currently off the screen. If you move the cursor a little past the top or bottom of the typing area, the document scrolls up or down. In our experience, however, the document scrolls so quickly that you can have difficulty getting where you want to be. If you're moving text to a place in the document that you can't see, you may want to stick with the cut-and-paste method.

Unit 5 Quiz

For each of the following questions, circle the letter of the correct answer or answers. Remember, we may include more than one right answer for each question!

1. **This button ...**

   A. Does the same thing as Ctrl+X.

   B. Does the same thing as Edit⇨Cut.

   C. Uses pinking shears on your printed document.

   D. Denotes that this document is good only for children's art projects.

   E. Deletes selected text from your document and puts it in the Clipboard.

2. **This button ...**

   A. Does the same thing as Ctrl+C.

   B. Does the same thing as Edit⇨Copy.

   C. Puts a dotted line around the selected text.

   D. Changes the type in the document from black to blue.

   E. Copies selected text to the Clipboard.

3. **This button ...**

   A. Does the same thing as Ctrl+V.

   B. Does the same thing as Edit⇨Paste.

   C. Turns the document into stew.

   D. Makes the printed document sticky, for use in collages.

   E. Pastes text from the Windows Clipboard to the document, starting at the cursor.

4. **The Windows Clipboard ...**

   A. Makes you look good at meetings.

   B. Is a place to hold text that you want to copy or paste.

   C. Is a feature of Windows that allows you to move or copy information from one Windows-based program to another.

   D. Is where text goes when you cut it from your document.

   E. Is usually invisible, but very useful.

5. **Text can be selected by ...**

   A. Using the mouse by clicking at the beginning of the text and dragging the mouse pointer to the end of the text.

   B. Choosing Edit⇨Select from the menu bar.

   C. Using a QuickMenu — that is, right-clicking in the left margin of the document and then choosing Select Sentence, Select Paragraph, Select Page, or Select All from the QuickMenu that appears.

   D. Double-, triple-, or quadruple-clicking to select a word, sentence, or paragraph (respectively).

   E. Holding down the Shift key while pressing the cursor movement keys: ↑, ↓, ←, →, PgUp, PgDn, Home, and End.

6. **In the Mary Martin version of *Peter Pan*, what happens when the title character comes back for Wendy?**

   A. She happily follows him to Neverland and lives there as a child forever.

   B. She has grown up and can't go with Peter to Neverland.

   C. Wendy's daughter Jane goes with Peter Pan for an adventure.

   D. Peter challenges Wendy's brother John to an arm wrestling match.

   E. She calls the police.

Notes:

Unit 5 Exercise

1. Open Favorite.101.WPD. It contains a list of toys.

2. At the bottom of the list, add any other toys that you like (adult toys count).

3. If the list contains any toys that you don't enjoy, select and delete the items.

4. Move your favorite toy to the top of the list.

5. Save the document.

Finding and Replacing Text

Objectives for This Unit

✓ Searching for words or phrases

✓ Refining searches

✓ Replacing text with different text

Prerequisites

▶ Using dialog boxes (Lesson 2-1)

▶ Opening documents (Lesson 2-2)

on the CD

▶ Paint-By-Numbers.101.WPD

If you've ever needed to replace multiple instances of a word in a document or wondered where a certain word was in a document, you need to know how to use the WordPerfect search feature.

Searching for text is nearly hassle free — however, using the replace feature can royally screw up your document if you don't do exactly what you need. Someone once called us to tell us that she had replaced all her spaces with nothing — she had used the search and replace feature to remove all the spaces in her document. With all the spaces gone, each paragraph in the document is one long word — so be careful when you replace text. Make sure that you save your document before you do a major search and replace job so that you can retrieve the saved version if you need to.

WordPerfect can even find and replace formatting. For example, you can replace all the formatting codes that center-align text with codes that right-align text. For information about finding and replacing WordPerfect formatting codes, see Unit 9.

Lesson 6-1 # Searching for Words or Phrases

on the test

The way to search for a word or phrase in WordPerfect is to use the Find and Replace Text dialog box. Even when you are searching for text and aren't planning to replace it, this is still the dialog box you need to use. To begin a search, display the dialog box in one of the following ways:

◗ Press F2.

◗ Press Ctrl+F.

◗ Choose Edit⇨Find and Replace from the menu bar.

Figure 6-1 shows the Find and Replace Text dialog box.

on the CD

You can use the document Paint-By-Numbers.101.WPD to learn how to search. See Figure 6-2 for a look at the document. You start by searching for the first use of the word *number*.

1 **Open Paint-By-Numbers.101.WPD. Make sure that the cursor is at the top of the document.**

The fastest way to move the cursor to the top of the document is to press Ctrl+Home. This action insures that you find the first instance of the text that you're looking for. For example, if you want to find the first instance on the fifth page, you move the cursor to the top of page 5.

extra credit

A caveat: the Find and Replace dialog box has an option (Option⇨Begin Find and Top of Document) that forces every search to begin at the top of the document regardless of where the cursor is. This option can be turned on and off by using the Find and Replace dialog box menu. By default, this option is turned off and WordPerfect starts searching at the cursor.

2 **Press Ctrl+F or F2 to display the Find and Replace Text dialog box.**

If you prefer, choose Edit⇨Find and Replace from the menu.

WordPerfect displays the Find and Replace Text dialog box (refer to Figure 6-1). For the time being, the important thing to notice is that the Find box is highlighted, ready to receive your input.

3 **Type number in the Find box.**

Your cursor is already in the Find box, so all you need to do is type the word.

4 **To find the word, press Enter or click the Find Next button.**

WordPerfect highlights the first occurrence of that word in the document after the cursor (see Figure 6-3). Notice that the word that WordPerfect finds is actually *Numbers*, not *number*. Because you didn't tell WordPerfect if capitalization was important, or if you were looking for the whole word *number*, WordPerfect finds any occurrence of those six letters in that order. You learn how to look for specific capitalization and only the whole word in the next lesson.

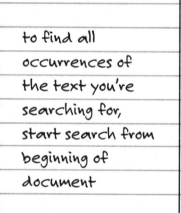

Notes:

to find all occurrences of the text you've searching for, start search from beginning of document

Ctrl+F to search for word or phrase

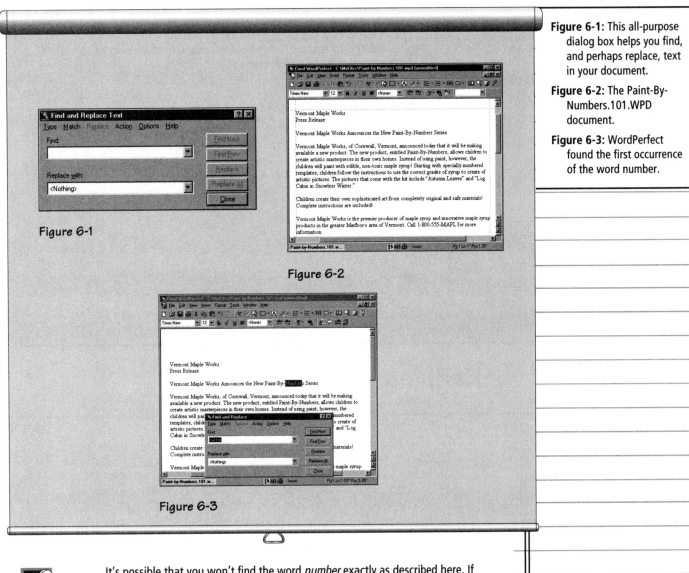

Figure 6-1

Figure 6-2

Figure 6-3

Figure 6-1: This all-purpose dialog box helps you find, and perhaps replace, text in your document.

Figure 6-2: The Paint-By-Numbers.101.WPD document.

Figure 6-3: WordPerfect found the first occurrence of the word number.

heads up

It's possible that you won't find the word *number* exactly as described here. If you or someone else used one of the myriad of Find and Replace options, that option may still be on. If your Find and Replace dialog box doesn't match the one in Figure 6-1 (perhaps you have Whole Word or Case Sensitive or something else immediately below the F̲ind box) look at Table 6-1 to figure out how to turn the option off.

5 To find more occurrences of the word *number,* continue to press Enter or click F̲ind Next.

Notice that WordPerfect doesn't care if the word is capitalized.

When the last occurrence of the word *number* in the document has been found, WordPerfect displays the message `"number" Not Found` and asks you to acknowledge that fact by clicking OK. This message means that, in the direction that WordPerfect is searching (from the top of the document to bottom, in this case), the word *number* does not appear between the cursor and the end of the document.

on the test

on the test

Progress Check

If you can do the following, you've mastered this lesson:

❑ Search for the first instance of a word in a document.

❑ Search for all instances of a word in a document.

6 **Click OK to acknowledge that no more occurrences of the word** *number* **exist in the document.**

You're finished searching.

7 **Click Close to close the Find and Replace Text dialog box.**

WordPerfect takes you back to your document. The cursor immediately follows the last instance of "number" in the document.

To find text in your document, use the Find and Replace Text dialog box. Type the text that you're looking for in the Find box and press Enter. You can keep looking for the text by clicking the Find Next button in the Find and Replace Text dialog box.

When you display the Find and Replace Text dialog box, WordPerfect remembers what you searched for last time and suggests it again. If you want to search for a word that you've searched for before, click the arrow on the right side of the Text dialog box to display a list of the last few words or phrases that you searched for.

Lesson 6-2   Refining Your Search

In a long document, finding what you're looking for can take awhile. You have at least two ways to make finding what you're looking for a little easier: One is to be smart about your search, and the other is to tell WordPerfect as much as you know about what you're searching for — and that may mean using the WordPerfect search features. So what does being smart mean? It means:

 ♦ Not searching for text where you know you won't find it. That is, don't start looking at the top of a 20-page document if you know that what you're looking for is in the last section. Move your cursor to the top of the last section and start your search there.

 ♦ Searching for a whole phrase, when you know it — not just a word. You can even include punctuation.

 ♦ Telling WordPerfect if capitalization is important.

 ♦ Telling WordPerfect if the text you're looking for is a whole word or just a string of letters.

Table 6-1 lists the specifics of how to refine a search using the Find and Replace Text dialog box. The Find and Replace Text dialog box has its own little menu bar at the top of the dialog box. You can choose commands from this menu bar to control how searching works. This lesson shows you how to use these commands.

Table 6-1	Search Options
To Find This . . .	*Do This in the Search and Replace Text Dialog Box*
A phrase	Type the whole phrase with punctuation in the Find and Replace Text dialog box.
The word, the whole word, and nothing but the word	Choose Match⇨Whole Word from the dialog box menu. A check mark appears next to this option on the dialog box menu when this option is selected.
Something anywhere in the document, regardless of where the cursor is	Choose Options⇨Begin Find at Top of Document, or Options⇨Wrap at Beg./End of Document. A check mark appears next to this option on the dialog box menu when this option is selected.
Something above (before) your cursor	Click the Find Prev button.
Something below (after) your cursor	Click the Find Next button.
A match with specific capitalization	Choose Match⇨Case from the dialog box menu. A check mark appears next to this option on the dialog box menu when this option is selected.
The text in a specific font or in a particular text style	Choose Match⇨Font from the dialog box menu and specify the font or text style in the Match Font dialog box.

Nothing extraneous, please

You may notice, especially when you're searching for a short word, that WordPerfect finds your search word within other words. If, for example, as in Lesson 6-1, you're looking for the word *number*, WordPerfect may also find that combination of letters in *number*s and *number*ed. Sometimes the results of a search will surprise you: WordPerfect will find *man* in wo*man* and *man*gy, for instance.

One way to solve this problem is to type a space before or after the word in the Find box. When searching for *man* preceded by a space, WordPerfect won't find wo*man*, but will find *man*ager and *man*gy. Searching for *man* followed by a space still doesn't work perfectly, because WordPerfect finds wo*man*. And adding a space after the word causes WordPerfect to miss the word when it is followed by punctuation, such as a period or a comma.

Luckily, WordPerfect has a feature that lets you tell it to find a string of letters only when they form an entire word and not when they form part of a larger word.

Notes:

on the CD

In Find and
Replace dialog
box, Match→Whole
Word to find whole
words only

In these steps, you find *art* in Paint-By-Numbers.101.WPD only when it's a word, not when it's part of a word.

1 **Open the Paint-By-Numbers.101.WPD document, if it's not still open from the preceding lesson.**

2 **Move the cursor to the top of the document by pressing Ctrl+Home.**

WordPerfect will start its search from the current location of the cursor — in this case, the top of the document.

3 **Open the Find and Replace Text dialog box by pressing F2 or Ctrl+F.**

If you prefer, you can choose Edit⇨Find and Replace from the menu.

4 **Type *art* in the Find box.**

This part is the same as if you were looking for any instance of *art*.

5 **Click Find Next a few times.**

WordPerfect finds the letters *art* within the words *artistic* and *starting*.

click in the
document during
a search to move
the cursor

6 **Click in the document to tell WordPerfect that you want to work there, and then press Ctrl+Home to move back to the top of the document.**

The Find and Replace Text dialog box remains visible while you do this step. Moving back to the top of the document is one way to ensure that the next search includes the whole document.

7 **Choose Match⇨Whole Word from the menu bar in the dialog box.**

The phrase *Whole Word* appears under the Find box in the dialog box to let you know that WordPerfect is looking only for the word *art*.

8 **Press Enter or click Find Next to find the whole word *art*.**

WordPerfect highlights the first (and only) time that the word *art* is used in the document.

9 **Press Enter or click Find Next to find the next occurrence of the whole word *art*.**

WordPerfect tells you that "art" is not found.

10 **Press Enter or click OK to close the message box, and then click Close or press Esc to close the dialog box.**

The dialog box closes, and the text that the search found is highlighted.

Using the Find and Replace Text dialog box menu bar lets you be more specific about what you're looking for. The Match⇨Whole Word command tells WordPerfect that you want the text in the box only when it's a whole word, not when the letters appear as part of another word.

heads up

The Whole Word setting remains in effect until you turn it off. The next time that you use the Find and Replace Text dialog box, you'll see that the words *Whole Word* still appear beneath the Find text box. To turn off the Whole Word setting, choose the Match⇨Whole Word command from the dialog box menu bar again.

Using the Whole Word setting is one way to specify your searches so that you find what you're looking for more quickly. Don't forget to read Table 6-1 to find other ways.

heads up

You can work in your document while the Find and Replace dialog box is open — just click the document to edit the text or move the cursor. Then click the dialog box to make it active again and continue your searching.

Recess

If you need to look for something other than text, such as your kids, your keys, or your sanity, exit WordPerfect without saving the document. When you're ready to start again, open Paint-By-Numbers.101.WPD.

Replacing What You've Found   Lesson 6-3

WordPerfect makes it easy to find all instances of a word or phrase and replace it with a word or phrase. For example, while working on your forthcoming novel, you write a magnificent chapter in which the main character eats a brownie. You then realize that in an earlier chapter, you wrote that she's allergic to chocolate. You decide to replace *brownie* with *butterscotch bar* throughout the chapter.

Replacing one word or phrase with another is called *global search and replace* in computer lingo. WordPerfect makes it a breeze, using the same Find and Replace Text dialog box that you use when searching for text. You type the text to be replaced in the F<u>i</u>nd box and the text to replace it with in the Replace <u>w</u>ith box. You then click the <u>R</u>eplace button, which tells WordPerfect to find the first instance of that text and ask you whether you want to replace it with the text in the Replace <u>w</u>ith box. WordPerfect shows you each place in which it finds the F<u>i</u>nd text and lets you decide if the text should be replaced.

on the test

If you want to replace all instances of a word or phrase without WordPerfect asking about each one, you can click the Replace <u>A</u>ll button, which takes the choice out of your hands, and replaces all instances of the F<u>i</u>nd text with the Replace <u>w</u>ith text.

Although WordPerfect is trustworthy, it does *exactly* what you tell it to do, which can backfire dreadfully. Watch out when you use the Replace <u>A</u>ll button, because you can easily make mistakes. For example, you may forget to use the <u>M</u>atch⇨<u>W</u>ord command when you're replacing text like *in* with *inside*. You can end up with words like *Winsidedows 95, providinsideg,* and *insideformation*. As much as you may like these new words, they are probably not exactly what you had in mind.

Notes:

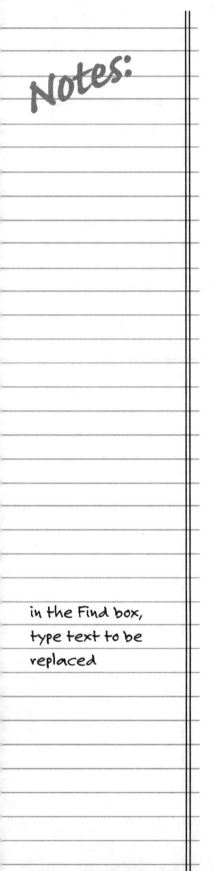

Notes:

on the test

Following are three ways to avoid making hash out of your document when you're replacing text:

- Save your document before you use the Find and Replace Text dialog box to replace text. If you need to retrieve the text, close the current document *without* saving the document, and open the saved version.

- Use the <u>F</u>ind Next button to find a few instances of the text that you want to replace, to make sure that WordPerfect finds the text you had in mind.

- Use the <u>R</u>eplace button, not the Replace <u>A</u>ll button, to do the replacement instance by instance, unless you're *sure* you really want to replace all occurrences of the word.

The Vermont Maple Works has found out that it can't call its new product Paint-by-Numbers for copyright reasons. Instead, they'll call it Paint-By-Letters. You're going to find every instance of *Number* in the press release and replace it with *Letter*.

on the CD

1 Open the Paint-By-Numbers.101.WPD document (if it isn't already open).

2 Save it immediately as Paint-By-Letters.WPD, using the <u>F</u>ile⇨Save <u>A</u>s command.

This step insures that you won't accidentally replace the document that you've been working on with the new document that you want to create. (You could also have opened the document as Read Only.) If the Save As dialog box and Read Only are unfamiliar, review Lesson 2-2.

3 Move the cursor to the top of the document by pressing Ctrl+Home.

Start at the top of the document to be sure that you find all occurrences of the word or phrase that you're looking for.

4 Open the Find and Replace Text dialog box by pressing F2.

The last word that you looked for is still in the F<u>i</u>nd box, even if you looked for it in a different document (unless you closed WordPerfect, in which case the F<u>i</u>nd box is empty). The contents of the F<u>i</u>nd box are highlighted, so whatever you type replaces it.

in the Find box, type text to be replaced

5 Type number in the F<u>i</u>nd box and then press Tab to move to the Replace <u>w</u>ith box.

Be sure not to type a space after the word. (Occasionally, you may want to look for the space, but not in this case.)

6 Type letter in the Replace <u>w</u>ith box.

Be sure not to include any spaces in the Replace <u>w</u>ith text.

7 Make sure that the Whole Word setting is turned off.

heads up

If *Whole Word* appears beneath the F<u>i</u>nd box, choose Match⇨<u>W</u>hole Word from the dialog box menu bar to turn off this setting. You want to replace *numbers* with *letters* and *numbered* with *lettered,* as well as replacing plain old *number* with *letter*. This might not always be true when you're doing a find and replace, but it will have the desired result in this case. If the Whole Word setting is left on, only the word *number* will be replaced. *Numbers* and *numbered* and any other word forms would be left as is.

8   **In the Replace with box, type** letter.

9   **Press Enter or click Find Next.**

WordPerfect highlights the first instance of *number,* which is on the title line.

10   **Click the Replace button.**

WordPerfect replaces *Number* with *Letter.* The *s* at the end of *numbers* is unaffected, so it is on hand to turn *letter* into *letters.* You may be pleased and surprised to see that WordPerfect is smart enough to match capitalization when it replaces a word; that is, because *numbers* was capitalized, WordPerfect capitalizes *letters.*

11   **Continue through the document, deciding whether or not to replace each instance of** number **with** letter.

In this case, you can click to replace each time *number* is found. Replacing them all with *letter* makes sense. If you find an instance of the Find word that you don't want to replace, click the Find Next button to skip the found word.

12   **Save the completed document by pressing Ctrl+S; then close the document by pressing Ctrl+F4.**

You may want to review the document before you close it. It may be hard to know exactly what you've found and replaced until you've finished the process.

By specifying a word in the Replace with box, you can replace one word in your text with another.

You aren't limited to replacing single words. You can replace a phrase or punctuation, using the Find and Replace Text dialog box. In Unit 8, you find out how to replace formatting, too (for example, changing all bold to italics).

heads up

You can undo any replacements you make by using the Undo button or Ctrl+Z. Changes are undone one at a time, so if you used the Replace All option, you may have to Undo quite a few changes to get the document back the way you want it.

extra credit

Swapping two terms

You may need to search and replace in several steps. For example, if you've written an article comparing butterscotch bars and brownies and then realize that you have them mixed up and need to replace every instance of *butterscotch bars* with *brownies* and vice versa, you need to swap the terms in three steps. If you use the search and replace feature to replace all instances of *butterscotch bars* with *brownies,* you have no way of telling the difference between the *brownies* that are supposed to get changed back to *butterscotch bars* and those that should remain *brownies.* You would have an article that was only about brownies, with no mention of butterscotch bars at all!

(continued)

---

in the Replace with box, type text to replace with

Notes:

(continued)

Instead, you need to follow these steps:

1. Replace all instances of *brownies* with text that won't appear anywhere else in your document — something like *xbrownies.* Now the article is about xbrownies and butterscotch bars.

2. Replace all instances of *butterscotch bars* with *brownies.* Now the article is about xbrownies and brownies.

3. Replace all instances of *xbrownies* with *butterscotch bars.* Now the article is about butterscotch bars and brownies again.

extra credit

Replacing all forms of a word with a different word

WordPerfect 8 has an ultra-cool feature: You can find and replace all forms of a word. For example, you can replace all references to *driving* in your novel to *piloting* (you want to add that science-fiction flavor). That switch means that *drove* becomes *piloted, driving* becomes *piloting,* and so on.

To tell WordPerfect that you want to deal with word forms, choose Type⇨Word Forms from the menu bar in the Find and Replace Text dialog box. WordPerfect displays the phrase *Word Forms* below the

Find box to remind you of what you're doing.

When you're replacing word forms, confirming each replacement rather than using the Replace All button is a good idea — WordPerfect isn't smart enough not to change a noun into a verb, and you may find that your substitution makes no sense. Occasionally, you can choose the form of the Replace with word — just pick the one that you want and click Replace to continue.

☑ **Progress Check**

If you can do the following, you've mastered this lesson:

❑ Search for all occurrences of a word in a document, and replace it with a different word.

❑ Search for all occurrences of a phrase, and replace it with a different phrase.

Unit 6 Quiz

For each of the following questions, circle the letter of the correct answer or answers. Remember, we may give you more than one right answer for each question!

1. **The Find and Replace Text dialog box can be used to...**

   A. Find text in your document.

   B. Find text in your document and replace it with other text.

   C. Find a word or phrase.

   D. Find a character, such as an asterisk.

   E. Replace all the occurrences of *I* in your document with *Elvis.*

2. **Global search and replace is...**

    A. When you look all over the world for something.

    B. When WordPerfect looks through a document replacing one word or phrase with another.

    C. A convenient way to fix a mistake that you've made consistently throughout a document, such as spelling someone's name wrong.

    D. A dangerous command that can foul up your document if you aren't careful.

    E. Something you do with the Find and Replace Text dialog box.

3. **Before clicking the Replace or Replace All button on the Find and Replace dialog box, a good idea is to...**

    A. Think twice: Are you sure that you want to make the change?

    B. Save your document, just in case.

    C. Check that the sentence will read correctly after the replacement is made.

    D. Check to see if the Whole Word setting is turned on.

    E. Utter a brief prayer to the word processing gods.

4. **A good way to display the Find and Replace Text dialog box is to...**

    A. Press F2.

    B. Press Ctrl+F.

    C. Press Alt+E and then F. Try it!

    D. Press and release the Alt key, and then type *ef*. Again, try it!

    E. Position the mouse pointer on each of the buttons on the Toolbar in turn and read the description of the button that appears, to see if any of them displays the Find and Replace Text dialog box. After you determine that there is no button for this command, give up and press F2.

5. **Options on the Find and Replace dialog box allow you to tell WordPerfect to...**

    A. Search for any form of the word in the Find box.

    B. Search for only the whole word, not just the letters as they appear in the Find box.

    C. Search for the word in the Find box with capitalization as you've typed it.

    D. Search for your keys.

    E. Search the document before the cursor.

Unit 6 Exercise

1. Write a letter to your favorite kitchen store, enumerating all the uses you have found for their latest kitchen tool. Explain how you use this tool for a variety of different tasks. Make up tasks if you have to!

2. Save the document as Kitchen Tool.WPD.

3. Use the Find and Replace Text dialog box to replace all instances of the kitchen tool, such as *rolling pin,* with *hammer.*

4. Experiment with a way to totally ruin a document with the Find and Replace Text dialog box, so that you won't ruin an important document.

   Use the Find and Replace Text dialog box to replace all the spaces in your document with nothing. Replace the contents of the F‌ind box with a single space, delete the contents of the Replace w‌ith box, and then click Replace A‌ll.

5. Wow! A document with no spaces is totally unintelligible! Close the document without saving it. (Alternatively, you could click Undo lots of times to undo all the changes you made when you clicked Replace A‌ll.)

6. Open the Kitchen Tool.WPD document, which should be the version of the memo that describes your kitchen tool that you saved in Step 2, with the spaces intact.

Writing Tools to Improve Your Spelling, Grammar, and Word Choice

Objectives for This Unit

✓ Checking your spelling

✓ Automatically correcting common mistakes

✓ Using the Thesaurus to improve word choice

✓ Checking grammar

Prerequisites

▶ Using dialog boxes (Lesson 2-1)

▶ Opening documents (Lesson 2-2)

▶ Application .101.WPD

on the CD

▶ History of Circuses.101.WPD

*O*ne reason many people switch from a typewriter to a computer is to take advantage of a computer's smarts so that their letters, memos, reports, and other documents look slicker and more professional. This unit is the one in which you learn how to take advantage of smart features of WordPerfect. WordPerfect can

▶ Check your spelling (even without you asking!).

▶ Automatically correct common mistakes as you type.

▶ List synonyms and antonyms of a word so that you can hone in on exactly the word that will get your point across.

▶ Check your grammar.

These tools are useful when finishing off your own document or editing someone else's document.

Notes:

You should always check the spelling in a document before you print it. WordPerfect 8 lets you choose between Spell-as-You-Go and the more conventional Spell Checker. Both work by comparing the words in your document against a dictionary that comes with WordPerfect. If a word in your document isn't in the WordPerfect dictionary, like someone's last name or the name of your town, WordPerfect flags the word as misspelled. In this unit, you learn how to add words to the WordPerfect dictionary so that WordPerfect doesn't keep stopping for perfectly spelled words.

An even cooler feature is QuickCorrect. QuickCorrect works for you whether you know it or not — so you may as well learn to get the full power of it. As you type, QuickCorrect is on the lookout for misspelled words. As soon as you type the space or punctuation following a misspelled word, WordPerfect corrects the misspelled word, without asking and without any further ado. You can control which words appear on the QuickCorrect list of misspelled words.

Many people don't use the other two features — the Thesaurus and Grammatik — very often, but *you* may. Learn to use them and then see if they're useful for the word processing work that you do.

Spell check, the Thesaurus, and Grammatik are all tabs on the Writing Tools dialog box, so when you're editing your document you can easily switch from one writing tool to another. As you start to use the Writing Tools dialog box, it will appear in one of two ways — it may replace half of the WordPerfect window, as in Figure 7-3, making the typing area smaller, or it may appear as a regular dialog box, as shown in Figure 7-5. You can move it from one to the other by clicking and dragging when the mouse pointer turns into a four-way arrow.

In addition to the Writing Tools dialog box, the Prompt-As-You-Go box, at the far right of the Properties bar, prompts you to correct your spelling or grammar, or offers you synonyms to the selected word, depending on where the cursor is.

Lesson 7-1   Checking Your Spelling

When you use WordPerfect to write your documents, you don't have to be able to spell perfectly, because the WordPerfect Spell Checker can check your words against its dictionary. You should be aware, however, that the speller can't check the context of a word — it may think that *there* looks fine when what you actually meant to type was *their*. The Spell Checker compares your words with words in its dictionary, which contains no definitions. The Spell Checker is very good at finding misspellings of common words, and can suggest to you what you actually meant to type. It can be tiresome, however, when you frequently use words that are not in the WordPerfect dictionary. Fortunately, you can add words to the dictionary to avoid that annoyance.

WordPerfect has two spell checkers that work off of the same dictionary. One checks spelling as you type, and the other you run after you are finished typing your document. We think Spell-As-You-Go is such a nifty feature that no one should ever need the regular Spell Checker again, but you may be annoyed by those little squiggly lines it places under words it considers misspelled. You may also decide that checking the spelling of your whole document at once is more efficient than taking the time to fix spelling one word at a time. What this boils down to is that checking spelling is so easy with WordPerfect that there's no excuse for having misspelled words in your documents. Here are your spell checking choices:

▶ Leave Spell-As-You-Go on. It should be on if you haven't turned it off. Each time you see a word with a squiggly red lines under it, right-click the word and choose the correct spelling, add it to the dictionary, or tell WordPerfect that using that spelling in this document (Skip in Document) is all right. If the correct spelling does not appear in the list, double-click the word to select it and type the correct spelling.

▶ Turn Spell-As-You-Go off, and instead use the Spell Checker after you've finished writing and editing your document. Click the Spell Check button to run the Spell Checker.

▶ Leave Spell-As-You-Go on, and also run the Spell Checker when you're finished writing and editing — that way, you can correct spelling as you write, and by using the Spell Checker you make sure you don't miss any misspelled words.

▶ Turn Spell-As-You-Go off, forget to use the Spell Checker, and let the world know that you are a word processing beginner (not a problem in itself, but probably not worth broadcasting, either).

Taking advantage of Spell-As-You-Go

Spell-As-You-Go is your authors' favorite WordPerfect feature. You can fix your spelling whenever you like, and you're unlikely to miss a misspelled word. Spell-As-You-Go allows you not only to fix the spelling of a misspelled word, but also to tell WordPerfect that a word is correctly spelled, either in general, or just for this document. Figure 7-1 shows the Spell-As-You-Go menu that you display by right-clicking a misspelled word. Here's how you can use the Spell-As-You-Go menu:

▶ Click the correctly spelled word to use it in place of the misspelled word in your document. After you do, the Spell-As-You-Go menu goes away.

▶ You may have the option of clicking the More choice to see more correctly spelled words.

▶ Add a word to the Spell Check dictionary. From then on, WordPerfect will not mark that word as misspelled.

▶ Skip in Document. WordPerfect will never mark this word misspelled in this document, although it will continue to mark it in other documents. (It adds the word to a supplementary dictionary that is attached to only the document that you are working on.)

Spell Check button

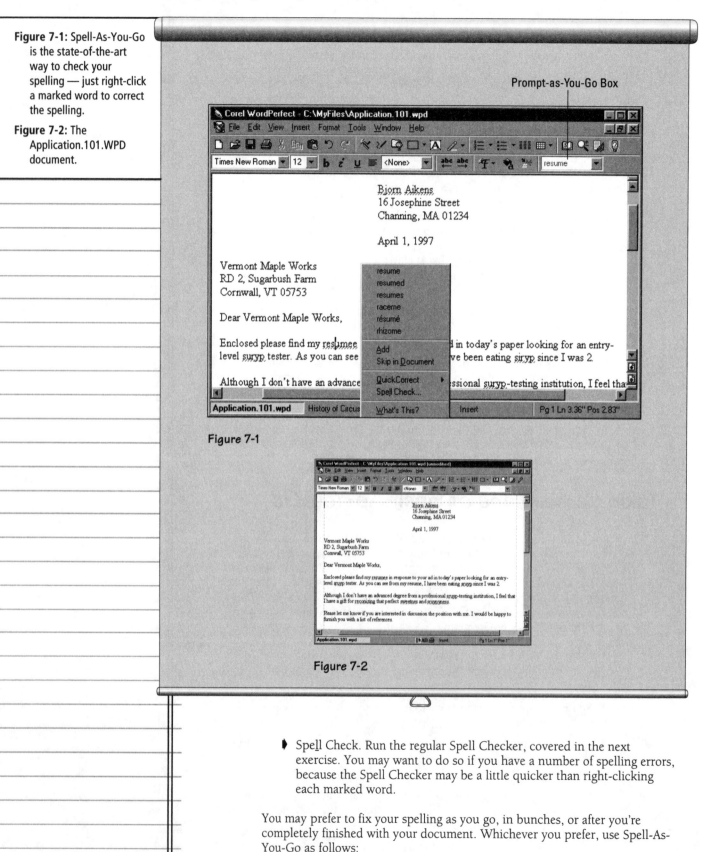

Prompt-as-You-Go Box

Figure 7-1

Figure 7-2

▶ Spell Check. Run the regular Spell Checker, covered in the next exercise. You may want to do so if you have a number of spelling errors, because the Spell Checker may be a little quicker than right-clicking each marked word.

You may prefer to fix your spelling as you go, in bunches, or after you're completely finished with your document. Whichever you prefer, use Spell-As-You-Go as follows:

on the CD

1 Make sure that Spell-As-You-Go is on.

Choose Tools⇨Proofread. If a bullet (a dot) appears next to the Spell-As-You-Go option, press Esc twice. If the bullet does not appear, choose Spell-As-You-Go to turn the feature on.

2 Open Application.101.WPD, a letter from Bjorn Aikens to the Vermont Maple Works applying for a job.

You see the letter in Figure 7-2.

3 Find the word resumee **with a squiggly red line under it.**

4 Move your mouse to resumee **and right-click the word.**

A small menu appears (refer to Figure 7-1) with alternative correct spellings to *resumee* at the top, and additional options at the bottom.

5 Choose one of the correct spellings. We prefer resume **without the accents, although the version with accents is also correct.**

WordPerfect replaces *resumee* with *resume* (or whichever spelling you chose). The squiggly red line under the word disappears.

6 Right-click Bjorn.

The Spell-As-You-Go menu appears.

You may not want this word in your permanent dictionary, but the spelling is correct in this context, and making the squiggly red line disappear would be nice.

7 Click Skip in Document.

WordPerfect removes the squiggly red line under *Bjorn*. If you use *Bjorn* in another document, WordPerfect will mark it as misspelled. If your name is Bjorn, you probably want to Add the word to the dictionary, because seeing it marked as misspelled may be a little demoralizing — it makes you feel like you don't really exist.

8 Close the document without saving changes.

You'll use this document again with the more conventional Spell Checker.

If you really don't like the Spell-As-You-Go feature, you can turn it off by choosing Tools⇨Proofread⇨Off from the menu. A bullet next to Spell-As-You-Go means the feature is turned on.

on the test

An alternative to right-clicking words marked as misspelled is to use the Prompt-As-You-Go box on the Property bar. When the cursor is in a misspelled word, a correctly spelled word appears in red in the Prompt-As-You-Go box. To correct the misspelled word, display the Prompt-As-You-Go drop-down list and choose the word you want to use.

Using the WordPerfect Spell Checker

If you prefer to do all your spell checking at once, use the Spell Checker. To run the Spell Checker:

Notes:

| resume ▼ |

Prompt-As-You-Go
box on the Property
bar

click Spell Check
button

Notes:

♦ Click the Spell Check button on the toolbar — the button that shows an open book with a red S on one page.

♦ Choose Tools ➪Spell Check from the menu.

♦ Press Ctrl+F1.

♦ Choose Spell Check from the Spell-As-You-Go menu.

WordPerfect displays the Spell Checker dialog box (as shown in Figure 7-3), finds the first word that it doesn't recognize, and waits for you to decide what to do with it. (Notice that you have access to Grammatik and Thesaurus through the tabs at the top of the dialog box.) Here are your options:

♦ The word is spelled wrong, but WordPerfect figured out the correct spelling. Click Replace to replace the misspelled word with the correct spelling.

♦ The word is spelled wrong, and WordPerfect guessed wrong about the correct spelling. Replace the misspelled word by selecting a word from the list of WordPerfect suggestions. Click the word you want and then click Replace. You can also double-click the replacement word, or you can replace the word by selecting the word in the Replace with box and typing the new word in its place. To get a larger list of possible spellings, click Suggest.

♦ The word is spelled right, but you want to see other instances of the same word. Skip the word this one time by clicking Skip Once. If WordPerfect finds the same word again, it will ask you what you want to do.

♦ The word is spelled right and should be ignored. Click Skip All to skip the word every time it's found during this running of the Spell Checker.

♦ The word is spelled right and should be added to the dictionary. If this is a word that you want to add to the dictionary, click the Add button at the bottom of the dialog box.

♦ You frequently misspell this word, and want it fixed automatically. If you frequently misspell a word, you can click Auto Replace, which adds the word to the list of words that WordPerfect automatically corrects as you type. (See Lesson 7-2, on QuickCorrect.)

on the CD

Check the spelling in Application.101.WPD again, this time using the Spell Checker.

1 **Open Application.101.WPD.**

Refer to Figure 7-2 for a look at the document.

2 **Start the Spell Checker by clicking the Spell Check button, pressing Ctrl+F1, or choosing Tools➪Spell Check from the menu.**

WordPerfect opens the Spell Checker dialog box. In the document, WordPerfect highlights the first word that it doesn't recognize, Bjorn's name. The Spell Checker dialog box indicates that WordPerfect didn't find this word in its dictionary. It suggests another spelling, *Born.*

Ctrl+F1 starts Spell
Checker

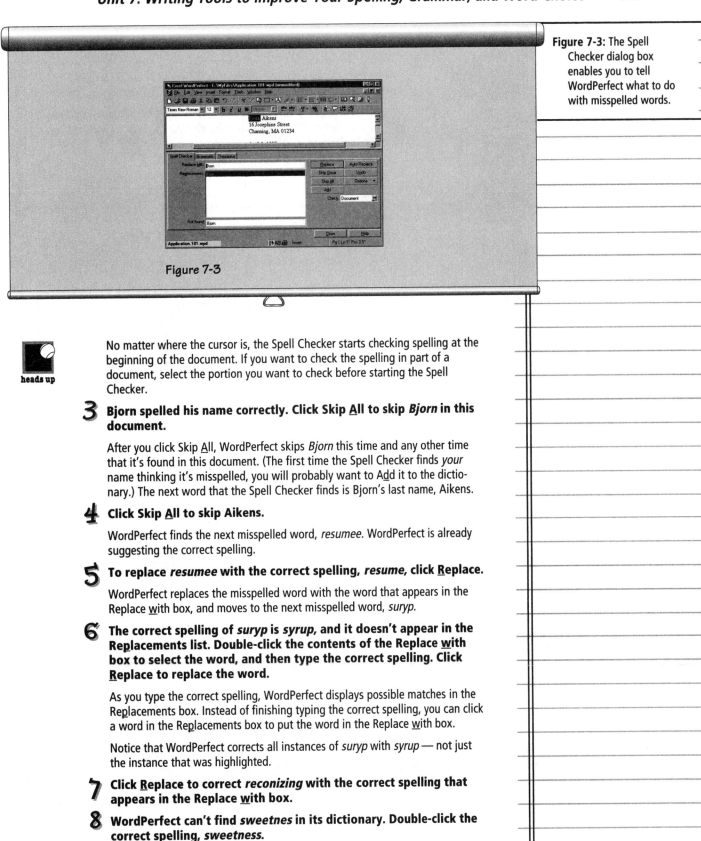

Figure 7-3

No matter where the cursor is, the Spell Checker starts checking spelling at the beginning of the document. If you want to check the spelling in part of a document, select the portion you want to check before starting the Spell Checker.

3 Bjorn spelled his name correctly. Click Skip All to skip *Bjorn* in this document.

After you click Skip All, WordPerfect skips *Bjorn* this time and any other time that it's found in this document. (The first time the Spell Checker finds *your* name thinking it's misspelled, you will probably want to Add it to the dictionary.) The next word that the Spell Checker finds is Bjorn's last name, Aikens.

4 Click Skip All to skip Aikens.

WordPerfect finds the next misspelled word, *resumee*. WordPerfect is already suggesting the correct spelling.

5 To replace *resumee* with the correct spelling, *resume*, click Replace.

WordPerfect replaces the misspelled word with the word that appears in the Replace with box, and moves to the next misspelled word, *suryp*.

6 The correct spelling of *suryp* is *syrup*, and it doesn't appear in the Replacements list. Double-click the contents of the Replace with box to select the word, and then type the correct spelling. Click Replace to replace the word.

As you type the correct spelling, WordPerfect displays possible matches in the Replacements box. Instead of finishing typing the correct spelling, you can click a word in the Replacements box to put the word in the Replace with box.

Notice that WordPerfect corrects all instances of *suryp* with *syrup* — not just the instance that was highlighted.

7 Click Replace to correct *reconizing* with the correct spelling that appears in the Replace with box.

8 WordPerfect can't find *sweetnes* in its dictionary. Double-click the correct spelling, *sweetness*.

on the test

You have to use the scroll bar to find the correct spelling. You can also click *sweetness* once and then click the Replace button, or simply double-click *sweetness*.

9   **WordPerfect can't find *surypness* in the dictionary, either. Type the word *syrupyness* in the Replace with box and click the Replace button.**

Even the correct spelling isn't in the dictionary.

extra credit

Adding and deleting words from the dictionary

You can add a word to the dictionary if you think you're likely to use it again. Just click the Add button in the Spell Checker dialog box or the Add option on the Spell-As-You-Go menu to add a word to the *supplemental dictionary* — that is, the list of words that are spelled correctly and that you don't want WordPerfect to flag as misspelled in any document.

You may find, however, that you're happily clicking along, adding words to the dictionary so that WordPerfect doesn't annoy you by stopping at perfectly spelled words, and then bang! You add a word that you didn't look at carefully and that was indeed misspelled. Now it's in the dictionary! What do you do?

When you add words, you're actually adding them to a supplementary dictionary, and that's where you need to delete them. Incidentally, this is the same dictionary from which QuickCorrect works. Following is how to edit additions to the dictionary:

1. **Run the Spell Checker.**

2. **Click the Options button on the Spell Checker tab of the Writing Tools dialog box. Choose User Word Lists from the drop-down menu.**

   The User Word List dialog box appears.

3. **Click the word list that you want to edit (probably WT80US.UWL, if it's not already highlighted) in the Word lists box.**

   The Word list contents box at the bottom now displays the words in that document in alphabetical order. Words beginning with symbols come before words beginning with letters.

   Notice that, instead of WT80US.UWL, you can pick the document word list to edit words that you have told WordPerfect to skip for the current document.

4. **Type the first few letters of the word you entered into the dictionary by mistake in the Word/Phrase box.**

   The word you are looking for should appear in the box below. You may want to use the scroll bar or the up and down arrow keys to find the misspelled word.

5. **Click the misspelled word, and then click Delete Entry.**

6. **Click Close to return to the Spell Checker dialog box.**

Notes:

10 Click the Skip **O**nce button to skip the word you just typed, syrupyness.

No, it's not in the dictionary, but you want to use it anyway.

WordPerfect can't find any more misspelled words and replies with, `Spell Check Completed. Close Spell Checker?`

11 Click the **Y**es button.

After the spell checking is complete, you don't need to keep the Spell Checker dialog box open. You can work around the dialog box, but it will probably get in your way.

12 Click the **C**lose button to close the Spell Checker dialog box at any time.

You're finished with this document for now, so go ahead and close it, using the File⇨Close command. Save it with the corrected spelling.

Recess

Now that you've checked the spelling in your document, you may want to rest for a spell. Save your document and then close WordPerfect by choosing File⇨Exit from the menu bar. Come back soon to find out how to tell WordPerfect to correct misspelled words as you type them!

☑ **Progress Check**

If you can do the following, you've mastered this lesson:

❑ Use Spell-As-You-Go to correct spelling.

❑ Use the Prompt-As-You-Go box to correct spelling.

❑ Use the more traditional Spell Checker to correct the spelling of words in your document.

❑ Add words to your dictionary that you use but that don't appear in the WordPerfect dictionary.

QuickCorrecting Mistakes Automagically

Lesson 7-2

QuickCorrect is one of WordPerfect's snazziest features. It's a wonderful feature but, like anything automatic, can be annoying if you don't know how to make it do what you want.

QuickCorrect automagically corrects spelling errors and typos as you type. For example, if you type two capital letters at the beginning of a word, QuickCorrect makes the second letter lowercase. If you tell it to, QuickCorrect automatically expands abbreviations to full words. For example, if you've added the abbreviation VMW (for Vermont Maple Works) to QuickCorrect, whenever you type *VMW*, QuickCorrect can change it to *Vermont Maple Works*. QuickCorrect can also insert typographical or other symbols into your document so you don't have to use WordPerfect commands each time.

on the test

QuickCorrect is similar to the WordPerfect Spell Checker because it corrects mistakes, but with one big difference: Spell Checker only fixes things when you tell it to, whereas QuickCorrect works any time that you're typing. Here's how QuickCorrect works: As soon as you type the space or punctuation after a word, QuickCorrect checks whether the word is on its list of misspelled words and abbreviations. If the word you typed appears on its list, QuickCorrect replaces it with the correctly spelled word or the unabbreviated version.

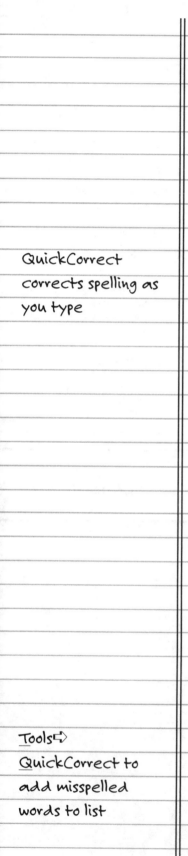

QuickCorrect corrects spelling as you type

heads up

QuickCorrect does not correct anything you haven't typed — typing a space or punctuation is what makes QuickCorrect kick in, so if you don't type a space or punctuation after the word, no automatic correction takes place.

WordPerfect comes with a list of commonly misspelled words already entered into the QuickCorrect list, along with the correctly spelled versions of each. You can add your own entries to the QuickCorrect list, including words that you frequently misspell and abbreviations that you want QuickCorrect to spell out.

QuickCorrect at work

When QuickCorrect works, it works silently and efficiently. Test it out in a new, blank document:

1   Close all the documents so that you see a new, blank document.

Adventurous readers, you can click the New Document button instead to create a new, blank document without closing the other document(s) that you're using.

2   Type the following sentence exactly as it appears here:

```
teh wierd aquaintance has asma, as was aparent on
            that ocasion in febuary.
```

As you type, QuickCorrect puts a capital letter on the beginning of the sentence and corrects the spelling of every incorrect word. However, it also has limitations.

3   Type the following sentence exactly as it appears here:

```
hte strang man she's engagd to siezed the oportunity
        to return when she greived about loseing him.
```

Although WordPerfect marks all the misspelled words, it only manages to make one correction: It puts a capital on the beginning of this sentence. QuickCorrect knows how to correct *sieze* and *greive*, but not when they're in the past tense. The other misspellings are simply not in the QuickCorrect list.

All you need to do is type and make errors that QuickCorrect knows about — WordPerfect fixes those errors automatically as you type.

Making QuickCorrect work for you

QuickCorrect doesn't always correct errors that you think it should. Fortunately, you can add your favorite typos to the list so that QuickCorrect knows how to fix those, too. QuickCorrect runs whenever WordPerfect runs, so any changes that you make to the QuickCorrect word list apply to any document that you create.

Tools⇨ QuickCorrect to add misspelled words to list

Add a typo to the QuickCorrect list of words to correct by following these steps:

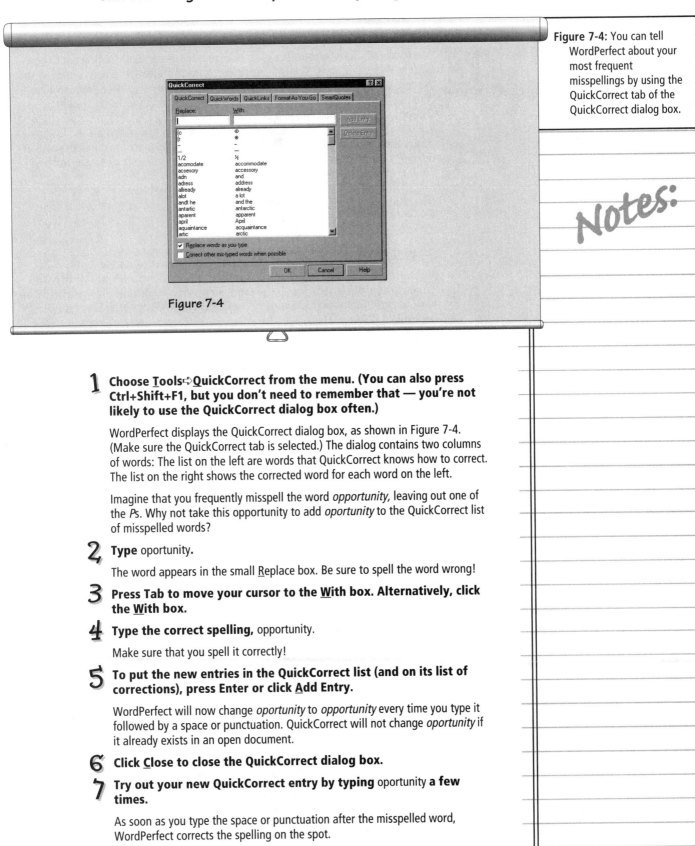

Figure 7-4

Figure 7-4: You can tell WordPerfect about your most frequent misspellings by using the QuickCorrect tab of the QuickCorrect dialog box.

Notes:

1 **Choose Tools⇨QuickCorrect from the menu. (You can also press Ctrl+Shift+F1, but you don't need to remember that — you're not likely to use the QuickCorrect dialog box often.)**

WordPerfect displays the QuickCorrect dialog box, as shown in Figure 7-4. (Make sure the QuickCorrect tab is selected.) The dialog contains two columns of words: The list on the left are words that QuickCorrect knows how to correct. The list on the right shows the corrected word for each word on the left.

Imagine that you frequently misspell the word *opportunity,* leaving out one of the *P*s. Why not take this opportunity to add *oportunity* to the QuickCorrect list of misspelled words?

2 **Type** oportunity.

The word appears in the small Replace box. Be sure to spell the word wrong!

3 **Press Tab to move your cursor to the With box. Alternatively, click the With box.**

4 **Type the correct spelling,** opportunity.

Make sure that you spell it correctly!

5 **To put the new entries in the QuickCorrect list (and on its list of corrections), press Enter or click Add Entry.**

WordPerfect will now change *oportunity* to *opportunity* every time you type it followed by a space or punctuation. QuickCorrect will not change *oportunity* if it already exists in an open document.

6 **Click Close to close the QuickCorrect dialog box.**

7 **Try out your new QuickCorrect entry by typing** oportunity **a few times.**

As soon as you type the space or punctuation after the misspelled word, WordPerfect corrects the spelling on the spot.

on the test

You can add a new item to the QuickCorrect list — or just check what's there already — by choosing Tools➪QuickCorrect and putting the new words in the Replace and With boxes. You can also delete items by selecting them and clicking Delete Entry, or change the way QuickCorrect works by clicking Options. Options that you can change include telling QuickCorrect whether or not to capitalize the first letter of a sentence, correct a word when the first two letters are capitals, change a double space to a single space, make the spaces at the end of sentences consistent, and change the appearance of single and double quotes.

Now you know how to customize WordPerfect to respond to the typos that you tend to make. QuickCorrect is an easy way to save editing time — typos disappear before you can correct them.

While you're at it, you can also add abbreviations that you'd like to use while typing so that QuickCorrect automatically replaces them with full words. You can create abbreviations for all the long, awkward words and phrases that you have to type, including company names, addresses, phone numbers, and long boilerplate phrases. Using QuickCorrect for your own abbreviations is a great time-saver!

When you add an abbreviation to the QuickCorrect list, make sure that you will use the abbreviation only as an abbreviation. Otherwise, QuickCorrect will replace it with the word you specified. For example, suppose that you decide to abbreviate *maple syrup* as *ms*; when you type *MS* as an abbreviation for *Mississippi* in an address, QuickCorrect replaces it with *MAPLE SYRUP* (QuickCorrect matches your capitalization)! So choose a more obscure abbreviation that you want WordPerfect to replace. Add an abbreviation and the full word(s) that you want to replace it with to the QuickCorrect list the same way you add a frequent typo and its correct spelling.

Note: To turn QuickCorrect off, display the QuickCorrect dialog box and click the Replace words as you type choice, so that a check mark appears. You may want to leave QuickCorrect running all the time because it's so helpful. If you just occasionally don't want the correction QuickCorrect made, you don't have to turn off the feature — to correct a correction, cursor back and edit the word; then don't type a space or punctuation at the end of the word. QuickCorrect won't kick in and make changes.

You're finished with the silly sentences that you used to test QuickCorrect. Close the document without saving it. Don't worry: WordPerfect will remember the changes that you made in the QuickCorrect dialog box.

QuickCorrect can replace abbreviation with what it stands for

☑ **Progress Check**

If you can do the following, you've mastered this lesson:

❑ Let WordPerfect automagiclly correct typos and misspellings as you type.

❑ Add a misspelled word to the QuickCorrect list.

❑ Create an abbreviation that QuickCorrect automatically spells out.

Finding Just the Right Word

The Thesaurus — sounds like a dinosaur, doesn't it? "The mighty Thesaurus lumbered across the Jurassic plains." Well, the Thesaurus in book form is becoming a dinosaur, as it is replaced by the online Thesaurus. The WordPerfect Thesaurus is a great online (that means that you don't have to go to your bookshelf) reference to use when you can't quite think of the word you want. You tell WordPerfect a word, and it suggests other words that have similar meanings.

To run the WordPerfect Thesaurus:

▶ Choose Tools⇨Thesaurus from the menu.

▶ Press Alt+F1.

▶ Click the Thesaurus tab on the Writing Tools dialog box (that's the dialog box you see when you're using the Spell Checker, Grammatik, or the Thesaurus — sometimes you can't see its name).

on the test

Or you can check out the Prompt-As-You-Go box on the Property bar. When the cursor is in a correctly spelled word, the Prompt-As-You-Go box displays a synonym for the word. Click the arrow to see more synonyms. Click a word from the Prompt-As-You-Go drop-down list to replace the word the cursor is in with the word from the drop-down list.

on the CD

Give it a try using the Application.101.WPD document. Open the document now.

1 Select the word gift **in the second paragraph.**

You can move your cursor there with the mouse or cursor keys, or you can choose Edit⇨Find and Replace to find the word.

2 Run the mighty Thesaurus by choosing Tools⇨Thesaurus from the menu bar or pressing Alt+F1.

The Thesaurus dialog box opens (see Figure 7-5), and options for replacing *gift* are listed. You have to use the scroll bar to see them all — they go on and on!

Hmmm . . . . None of the words you can see at first looks right. *Accomplishment* may be a move in the right direction — so you want to find other words like *accomplishment.*

3 To find synonyms for accomplishment, **double-click the word, or click it once and then click Look Up.**

Synonyms for *accomplishment* appear. A list of antonyms (words that mean the opposite) appears at the bottom of the list of synonyms.

As you may guess, you can go on like this for a while, double-clicking words to see their synonyms.

Alt+F1 for
Thesaurus

Thesaurus shows
synonyms for
selected word

Figure 7-5: The WordPerfect Thesaurus helps you find just the right word.

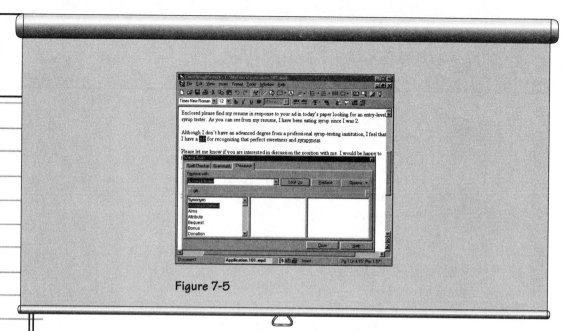

Figure 7-5

Progress Check

If you can do the following, you've mastered this lesson:

❑ Find synonyms for a selected word.

❑ Replace a word with a synonym.

4 Continue to explore the synonyms available. After you find the word that you want to use (we like *talent*), click the word to put it in the Insert box, and then click Insert to replace the selected word in the text.

Or if you decide that your word choice was fine after all, click Close to close the Thesaurus and keep the selected word *(gift)* as is.

heads up

The Prompt-As-You-Go box is another way to find a synonym — if the word the cursor is in in the Prompt-As-You-Go box shows synonyms rather than correct spellings. Click the box to see the list; select a word to replace the word the cursor is in with the word on the list. Although you can use Prompt-As-You-Go to find synonyms, the Thesaurus offers you many more options.

Lesson 7-4

Checking Your Grammar with Grammatik

on the test

Grammatik is a grammar program that comes with WordPerfect. It's not as good as Sheila, who occasionally edits our stuff before the IDG people do, but it gives you a way to review your document for common grammatical errors. Computers are smart, but they can only do what they're told. Grammatik follows certain rules for judging grammar that can be changed to suit your style, but it doesn't catch every error.

You run Grammatik (display the Grammatik dialog box) by

▶ Choosing Tools⇨Grammatik from the menu

▶ Pressing Alt+Shift+F1

▶ Clicking the Grammatik tab on the Writing Tools dialog box

At the bottom of the Grammatik dialog box, the Checking Style box lets you tell Grammatik what type of document you're checking. If you tell Grammatik that you're writing a formal memo or letter, it applies higher standards than if you are doing a quick grammar check on a more casual document.

Using Grammatik

Find out what Grammatik thinks of the grammar in Application.101.WPD, the cover letter you saw back in Figure 7-2. If you just finished Lesson 7-3, it should still be open.

1 Move to the beginning of the document.

Press Ctrl+Home — but you knew that, right?

2 Run Grammatik by choosing Tools⇨Grammatik from the menu or pressing Alt+Shift+F1.

The Grammatik dialog box opens, as shown in Figure 7-6, and presents you with the first problem that it finds.

You can decide how Grammatik should check your document. Click the Options button and select Checking style. The style chosen is probably Quick Check. Notice you can choose the checking style that matches the formality of the document you're creating. If you want to know which rules Grammatik is applying for a given style, click the style name, and then click the Edit button on the Checking Styles dialog box. You can turn a rule on or off by clicking the check box next to the rule name to toggle the check mark on or off.

3 The first problem Grammatik finds is the use of the numeral *2*. Grammatik suggests replacing *2* with *two*, and explains why at the bottom of the dialog box. Click Replace to accept Grammatik's changes.

The next problem Grammatik finds is a word that is not in the dictionary: *syrupyness.*

4 You may want to replace this word if you can think of a better one. You can edit the sentence in the document, or you can click Skip Once to skip the problem.

If you correct the problem in the document, you'll need to click the Resume button on the Writing Tools dialog box to continue the grammar check.

5 The last error Grammatik finds is a misused word. It's really a typo that is a correctly spelled word. To fix the problem, click in your document and replace discussion **with** discussing.

Grammatik lets you work in your document if you need to. After you're finished, click the Resume button.

6 Click the Resume button.

Grammatik finds no more grammar problems and displays a dialog box asking if you want to close Grammatik.

7 Click Yes to close Grammatik.

The Grammatik dialog box fades gently into the mist. (Wordy. Consider simplifying.)

Notes:

Tools→Grammatik to start Grammatik

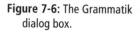

Figure 7-6: The Grammatik
dialog box.

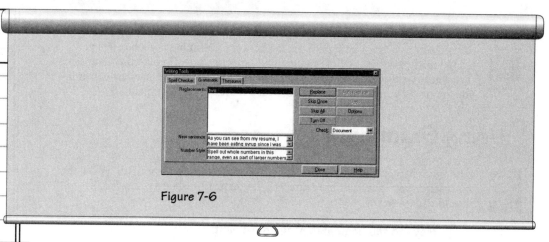

Figure 7-6

8 **Save your changes, and then close the document.**

Grammatik is an easy way to edit your document — you may not always agree
with its suggestions, but it may give you ideas of how to improve your text.
Just remember: It's only a mindless electronic editor, but it's easily better than
nothing!

Recess

Because you've already closed the document that you were using, just close
WordPerfect unless you have real work to do. Otherwise, go ahead and try the
quiz.

Unit 7 Quiz

For each of the following questions, circle the letter of the correct answer or
answers. Remember, we may have included more than one right answer for
each question!

 1. After you click this button, WordPerfect...

A. Types a small red *s* in your document.

B. Types a small red check mark in your document.

C. Checks the spelling of your document or, if text is selected, of the
selected text.

D. Compares each word in your document with the list of words in its
dictionary.

E. Displays the Spell Checker dialog box.

2. **When the WordPerfect Spell Checker finds a word that is misspelled, you can...**

    A. Choose the correctly spelled word from the list of suggestions and click <u>R</u>eplace.

    B. Double-click the correctly spelled word in the list of suggestions.

    C. Click the <u>S</u>uggest button to see other possible spellings.

    D. Type the correct spelling in the Replace <u>w</u>ith box and click <u>R</u>eplace.

    E. Click the <u>C</u>lose button to forget about the whole idea of checking your spelling. Eat lunch instead.

3. **If WordPerfect thinks a word is spelled wrong but it's not, you can...**

    A. Click Skip <u>O</u>nce to ignore this word this one time. If WordPerfect finds the same word later in the document, it complains about it again.

    B. Click Skip <u>A</u>ll to skip this word for the rest of the document. WordPerfect ignores the word for the rest of this session with the Spell Checker.

    C. Click the A<u>d</u>d button to add this word to the dictionary so that WordPerfect considers it to be a correctly spelled word from now on.

    D. Click the A<u>u</u>toReplace button to add the misspelled word and the suggested correction in the Replace <u>w</u>ith box to the QuickCorrect list of misspelled words.

    E. Jump up and down and yell at WordPerfect because it's not as smart as it thinks it is.

4. **The WordPerfect Thesaurus . . .**

    A. Suggests words that have the same or similar meanings to the word that you select.

    B. Suggests words that mean the opposite of the word that you select.

    C. Suggests the kinds of words that your sixth-grade English teacher used to use.

    D. Suggests words that will make your document sound impressive and erudite.

    E. Suggests a dinosaur that would be appropriate to mention in your document.

5. **In the classic song "Let's Call the Whole Thing Off," the two people pronounce the following words differently:**

    A. Tomato.

    B. Potato.

    C. Either.

    D. Aunt.

    E. Neither.

Notes:

6. **The purpose of Grammatik is to...**

   A. Make you wish that you had done your English homework during high school.

   B. Fix grammatical errors in your document.

   C. Find incorrect or awkward wording and replace it with better word choices.

   D. Get rid of wording that will make people roll their eyes when they read your document.

   E. Simulate your Grandma.

Unit 7 Exercise

on the CD

1. Open the document History of Circuses.101.WPD.

2. Fix any spelling errors, assuming that names are spelled correctly.

3. Find a better word for *scintillating*.

4. Run Grammatik to check grammar in the document.

5. Save the improved document with the same name.

Part II Review

Unit 5 Summary

‣ **Selecting text:** Select text by painting it with the mouse (clicking and dragging), by using the Shift key with the cursor movement keys, or by using the mouse button to click on the text or in the margin.

‣ **Deleting text:** Delete a bunch of text by selecting it and pressing Delete.

‣ **Undo Command:** Undo what you just did by pressing Ctrl+Z or choosing Edit⇨Undo from the menu bar.

‣ **Copying text:** Copy text to the Clipboard by selecting it and pressing Ctrl+C, or clicking on the Copy button on the toolbar. Copy text from the toolbar to the point where the cursor is by pressing Ctrl+V, or clicking on the Paste button on the toolbar. Alternatively, select the text and then hold down the Ctrl key while clicking on it and dragging it to its new position.

‣ **Moving text:** Move text by selecting it, cutting it to the Clipboard by pressing Ctrl+X, or clicking on the Cut button on the toolbar. Insert text in its new position by moving the cursor to that position and pressing Ctrl+V, or clicking on the Paste button on the toolbar. Alternatively, select the text, then click on it, and drag it to its new position.

Unit 6 Summary

‣ **Searching for words or phrases:** Press F2 to search for a word or phrase (by using the Find and Replace Text dialog box).

‣ **Continue searching:** Click on Find Next to continue the search.

‣ **Searching for whole words:** Use the Match⇨ Whole Word option from the dialog box menu when you are looking only for a whole word, and not for a portion of a word.

‣ **Replacing words or phrases:** Use the Replace All button when you want to replace all instances of the word or phrase in the Find box with the word or phrase in the Replace With box. Always save your document before doing a global search and replace.

Unit 7 Summary

‣ **Correcting spelling:** Right-click on a word with a squiggly red line under it to correct its spelling using Spell-As-You-Go.

‣ **Using Spell Check:** Click on the Spell Check button on the Toolbar or choose Tools⇨Spell Check to check the spelling of a document using Spell Check.

‣ **Adding words to the dictionary:** Use the Add button on the Spell Checker tab of the Writing Tools dialog box or the Add option on the Spell-As-You-Go menu to add words you frequently use to the WordPerfect dictionary.

‣ **QuickCorrect:** Add commonly misspelled words and abbreviations for commonly used words or phrases to QuickCorrect. Display the QuickCorrect dialog box by choosing Tools⇨QuickCorrect from the menu.

‣ **Thesaurus:** Use the Thesaurus to find a better word: Select a word and choose Tools⇨ Thesaurus to let the WordPerfect Thesaurus suggest alternative words.

‣ **Grammatik:** Use Grammatik to check your grammar when you don't have an editor in the family: Click on the Grammatik button on the Toolbar or choose Tools⇨Grammatik from the menu bar.

Part II Test

The questions on this test cover all of the material presented in Parts I and II, Units 1-8.

True False

T   F   1. QuickCorrect can be used to expand abbreviations.

T   F   2. There is only one way to select text.

T   F   3. The WordPerfect Grammatik feature helps make your writing more like Stephen King's.

T   F   4. The Edit⇨Find and Replace command can be used to remove all the spaces from your document.

T   F   5. Mister Rogers is a Presbyterian minister.

T   F   6. Spell-checking your doumnets is a good idea.

T   F   7. You can move text by selecting it and using the mouse to drag it to its new position.

T   F   8. The Clipboard is where Windows stores your grocery list.

T   F   9. You can use the WordPerfect search feature to find your car keys.

T   F   10. If WordPerfect doesn't know how to spell a word, you can add it to the dictionary.

Multiple Choice

For each of the following questions, circle the correct answer or answers. Remember, there may be more than one right answer for each question!

11. **What's the default document directory?**

A. The directory where WordPerfect stores documents, unless you change to a different directory.

B. C:\ MyFiles.

C. Where the bank looks when WordPerfect defaults on a loan.

D. Whatever you want it to be.

E. WordPerfect\Default\Directory.

12. **How do you copy some text from one part of your document to another?**

A. Select the text, hold down the Ctrl key, and drag the text to the new location.

B. Select the text, press Ctrl+C, move the cursor to the new location, and press Ctrl+V.

C. Print the document and photocopy the section that needs to be copied and cut and paste the document to look like you want it to.

D. Select the text, click on the Copy button on the toolbar, move the cursor to the new location, and click on the Paste button on the toolbar.

E. Click your heels three times and wish for a tornado to move the text to the new location.

13. **What does K.I.S.S. stand for?**

A. Kill Innocent Single Snakes.

B. Keep It Simple, Stupid.

C. What do you mean, "stand for"? Isn't "kiss" a word?

D. Keep It Simple, Smarty.

E. Korea, Indonesia, Samoa, and Singapore.

14. **What does Ctrl+X do?**

A. The same thing as the Cut button on the toolbar.

B. Erases the selected text and stores it on the Windows Clipboard for later use.

C. Capitalizes the text.

D. Replaces all the characters in the document with Xs.

E. Displays an episode of *The X-Files*.

15. **QuickCorrect makes a correction (if the word you typed is in its list)**

A. When you type a period after the incorrect word.

B. When you type a space after the incorrect word.

C. When you open a WordPerfect document.

D. Any time you make a spelling error while using Windows.

E. When you hit Enter after an incorrect word.

Part II Test

16. **When the WordPerfect spelling checker finds a word it doesn't know, what can you do?**

    A. Add it to the dictionary.
    B. Replace it with a correctly spelled word.
    C. Skip it just this once.
    D. Skip it whenever it occurs, but just in this document.
    E. Burst into tears.

17. **Which of the following things can the WordPerfect Edit⇨Find and Replace command do?**

    A. Replace your kids with kids who clean up the house and set the table without being asked.
    B. Replace one whole word with another whole word.
    C. Replace all the incorrectly spelled words with correctly spelled words.

    D. Replace a word or phrase with another word or phrase.
    E. Replace all the spaces in your document with question marks. (But save the document first!)

18. **Which aren't actually as bad as they sound?**

    A. English muffins with strawberry jam and cheddar cheese (melt the cheese).
    B. Lentils.
    C. Black beans, especially in feijoada, the Brazilian national dish.
    D. Cottage cheese and ketchup. (President Nixon was reported to have loved it.)
    E. Checking grammar in your WordPerfect documents.

Matching

19. **Match the following toolbar buttons with the corresponding commands:**

    A.   1. Edit⇨Copy

    B.   2. Edit⇨Paste

    C.   3. Edit⇨Undo

    D.   4. Edit⇨Cut

    E.   5. Tools⇨Spell Check

20. **Match the descriptions with the buttons on the toolbar:**

    A. Displays the Print dialog box   1.

    B. Inserts the information from the Clipboard at the cursor   2.

    C. Displays the Open File dialog box   3.

    D. Copies the selected text to the Clipboard   4. [icon]

    E. Checks the spelling in the document   5. [icon]

21. **Match the following keyboard shortcuts with the corresponding feature.**

    A. Ctrl+X   1. Save
    B. Ctrl+S   2. Cut
    C. Ctrl+V   3. Undo
    D. Ctrl+C   4. Paste
    E. Ctrl+Z   5. Copy

22. **Match the following characters with their TV shows:**

    A. Mulder   1. *The Simpsons*
    B. Mark Green   2. *The X-Files*
    C. Capt. Janeway   3. *Sesame Street*
    D. Bart   4. *Star Trek: Voyager*
    E. Oscar   5. *ER*

Part II Lab Assignment

Vermont Maple Works is branching out — they've decided that a stuffed animal mascot would be a good addition to their product line. In this assignment, you will write instructions for the design criteria for stuffed animals to be manufactured for Vermont Maple Works.

Step 1: Write the first draft

Starting with a blank document, write instructions for how to design teddy bears. Mention size, color, accessories, and facial expression.

Vermont Maple Works
Design Criteria for Teddy Bears

1. Teddy bears should be no more than three feet (36 inches) high, so they won't be too scary for small children.

2. Teddy bear colors are limited to white, brown, and pastels, so they look cheery.

3. Teddy bears may come with accessories, such as clothing, hats, bags, flags, etc. Attached accessories must be washable. Detachable accessories do not have to be washable. All accessories that come with Teddy bears should be safe for children aged three and under (nothing that can be swallowed, such as buttons).

4. Teddy bear facial expressions must be pleasant or blank. No ferocious Teddy bears, please!

5. Teddy bears should look well-fed without appearing obese. We are going for the "pleasantly plump" look.

Save the document as Teddy Bears.WPD.

Step 2: Change the subject of the document

Oops! You were *supposed* to write about design criteria for toy dinosaurs — the Maple Monster! Now they tell you! No problem — use the WordPerfect search-and-replace feature to change all the references to teddy bears to references to dinosaurs. Proofread the document after making the replacements to make sure that it still makes sense. Some adjustments may be needed.

Step 3: Switch the order of the topics

Move point 5 up to come after point 2, and renumber the points.

Step 4: Check your spelling

Spell check the document and save it again.

Adding Pizzazz

Part III

In this part . . .

We know you've been waiting anxiously to learn about the features in WordPerfect that will make you look like a real word processing pro. This part teaches you how to format your characters, paragraphs, pages, and even shows you how to untangle formatting mishaps.

Using a powerful word processor such as WordPerfect to produce documents that look like they could have been produced on a typewriter would be a shame. After all, WordPerfect makes controlling the fonts, spacing, centering, and justification of the text in your document easy. When you follow the lessons in this part of the book, you'll learn how to use boldface, italics, and different fonts to jazz up your characters, centering and indenting to jazz up your paragraphs, and headers and page formatting to jazz up your pages.

Formatting Fancy Characters

Objectives for This Unit

✓ Adding bold, italics, and underline to text that you've already typed

✓ Making text that you're about to type bold, italic, and underlined

✓ Changing the font and font size of text

✓ Capitalizing and decapitalizing (not to be confused with decapitating) chunks of text

✓ Copying nice-looking character formatting to less attractive text

Prerequisites

◗ Opening an existing document (Lesson 2-2)

◗ Selecting text (Lesson 5-1)

on the CD

◗ GTK Sample Products.101.WPD

◗ GTK Sample Products2.101.WPD

◗ GTK Sample Products3.101.WPD

You know how other people with word processors can do neat stuff with their characters? (We're not talking about character development, like having a better sense of humor or becoming more outgoing.) Some folks can spruce up their writing by making characters italic or bold, using different fonts and characters of different sizes — in short, their documents look pretty snazzy.

This part of the book shows you how to add some pizzazz to your documents. What's the point in using a powerful word processor like WordPerfect if your documents end up looking as if you typed them on an Underwood typewriter? You learn about using lots of different size and shapes for the characters in the document, as well as how to center text, make hanging indents, fool around with margins, and stick things in the margins (like page numbers, headers, and footers).

Notes:

We want to warn you, though, about using these new skills to excess — formatting should enhance the meaning of the text, not overwhelm it. *No one likes* to **read text** that has been ***overly formatted***!

You'll use the Property bar to format text. The Property bar appears immediately below the toolbar. The Property bar displays different *controls* (controls are options on a toolbar or dialog box) depending on what you are doing. When the cursor is in a table, for instance, you see different buttons than when text is selected. (You'll learn about tables in Unit 12.) The Property bar shows the controls that are displayed when the cursor is in regular text (not a table, for instance) and when text is selected. You'll be using the first five controls to format text in this unit.

Starting with this unit, the documents you work on will have to do with a company called Great Tapes for Kids. In this unit, you work on making the list of products for GTK look more appealing. We give you the text, and you do the formatting.

Lesson 8-1

Basic Formatting: Bold, Italics, and Underline

Bold button

Italics button

Underline button

The first kind of formatting we cover is what WordPerfect calls *text styles*, otherwise known as making text bold, italic, or underlined. The good news is that these are the easiest of formatting tricks. Why? Because WordPerfect gives you easy-to-use buttons on the toolbar for each text style. All you need to do is select the text and click the relevant button. Or, if you have a button phobia, you can use Ctrl+B, Ctrl+I, or Ctrl+U (nice mnemonic keystrokes for a change) to make text **bold**, *italic*, or <u>underlined</u>, respectively. If you're not confident about selecting text, have another look at Unit 5 to refresh your memory.

on the test

WordPerfect has two ways to make text bold, italic, or underlined, using either the toolbar buttons or the keyboard:

- ◆ If you haven't typed the text yet that you want to format, click the toolbar button or press the keys to turn on bold, italics, or underlining, and then type the text. Click the toolbar button or press the keys to turn the formatting off again.

- ◆ If you've already typed the text that you want to format, select the text and then click the toolbar button or press the keys to format it. After the text is selected, you can go on formatting it by clicking yet another button or using the keystroke command.

- ◆ If you decide that having your text bold, italic, or underlined obscures what you're trying to say, just select the text and click one of the three buttons again, or give the keystroke command again, to undo the formatting.

Formatting text you've already typed

on the CD

The document GTK Sample Products.101.WPD contains a sample of the product list for Great Tapes for Kids. You can make the document look more interesting by using bold to make the important stuff stick out, and then by experimenting with italics and underline. In the process, you learn to undo text style formatting.

1 Open the document GTK Sample Products.101.WPD.

The text is pretty good, but the document looks pretty boring. No one is going to get excited by the appearance of this list. You can make the document clearer by adding some formatting — after you've added some formatting, GTK Sample Products.101.WPD will look like Figure 8-1.

2 Select the fourth heading, *A little pig goes a long way*.

You can select it by using the mouse or the keyboard. Refer to Unit 5 for ways to select text.

3 Click the Bold button on the toolbar.

Take a look at the Bold button on the toolbar. The button appears pushed in when the cursor is in the bold text. The line is now . . . boldified? boldfacized? The characters look darker. To see what the text looks like when bold text is not selected, click once somewhere else in the document.

4 Now select the first line of the document, *Great Tapes for Kids — Product List*.

5 Click the Underline button on the toolbar.

The first line of the letter is underlined.

6 With the first line of the letter still selected, click the Italic button on the toolbar.

Hmm . . . It doesn't look very good that way. Time to undo it.

7 While the text is still selected, undo the italics by clicking the Italic button again.

Voilà! Back to just underlined text.

8 Select the word *Babe* in the first sentence of the description, and then italicize it.

Using these three types of formatting is as simple as selecting and clicking a button.

Formatting as you type

You can also tell WordPerfect how you want text to look before you type it. Click the appropriate text style button — or use the text style shortcut keys — before you start typing. After you're finished typing, turn the text style off in the same way. Try it:

Figure 8-2: The GTK Sample Products.101.WPD document the way it will look in a few exercises!

Notes:

Property bar ⌐

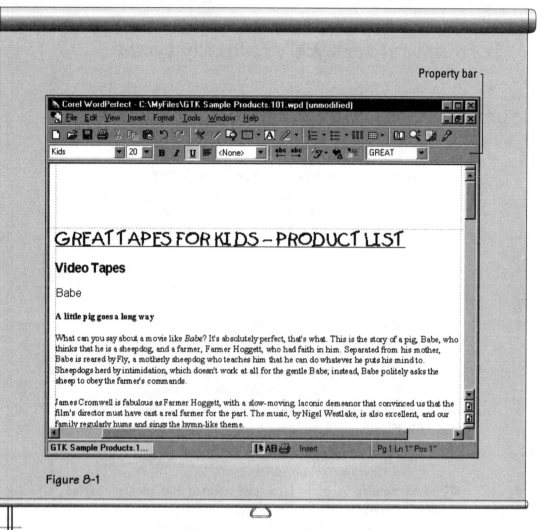

Figure 8-1

Ctrl+B turns boldface on/off

Ctrl+I turns italics on/off

Ctrl+U turns underline on/off

1 **Put your cursor at the end of the first line, *Great Tapes for Kids — Product List* heading and press Enter twice.**

You're going to add a subtitle.

2 **Press Ctrl+B or click the Bold button on the toolbar.**

Now any text you type is bold. The Bold button on the toolbar is pushed in.

3 **Type** *Video Tapes.*

The text appears in bold.

4 **Press Ctrl+B or click the Bold button again to turn bold off.**

The Bold button on the toolbar pops back out — that is, it doesn't look like it's pushed in. Now whatever you type won't be in bold.

5 **Press Ctrl+S to save your document, just in case the cat knocks your coffee onto your computer keyboard and shorts it out.**

If you prefer to format as you type, you can turn a text style on before you type, using Ctrl+B, Ctrl+I, or Ctrl+U, or by clicking buttons on the toolbar.

Note: You don't need to turn formatting off if you aren't going to type anything else where the cursor is. For example, if you turn on the underline text format, type underlined text, then move the cursor to another location in the document and start typing again, the underline text format isn't turned on at your new location (unless the text at the new location is also formatted with underlining). You can always tell whether bold, italics, or underline is turned on by looking at the buttons on the toolbar: If they look pushed in, that text format is turned on.

☑ Progress Check

If you can do the following, you've mastered this lesson:

- ❏ Format text that has already been typed.

- ❏ Format text as you type, using bold, italics, and underline.

- ❏ Remove italics, bold, and underline from formatted text.

Choosing Fonts and Font Sizes

Lesson 8-2

So what is a *font,* anyway? A font is a set of shapes for letters, numbers, and punctuation. In the old days, just a few fonts existed, with names like Times Roman, Courier, Prestige, and Elite. These days, if our computers are anything to go by, fonts are on a mission to take over the world. In fact, people have jobs thinking up new fonts!

Fonts are often broken down into two major categories: ones that have little thingies called *serifs* off the main strokes of the letters, and plainer ones (called *sans serif*) without the thingies. Serifs are the tiny flourishes that you probably don't use when you print, but you might add if you were doing calligraphy. You may need to brush up on your French to remember these names (*sans* means "without"). We can explain it better by example: The type that you're reading right now is a serif font, and the extra credit text, in the sidebars, is a sans serif font.

A font is a set of character shapes

Usually WordPerfect automatically uses a serif font called Times Roman (or a variation on that name, such as Times New Roman or Tms Roman) unless you tell it to use another font. Common sans serif fonts are Helvetica, Swiss, and Arial. Sans serif fonts are a good choice for headings in a document that uses Times Roman for body text because the headline fonts and the body text fonts are easily distinguishable but still readable, and they don't clash with each other. Figure 8-2 shows commonly used fonts.

Figure 8-2: Examples of commonly used fonts.

This text is in Times New Roman and looks like newspaper type.

This text is in Courier and looks like typewriter type.

This text is in Arial and looks like a highway sign.

This text is in Staccato 222 and is almost unreadable.

Figure 8-2

Notes:

Property bar:
buttons below
toolbar

Windows comes with a bunch of fonts, and so do WordPerfect and your printer. You can buy more fonts or get more with other software that you buy. In this lesson, you see how to display a list of the fonts that you can use in your WordPerfect documents.

Most fonts are *proportionally spaced,* which means that different characters take up different amounts of space on the line. A capital *W* is usually the widest letter, and a small *i* is usually the narrowest. Look at the difference in the width of those two letters on this page. *Fixed-space* or *fixed-pitch* fonts are like those on a typewriter: Each character takes up the same amount of space. A common fixed-pitch font is Courier. Proportionally spaced fonts look more modern, while fixed space fonts replicate the look created with a typewriter.

on the test

Fonts also come in sizes, which are measured in *points* or *pitch.* A point is $1/72$ of an inch high. Readable type is usually 10 or 11 points high. Headlines can be 14, 24, or even 36 points high. The larger the point size, the larger the font looks. You control font size with the Font Size button, the second option on the Property bar.

You can make a so-so document look terrific (and waste a lot of time trying) by changing the font and by putting headings in a font that's different from the one you used for the text — like we did with the sans serif fonts mentioned previously as headings for the Times Roman body text. This lesson describes different ways to fool around with fonts. You can change the font of selected text by using the Font Face button, the first button on the Property bar.

heads up

Not all fonts are alphabet characters. Some fonts, like Wingdings and Monotype Sorts, are special characters that you might use to spice up your documents.

Seeing what fonts you have

The easiest way to work with fonts is by using a button on the Property bar. The two controls you'll use to change font and font size have a downward-pointing triangle at their right ends, indicating that if you click the control, a list of options will drop down.

Tip: If no row of buttons appears below the toolbar, choose <u>V</u>iew⇨Toolbars from the menu bar and see if a check mark appears next to the Property bar option. If not, click the Property bar box to display a check mark and then click the OK button. The Property bar appears.

The first button on the Property bar is the Font Face button. WordPerfect went a little overboard in trying to be original when naming this button — *font face* sounds like some sort of insult. Font faces are usually called either fonts or typefaces. The button displays the name of the font currently in use (where the cursor is).

To see a list of fonts that are on your computer:

1 **Click the Font Face button.**

A list of fonts appears below the Font Face button. It's probably quite a long list.

2 **Scroll through the list of fonts, using the scroll bar along the right edge of the list.**

As each font on the list is highlighted, a box appears showing you what the font looks like.

3 **To make the list disappear, press Esc or click in the typing area of the WordPerfect window.**

So far, you haven't changed anything in your document. You just took a peek at fonts that are available for you to use.

Changing the font and size of selected text

Start playing with fonts by changing the font of one line of text. If GTK Sample Products.101.WPD isn't open, open it now. If you didn't do Lesson 8-1, open GTK Sample Products2.101.WPD.

Note: WordPerfect comes with the fonts we suggest, but it's possible they weren't installed on your system. If you don't have the fonts we suggest, use fonts that you do have. The point isn't to use particular fonts, but to practice changing the font of selected text.

1 **Select the first line of the document, *Great Tapes for Kids — Product List*.**

2 **Click the Font Face button.**

You see a list of available fonts. If the list is long, a scroll bar appears.

3 **Pick a new font for the line — try Kids if you have it, or Comic Sans MS, or EnviroD.**

We like a font that's fun and bold at the top of the document, and one that highlights the fact that these are products for kids, but you can choose the font you prefer. After all, choosing fonts is a fun part of having WordPerfect, and we have no intention of spoiling your fun.

After you click the font, the list closes, and the font of the selected text changes. The text stays selected, so you can try out a different font if you want to. Click the Font Face button again and pick another font from the list.

The text looks different now. In the next step you'll make it bigger to see what it really looks like.

Sidebar notes:

Times New Roman | 12

the Font Face and Font Size buttons on the Property bar

check to see what fonts are installed

Notes:

4 **If the first line, the title of the document, is no longer selected, select it again. Now make the selected text larger by clicking the Font Size button.**

It's next to the Font Face button, and why it's not called Font Face Size is your guess!

A list of font sizes appears, shown in points ($1/72$ of an inch).

5 **Choose point size 20.**

After you click the size, the list closes, and the size of the selected text changes.

6 **Select the second line of the document that reads Video Tapes.**

It's a first level heading in the body document. Wouldn't the headings look nicer if they stood out a little? In the next couple of steps, you'll format this heading to make it a different font and slightly bigger than it is now — maybe point size 14 or 16.

7 **Click the Font Face button and choose a font.**

You may want to choose the same font you used for the title, but you can choose another one if you want. Hmm . . . Looks kind of small. Make it bigger.

8 **Click the Font Size button and choose point size 14.**

The line still needs to be selected for the font size change to affect it. If you don't like the look of the heading, select some other size and/or font.

9 **Select the title of the video, *Babe.* Change the font to Arial and the font size to 13 points.**

If you have trouble with this step, review the unit up to this point. Knowing how to flex your formatting will make word processing much more fun!

10 **As you move your cursor around the document, take a look at the Font Face and Font Size buttons on the Property bar.**

They show which font and size are in use wherever your cursor is. When your cursor is on the first line of the document, the Font Face button displays Kids or Comic Sans MS or EnviroD or whatever font you chose, and the Font Size button shows 30.

Font Face and Font Size buttons show font and size in use at cursor position

That's it. All you have to do to pretty up the font of selected text is to choose the font and font size by using the buttons on the Property bar.

heads up

Incidentally, you change the font for the rest of the document after the cursor if you don't select text before selecting a font. We don't recommend that approach, though — see our suggestions later in this unit for safe formatting. If you do change the font without selecting text first, click the Undo button to undo your change.

Choosing a font for the whole document

on the test

The default font for the document is the font that is applied to all text, including headers, footers, and page numbers, unless you specify otherwise. Here's how to set the default font for a document.

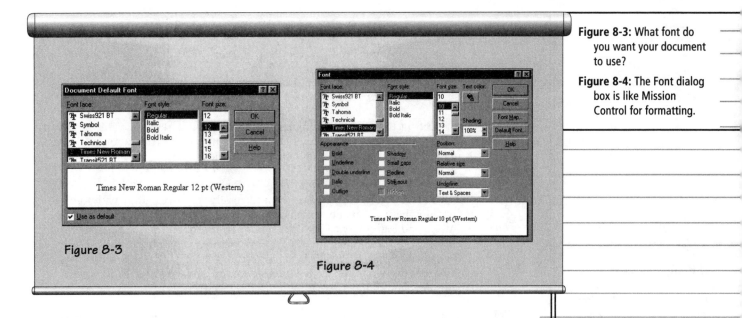

Figure 8-3: What font do you want your document to use?

Figure 8-4: The Font dialog box is like Mission Control for formatting.

Figure 8-3

Figure 8-4

1 **Make sure that no text is selected and then choose Format⇨Font from the menu bar.**

Unlike most commands that change a font, the location of your cursor is unimportant when you give this command.

This command affects the entire document, not just the text where the cursor is. WordPerfect displays the Font dialog box, where you can set additional attributes for selected text.

2 **Click the Default Font button on the right side of the Font dialog box.**

You see the Default Document Font dialog box in Figure 8-3. If text is selected in the document, this button will be *grayed out*, which means it's disabled — you can't click it.

3 **Select Times New Roman as the Font Face, 12 as the Font size, and Regular as the Font style.**

The text in the preview box displays how your text will appear. These will be the defaults for the document — any text not specially formatted will appear in 12 point Times New Roman.

The Font style enables you to set the default font to be italic, bold, or even bold italic. We have trouble thinking of a reason for the default text style to be bold, italic, or bold italic, though, but you might have one.

extra credit

You can change the default font of all documents by using the Use as default check box at the bottom of the Document Default Font dialog box. Click the check box to display a check mark when you want the default font to be used for other documents.

4 **Click the OK button to make the change.**

Any text that doesn't have a specified font (like the headings you formatted with new fonts in the last exercise) changes to the default font you just defined.

5 **Press Ctrl+S to save your document, just in case lightning strikes your building before you finish this unit.**

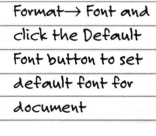

Format→ Font and
click the Default
Font button to set
default font for
document

☑ Progress Check

If you can do the following, you've mastered this lesson:

❑ Change the font and font size for selected text.

❑ Change the font and font size for the rest of the document.

❑ Set the default font and font size for the document.

In the GTK Sample Products.101.WPD memo, you formatted the first three lines with a new font, and they don't change. The rest of the document changes to the new font, even the line you formatted using the Bold button. Only text that has been formatted with a particular font does not change.

The Default Document Font dialog box enables you to set the default font for the whole document. You can then change fonts for selected text or for the rest of the document starting from where the cursor is by using the Font Face button on the Property bar.

Tip: In case you haven't guessed, you can easily get carried away with fonts (because they're so much fun) and overformat a document. Normally, we (Alison and Margy) try to use a maximum of three fonts in a document — usually a serif and sans serif font that complement each other (like Times Roman and Arial) — one for headings and one for regular text, with perhaps a third font thrown in for spice. But fonts are fun, so enjoy yourself and trust your judgment.

heads up

You've now learned a lot of ways to change the font of text in your document, so we want to give you some safe formatting guidelines. Ready?

♦ Set the default document font to one that will be used for most of the text in the document.

♦ Format selected text, like headings, by selecting the text and changing the font. Changing fonts in this way insures that the text after the heading reverts to the document default font.

♦ Don't change font and font size when no text is selected.

Recess

You've learned useful formatting skills so far in this unit. If you need to, take a break before coming back to do the second half of the unit.

Lesson 8-3

Changing Capitalization

dON'T YOU HATE IT WHEN YOU PRESS THE cAPS lOCK KEY BY MISTAKE? Having the option of changing the capitalization of your text saves you from having to retype. Or maybe you're trying to figure out if a title looks better in all caps or just with the initial letter of each word capitalized. WordPerfect gives you an easy way to try out these options.

on the CD

In the GTK Sample Products document, make the title all capital letters. If you don't already have the GTK Sample Products.101.WPD document loaded, open it now. If you haven't done any of the lessons in this unit, open GTK Sample Products3.101.WPD. Then follow these steps:

extra credit

The master panel for text appearance

If you are doing serious formatting and find yourself wishing for a place where you could specify exactly how you want your text to look, look no further than the Font dialog box, which appears in Figure 8-4. To view the dialog box, press F9 or choose Format⇨Font from the menu bar. The changes you make on the Font dialog box affect selected text.

In addition to changing the formatting of your text in ways you've already seen, you can also use some new formatting options. The Appearance part of the Font dialog box contains not only Bold, Italic, and Underline, but also Double Underline, Outline, Shadow, Small Cap, Redline, Strikeout, and Hidden (which you use for comments that you don't want printed).

You can create superscripts and subscripts by changing the Position setting. If you want your superscript or subscript in a smaller font, use the Relative size setting, which makes selected text smaller or larger than the text around it.

You can change the color of the text by using the Text color option. You may also want to use the Shading option to make text lighter.

Format to your heart's delight, and if you suddenly become frightened that you've done too much, just press Esc or click Cancel to forget the whole thing. Click OK to keep the changes that you've made. You can also undo changes by clicking the Undo button.

1 **Select the title at the top of the document.**

2 **Chose Edit⇨Convert Case from the menu.**

WordPerfect gives you three choices: Lowercase, Uppercase, and Initial Capitals, which pretty much cover the options.

3 **Choose Uppercase.**

WordPerfect changes the capitalization of your text. Some fonts are almost unreadable in all caps — if you don't like the looks of your title, while it's still selected, you can change the font (by clicking the Font Face button).

Tip: You can also press Ctrl+K to change selected text from uppercase to lowercase and back again.

When you need to change the capitalization of your text, the Edit⇨Convert Case command saves you from the boredom of retyping it, although you may still need to edit a few letters to get them right.

☑ **Progress Check**

If you can do the following, you've mastered this lesson:

❑ Change the capitalization of selected text.

❑ Impress your coworkers by showing them that they don't have to retype their text if they press the Caps Lock key by mistake.

Copying Character Formatting   Lesson 8-4

on the test

WordPerfect provides an easy way to format several different selections of text the same way — QuickFormat. QuickFormat is useful when you have more than one heading in a document: After you've formatted one of the headings to look good, you can format the other headings without going through all the steps again.

QuickFormat
button

Following are three ways to use QuickFormat:

 ▶ Click the QuickFormat button.
 ▶ Click the right mouse button anywhere in the typing area (not in the margins) to display the text QuickMenu and then choose QuickFormat.
 ▶ Choose Format⇨QuickFormat from the menu bar.

Using QuickFormat

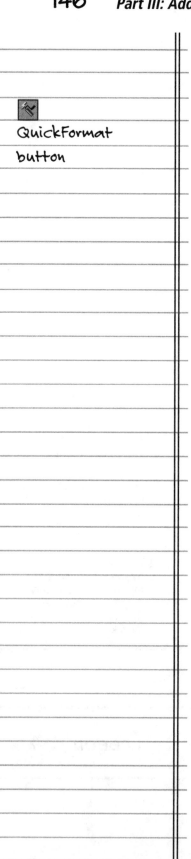

on the CD

You can use the QuickFormat option on the GTK Sample Products.101.WPD letter to copy formatting from one heading to other headings. If GTK Sample Products.101.WPD isn't open, open it now. If you haven't followed the first three lessons in this unit, open GTK Sample Products4.101.WPD instead, so your document has the same fancy formatting that it would have if you had followed the steps. Follow these steps:

1 **Select the *Video Tapes* heading that you formatted earlier.**

2 **While the heading is still selected, turn QuickFormat on by clicking the QuickFormat button on the toolbar.**

Alternatively, you can choose Format⇨QuickFormat from the menu bar, or click the right mouse button anywhere in the typing area and then choose QuickFormat from the QuickMenu that appears. Whichever method you use to start QuickFormatting, WordPerfect displays the QuickFormat dialog box, as shown in Figure 8-5.

Turning on QuickFormat means that you want WordPerfect to remember the format of the text that the cursor is in, because you want to format other text to look the same.

You have the option of copying character format only (Characters) or including paragraph formatting (Headings). Because you're formatting a heading, use the Headings choice. If you are copying the format of a piece of text that isn't a whole paragraph (meaning it doesn't have carriage returns before and after it), you can use the Characters option.

3 **Choose Headings and click the OK button.**

The dialog box closes, and the mouse pointer turns into a tall I with a paint-brush next to it, indicating that you can paint new text to look like your already prettified text.

4 **Select the next similar heading, *Audio Tapes*, to format.**

When you're copying a headings format, you need only to click somewhere in the paragraph (or line, in this case) to indicate that the format should be copied to the whole paragraph.

As soon as you select the text, WordPerfect immediately formats it the same way that the first heading is formatted. Very Quick! The mouse pointer still looks funny, though, with its tiny paintbrush. As long as the mouse pointer includes a paintbrush, WordPerfect is still ready to QuickFormat.

extra credit

Notice the QuickFormat on the Application Bar. This tells you which QuickFormat you're using to format text. If you know which QuickFormat you're using, you can format other text with it later.

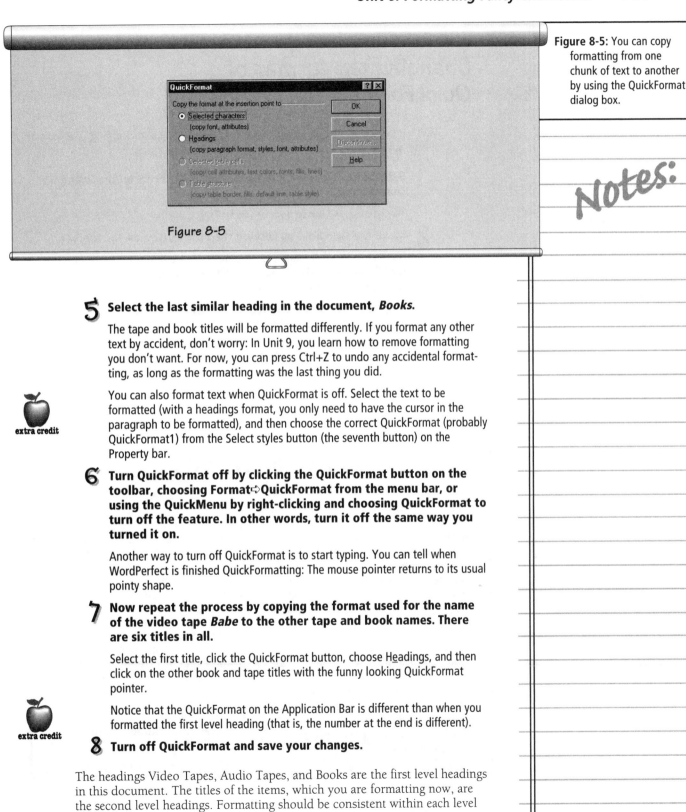

Figure 8-5: You can copy
formatting from one
chunk of text to another
by using the QuickFormat
dialog box.

Notes:

5 **Select the last similar heading in the document,** *Books*.

The tape and book titles will be formatted differently. If you format any other text by accident, don't worry: In Unit 9, you learn how to remove formatting you don't want. For now, you can press Ctrl+Z to undo any accidental formatting, as long as the formatting was the last thing you did.

You can also format text when QuickFormat is off. Select the text to be formatted (with a headings format, you only need to have the cursor in the paragraph to be formatted), and then choose the correct QuickFormat (probably QuickFormat1) from the Select styles button (the seventh button) on the Property bar.

6 **Turn QuickFormat off by clicking the QuickFormat button on the toolbar, choosing Format⇨QuickFormat from the menu bar, or using the QuickMenu by right-clicking and choosing QuickFormat to turn off the feature. In other words, turn it off the same way you turned it on.**

Another way to turn off QuickFormat is to start typing. You can tell when WordPerfect is finished QuickFormatting: The mouse pointer returns to its usual pointy shape.

7 **Now repeat the process by copying the format used for the name of the video tape** *Babe* **to the other tape and book names. There are six titles in all.**

Select the first title, click the QuickFormat button, choose Headings, and then click on the other book and tape titles with the funny looking QuickFormat pointer.

Notice that the QuickFormat on the Application Bar is different than when you formatted the first level heading (that is, the number at the end is different).

8 **Turn off QuickFormat and save your changes.**

The headings Video Tapes, Audio Tapes, and Books are the first level headings in this document. The titles of the items, which you are formatting now, are the second level headings. Formatting should be consistent within each level of heading, and using QuickFormat is an easy way to accomplish that.

Changing the format of QuickFormatted text

After you've used QuickFormat to format headings, you can change the format of one heading, and the format of the rest will change to match.

1 **Select one of the book or tape titles that are formatted using a QuickFormat.**

You have six to choose from — any will work.

2 **Make the title bold by clicking the Bold button on the toolbar.**

Have a quick look through your document. Notice that not only the format of the title you selected changed, but the format of the other titles you formatted with the same QuickFormat also changed.

3 **Close the GTK Sample Products.101.WPD document.** Be sure to save your changes, now that all the headings are formatted in a consistent way.

Using QuickFormat is a great way to consistently format a document. You simply format text and then copy the format to all the other text that should look the same. If you change your mind about how you want the text to look, just reformat it, and all the identically formatted text in the document also changes.

extra credit

Stylish concepts

Styles are one of WordPerfect's most powerful features. *Styles* are sets of formatting that you name. Styles enable you to create beautifully formatted documents with consistent formatting for all your headings, captions, quotations, and other specially formatted text. Styles also make formatting faster and easier. Styles are closely related to QuickFormat, but give you even more formatting control.

Styles are built in to WordPerfect. The heading styles are used often. For example, in the exercises you did in the last lesson in this unit, you could have formatted the headings using the styles Heading1 and Heading2. To get the styles to look like you want them to, you need to learn to edit a style.

You can apply a style by selecting the text to be formatted, and clicking the Select Style button on the Property bar. Select the style name from the drop-down list to format the selected text with that style.

WordPerfect has three kinds of styles:

▶ **Character:** Font formatting for selected text

▶ **Paragraph:** Paragraph spacing, font for the whole paragraph, line spacing for the paragraph, and other formatting that affects the entire paragraph

▶ **Document:** Formatting for the whole document, such as the default font

Unit 8 Quiz

For each of the following questions, circle the letter of the correct answer or answers. Remember, we may have included more than one right answer for each question!

 1. **What does this button do?**

   A. Types a B.

   B. Makes selected text look darker than usual.

   C. Tells WordPerfect that it's time for breakfast.

   D. Applies bold formatting to characters.

   E. Causes the spoken word "Bingo!" to come out of the computer's speaker.

2. **What is a font?**

   A. An old-fashioned fountain.

   B. A source; for example, this book is a font of information.

   C. A set of shapes for letters, numbers, and punctuation.

   D. A choice on the Font Face drop-down menu.

   E. The name of a WordPerfect dialog box.

3. **If you click the Font Face button and choose a different font when your cursor is in the middle of a document . . .**

   A. The default font for the document changes.

   B. The font changes from that point until another font code is encountered.

   C. The font changes for the line of text where the cursor is.

   D. You create a new font that is a combination of the document default font and the new font chosen.

   E. You'll get nothing for dinner.

4. **In WordPerfect, font size is measured in**

   A. Feet.

   B. 72nds of an inch.

   C. Points.

   D. Miles.

   E. Furlongs per fortnight.

Notes:

5. **Which button is this?**

   A. Paint Me a Picture.

   B. QuickFormat.

   C. Apply Wallpaper.

   D. Font Color

   E. Spell Check.

6. **What does QuickFormat do?**

   A. Guesses how you want to format your text and does it quickly.

   B. Quickly copies character and paragraph formatting.

   C. Remembers the formatting of the selected text and applies it to other text that you select.

   D. Formats your text like a duck.

   E. No one knows.

Unit 8 Exercise

1. Open the version of GTK Sample Products.101.WPD that you saved at the end of the last lesson in this unit. If you didn't complete the exercises, Open GTK Sample Products5.101.WPD.

2. Copy the formatting of the short description of *Babe*, **A little pig goes a long way,** to the description lines for the other products.

3. Find the name of a newspaper in the section with review quotes at the end of the description of **Babe.** Format the newspaper name with italics.

4. Copy the formatting of the newspaper name you just formatted to all the other newspapers and magazines listed in the document. The video and audio tapes have reviews with newspaper names cited; the books do not.

   Hint: This time you want to use the Selected characters option on the QuickFormat dialog box, because you are formatting part of a line and not the whole line, or heading.

5. Change the formatting of some text formatted with a QuickFormat. Perhaps the product type would look better underlined or formatted with a different font. Experiment to see if you can make the document look better.

6. Save the resulting document with a completely new name, like *My GTK Products.* Make a note of the name of the document in the margin.

Secrets of Formatting: Using Codes

Objectives for This Unit

✓ Knowing what formatting codes are

✓ Using the Reveal Codes window

✓ Deleting formatting codes

✓ Fixing formatting problems

✓ Editing formatting codes

Prerequisites

▶ Opening an existing document (Lesson 2-2)

▶ Using dialog boxes (Lesson 2-3)

▶ Making your text bold, italicized, and underlined (Lesson 8-1)

▶ Using different fonts and sizes (Lesson 8-2)

on the CD

▶ Mapleworks .WPD

▶ Mapleworks2 .101.WPD

▶ GTK Products .101.WPD

▶ GTK Products5 .101.WPD

▶ Catalog Request .101.WPD

▶ Flyer.101.WPD

We hear that the folks at WordPerfect were tempted to require membership in a secret club before allowing you to use any formatting commands, keystrokes, or buttons, but instead they settled for putting secret formatting codes in your documents. Just like a secret club, formatting codes have their hassles and benefits. The hassles include dealing with cryptic codes (quick, guess what *HRt* means!) and having to be careful where your cursor is when you give formatting commands (because you can't see where the formatting codes are unless you open up a special window to see them). The benefits of WordPerfect formatting codes include being able to clearly see how WordPerfect is formatting your document and being able to fix your documents when the formatting gets screwy (which is truly the WordPerfect advantage over its major competitor).

So what are these formatting codes, anyway? Formatting codes are what WordPerfect uses to turn special features on and off. WordPerfect has three kinds of formatting codes:

▶ **Character codes:** Represent a special character such as Tab or Enter.

Left Tab

This is a character code

Font: Arial Black

This is a single code

Bold ⟩Bold◇text⟨ Bold

These are paired codes (with the text they format between them)

◆ **Single codes:** Turn a feature on or change formatting starting at the point in the document where the formatting code is (for example, changing the font). WordPerfect usually inserts the formatting code wherever the cursor is when you give the command, click the button, or press the keys that create the formatting code. In some cases, WordPerfect sticks the formatting code at the beginning of the line, paragraph, page, or document where the cursor is.

◆ **Paired codes:** (WordPerfect calls these revertible codes — we won't.) One to turn a feature on and one to turn it off again. When you make text bold, for example, by using either the Bold button on the toolbar or pressing Ctrl+B, WordPerfect sticks two formatting codes into your document: one formatting code turns bold on, and another turns it off. If text is selected, WordPerfect puts the formatting codes at the beginning and the end of the selected text. If no text is selected, WordPerfect puts the formatting codes on either side of the cursor so that whatever you type next comes between the two formatting codes. Some formatting codes can be paired or single, depending on the method you use to format the text.

Don't get nervous — this detail sounds kind of technical, but the fact is that you rarely have to deal with formatting codes. Knowing how formatting codes work makes understanding how formatting commands work easier and gives you the power to untangle your document if the formatting goes awry.

Lesson 9-1

Seeing the Formatting Codes in Your Document

View→Reveal Codes to see formatting codes

WordPerfect provides you with a special little window at the bottom of the WordPerfect window in which to view all these special formatting codes. You may be staring in confusion at your WordPerfect screen, wondering where this window is — the answer is, it's not there yet. And the way to view it is a secret — just kidding! To see the Reveal Codes window, you choose View⇨Reveal Codes from the menu bar, making your screen look something like Figure 9-1. When you open the Mapleworks.WPD document, you see the regular view of the document in the typing area, and the formatting codes in the Reveal Codes window. In the Reveal Codes window, WordPerfect displays the text of your document, with the formatting codes and special characters visible. Each of the rectangles in the Reveal Codes window represents a code. The cursor appears as a red block in the Reveal Codes window. It corresponds with the cursor in the regular typing window — they move together.

In Unit 8, you learned how to create lots of different formatting codes to format your documents — formatting codes to turn bold, italics, and underline on and off and formatting codes to change the font. Most of the time, you don't need to look at them in the Reveal Codes window, but the formatting codes are hiding there, waiting for you to take a peek! Reveal your formatting codes in one of the following ways:

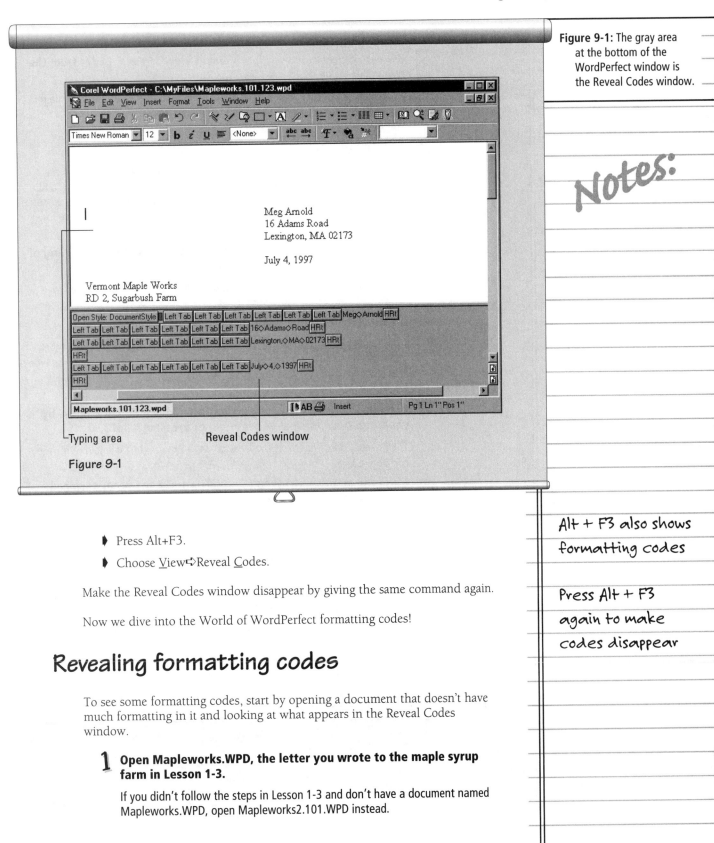

Figure 9-1: The gray area at the bottom of the WordPerfect window is the Reveal Codes window.

Notes:

Typing area

Reveal Codes window

Figure 9-1

Alt + F3 also shows formatting codes

Press Alt + F3 again to make codes disappear

▶ Press Alt+F3.

▶ Choose <u>V</u>iew⇨Reveal <u>C</u>odes.

Make the Reveal Codes window disappear by giving the same command again.

Now we dive into the World of WordPerfect formatting codes!

Revealing formatting codes

To see some formatting codes, start by opening a document that doesn't have much formatting in it and looking at what appears in the Reveal Codes window.

1 **Open Mapleworks.WPD, the letter you wrote to the maple syrup farm in Lesson 1-3.**

If you didn't follow the steps in Lesson 1-3 and don't have a document named Mapleworks.WPD, open Mapleworks2.101.WPD instead.

Notes:

2 **Reveal your secret codes by choosing View⇨Reveal Codes from the menu bar or by pressing Alt+F3.**

At the bottom of your WordPerfect window appears a gray area with some text and a lot of little boxes with letters in them. This area is the Reveal Codes window (you see it in Figure 9-1).

3 **Yell, "Aaarghhh!"**

Formatting codes can seem difficult in this day and age when computers are supposed to work for us! But look carefully at the Reveal Codes window, and you see that it's not so complicated — it's just another view of your document. Your text is there, but also you see lots of boxes, which are formatting codes. The red block is your cursor.

4 **Move down in the document until your cursor is at the beginning of the second paragraph in the body of the letter.**

Use your favorite method for moving around in a document. Be sure to move the cursor, not just the mouse pointer.

5 **Notice the formatting codes in this part of the letter.**

First, find your cursor in the Reveal Codes area. Notice that at the end of each line is a SRt code (*Soft return,* which is what WordPerfect puts in when you type past the end of a line). Also notice how hyphens appear — as -Hyphen codes (which seems a bit redundant).

6 **After you've seen enough, get rid of the Reveal Codes window by choosing View⇨Reveal Codes again or pressing Alt+F3.**

The Reveal Codes window disappears, and the WordPerfect window returns to its familiar state.

7 **Close the Mapleworks.WPD (or Mapleworks2.101.WPD) document by choosing File⇨Close from the menu bar.**

You haven't made any changes, so you don't need to save it.

The most popular formatting codes in WordPerfect

The Reveal Codes window lets you see how WordPerfect formats your document. So far, you've seen some basic formatting codes. Table 9-1 shows some of the formatting codes that you're most likely to run across in your documents and that you'll work with in the rest of this unit.

Table 9-1	Formatting Codes You See Frequently
Formatting Code	*Meaning*
HRt	Denotes a Hard return (you create it when you press Enter)
SRt	Denotes a Soft return (WordPerfect creates it automagically when text goes past the end of a line)

Formatting Code	Meaning
Tab	Indicates one of various types of tab stops that exist, as you see in Unit 11
Font	Specifies font (typeface) in use for text after the formatting code
Font Size	Specifies the size of the letters
Lft Margin	Defines white space on the left of the paper
Rgt Margin	Defines white space on the right of the paper
HPg	Denotes a Hard page break (you create it when you press Ctrl+Enter to start a new page)
SPg	Denotes a Soft page break (WordPerfect creates it when you type past the end of a page)
Just	Specifies whether text is flush left, centered, flush right, or justified
Bold	Makes text bold
Und	Makes text underlined
Italc	Makes text italicized

on the test

Many formatting codes are either *hard* or *soft*. This distinction is as follows:

- *Hard* codes are those that you type. WordPerfect never deletes these codes until you specifically tell it. For example, pressing Enter creates a *HRt* (Hard Return) code, and pressing Ctrl+Enter creates a *HPg* (Hard Page) code.

- *Soft* codes are usually created by WordPerfect to make the text flow properly. For example, the WordPerfect word wrap feature inserts Soft Return codes (*SRt*) when you type past the end of a line and Soft Page codes (*SPg*) when you type past the bottom of a page. WordPerfect may put them in and take them out at will. As you edit a paragraph, for example, WordPerfect inserts and deletes Soft Return codes so that your lines are all about the same length.

Looking at formatting codes

Most documents have more formatting codes than the Mapleworks.WPD letter because they contain more formatting (and you thought that Mapleworks had plenty!). Take a look at another document: GTK Sample Products.101.WPD (or GTK Sample Products5.101.WPD, if you didn't do Unit 8).

1 **Open GTK Sample Products5.101.WPD, which you see in Figure 9-2.**

Looks nice, doesn't it? This document includes lots of fancy fonts, using methods you learned in Unit 8.

2 **Display the Reveal Codes window by pressing Alt+F3 or choosing View⇨Reveal Codes from the menu bar.**

☑ Progress Check

If you can do the following, you've mastered this lesson:

❏ Reveal formatting codes.

❏ Recognize a formatting code from regular text in the Reveal Codes window.

❏ Learn more about a formatting code by positioning the red block cursor to the left of it.

❏ Change the size of the Reveal Codes window.

❏ Close the Reveal Codes window.

formatting codes with blunt points are paired

heads up

3 **Now take a deep breath and look at the formatting codes in this document.**

Move the cursor around to see more. (Remember, familiarity breeds contempt, which is probably better than what you're feeling right now!) You may immediately notice formatting codes you haven't seen before. Among them are Font (which tells WordPerfect which font to use), Font Size, and Und.

4 **Move your cursor around the document. Notice that some formatting codes have blunt points rather than being simple rectangles; these are paired formatting codes.**

The blunt points indicate beginnings of formatting (when the point faces right) and ends (when the point faces left).

5 **Make the Reveal Codes window bigger by clicking and dragging up the top border of the Reveal Codes window.**

Move your pointer around near the border between the typing area and the Reveal Codes window until the pointer turns into a double-ended arrow. Then click the mouse button and hold it down. You can now move the border up or down, making the Reveal Codes window larger or smaller. Release the mouse button to leave the window border where it is.

Intuitively, if you move the border all the way to the bottom of the typing area, the Reveal Codes window disappears. Counter-intuitively, if you move the border all the way to the top of the typing area, the Reveal Codes window still disappears, rather than taking up the whole window.

6 **Move your cursor back to the beginning of the document by pressing Ctrl+Home.**

Notice that you don't get to the beginning of the formatting codes; you just get to the beginning of the text.

7 **Move the cursor down two lines by pressing the down arrow twice.**

You are now at the beginning of the line with the heading *Video Tapes*.

When you move the cursor with the Reveal Codes window open, the cursor moves one step at a time through the *formatting codes*. Depending on where the cursor is, if you look in the typing area, you may have to press the right-arrow key several times before the cursor moves to the next letter.

8 **Move the cursor to the left, one character at a time, and notice that some formatting codes, when they're to the right of the cursor, expand to show you more detail.**

For example, when the cursor is to the left of the Para Style: Auto QuickFormat formatting code (which you created when you used this heading to QuickFormat the other headings), the formatting code expands to fully describe the formatting applied for this particular QuickFormat.

9 **After you've seen enough, get rid of the Reveal Codes window by choosing View⇨Reveal Codes from the menu bar or pressing Alt+F3.**

The Reveal Codes window disappears, leaving you with simple, comforting text.

10 **Close the document by choosing File⇨Close from the menu bar.**

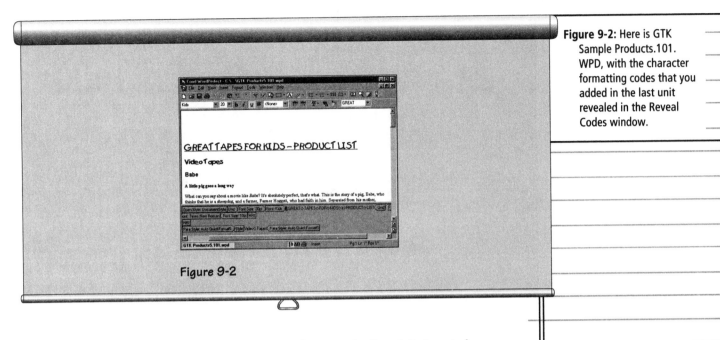

Figure 9-2

Figure 9-2: Here is GTK Sample Products.101. WPD, with the character formatting codes that you added in the last unit revealed in the Reveal Codes window.

You've looked at advanced formatting codes using the Reveal Codes window, moved your cursor in the Reveal Codes window, learned how to see more detail about a code, and expanded the Reveal Codes window.

Deleting Formatting Codes

Lesson 9-2

Understanding formatting codes is important because they really can make a mess of your document. If they're in the wrong places, formatting codes can create formatting havoc. Looking at them can help you figure out what happened.

Remember that WordPerfect usually inserts the formatting code where your cursor is when you give a formatting command. Formatting codes are inserted at the cursor when you give commands for margin changes, font changes, changes in tab settings, and other formatting commands. Entering formatting codes throughout the document can be useful, but sometimes the result is not what you expect. Looking at formatting codes helps you figure out what's up with your document in case you enter a formatting code in the wrong place. Better still, it may enable you to impress your colleagues by figuring out how to fix *their* documents.

If you find during the course of typing and editing your documents that something is formatted wrong or acts peculiar, you need to look at the formatting codes in your document. Maybe your tabs aren't acting like they used to, or suddenly you notice your left margin shifted a smidgen in the middle of your document. To fix the formatting in your document, you need to either delete a formatting code or alter it. This lesson describes how to delete formatting codes, and the extra credit sidebar describes how to alter them.

heads up

Saving your document before you do too much with formatting codes is a good idea — messing things up is easy. Save the document by pressing Ctrl+S. If you mess things up, close your document without saving and then open the document again. You get the version that you saved before you started playing with formatting codes.

Lesson 8-2 describes how to change fonts in the middle of your document. When you use the Font Face and Font Size buttons (or the Font dialog box), WordPerfect creates formatting codes named *Font* and *Font Size*. If a Font or Font Size code creeps into the middle of your document, it can make things look strange. And figuring out what's wrong can be hard!

Often, what you need to do is delete a misplaced formatting code. WordPerfect has at least three ways to do that when you have the Reveal Codes window open and you've found the formatting code that you want to delete:

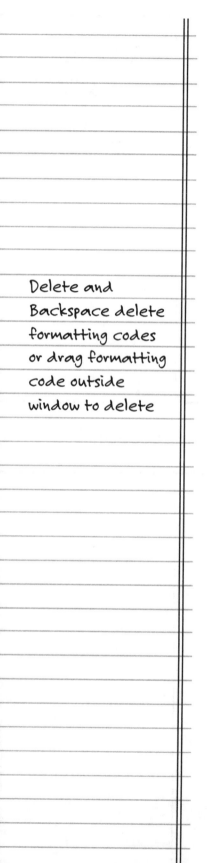

Delete and Backspace delete formatting codes or drag formatting code outside window to delete

- Move the cursor immediately before the formatting code and press Delete.
- Move the cursor immediately after the formatting code and press Backspace.
- Click the formatting code and drag it to somewhere outside the Reveal Codes window (formatting codes die from lack of oxygen when they leave the Reveal Codes window).

Deleting a misplaced formatting code

Now let's look at a document with an error in it — it's the Case of the Misplaced Code.

on the CD

1 **Open Catalog Request.101.WPD, which you see in Figure 9-3.**

2 **Notice that near the start of the second paragraph, the type size suddenly changes.**

The second paragraph in the body of the letter switches from 12- to 10-point type, right after the words *We hope*, and it looks terrible. Someone must have clicked the Font Size button by accident.

3 **Reveal codes by pressing Alt+F3 or choosing <u>V</u>iew⇨Reveal <u>C</u>odes or using your favorite method.**

4 **Move your cursor to the place where the font size changes.**

Look for the Font Size code where the type gets smaller, right after the words *We hope* in the second paragraph.

You know that you're looking for a font size code because you can see that the problem is new font size. Some formatting codes (those that control the way an entire paragraph looks) are always at the beginning of a paragraph, making them a little easier to find. Character formatting codes can appear anywhere in a paragraph, so they can be tricky to find.

The author of this letter may have wanted to change the font size for the whole letter but forgot to move the cursor to the beginning of the letter. You can fix the problem with a stroke of a key.

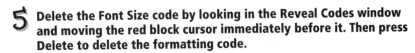

5 **Delete the Font Size code by looking in the Reveal Codes window and moving the red block cursor immediately before it. Then press Delete to delete the formatting code.**

The font size in the second part of the letter changes to match the font in the first part of the document.

Alternatively, you can also move the cursor to the position immediately after the formatting code and press Backspace. And perhaps the funnest way to delete a formatting code is to click it and drag it out of the Reveal Codes window.

6 **Close the document by choosing File⇨Close from the menu bar. Go ahead and save the changes to the document — you improved it significantly.**

Congratulations! You found a problem, looked for the formatting code that caused it, and deleted the formatting code.

Following are a few other notes about deleting formatting codes:

heads up

- ♦ When you're in the Reveal Codes window, you can easily delete a formatting code. When the Reveal Codes window isn't visible, WordPerfect usually doesn't let you delete formatting codes: It just skips over them and deletes the next visible character.

- ♦ When you delete a paired formatting code, you only have to delete one. The other disappears, too — it dies of grief, we suppose. For example, if you delete the Bold code at the beginning of a section of bold text, the Bold code at the end disappears, too.

extra credit

Searching for formatting codes

You may find that looking for formatting codes using your eyes and the Reveal Codes window is just too frustrating. WordPerfect offers another way. You can use Edit⇨Find and Replace to find a formatting code, or to find it and replace it with a different formatting code or with nothing.

After you see the Find and Replace Text dialog box, WordPerfect has two ways to look for formatting codes: using the Type⇨Specific Codes command and using the Match⇨Codes command, both chosen from the menu bar at the top of the Find and Replace Text dialog box.

If you want to look for a formatting code that contains specific settings, use the Type⇨Specific Codes command. For example, you can search for Font Size codes that set the size to 12-point and replace them all with Font Size codes that set the size to 14-point. If you want to look for a formatting code regardless of its specific settings, use the Match⇨Codes command. For example, you can search for all Font Size codes.

Both commands display additional dialog boxes where you can specify the formatting code that you're looking for and its settings.

---

delete one paired formatting code and both disappear

Figure 9-3: It looks like a bogus Font Size formatting code has crept into the Catalog Request.101.WPD document!

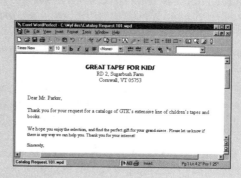

Figure 9-3

Notes:

Recess

Congratulations! You are now a member of the Mystical WordPerfect Formatting Codes Cabal. The secrets of the formatting codes are known only to an initiated few — use them wisely. In fact, you may want to quit WordPerfect and take a walk to let your head clear. Choose File➪Exit to leave the WordPerfect Formatting Codes Zone.

extra credit

Altering formatting codes

To create many formatting codes, you give a command that displays a dialog box. You choose settings on that dialog box and click OK — voilà! A formatting code! For example, you can create Font and Font Size codes using the Font dialog box.

What if you want to change the information in the formatting code? For example, if you create a Margin code that changes the margins to 1 inch on each side, and you want to change them to 1.5 inches later, how do you edit the formatting code?

By double-clicking most formatting codes, you can display the same dialog box you use to create the formatting code in the

first place (or the dialog box you bypassed by using a toolbar or Property bar button). By changing the settings in the dialog box, you change the formatting code. This procedure is better than creating a new formatting code with different settings, because you don't end up with extra formatting codes lying around in your document.

Don't use the double-clicking method to try changing paired formatting codes (for example, a line or two that has a different font) — WordPerfect just doesn't act the way you may think it does. Instead, select the text and apply the new formatting to it.

Unit 9 Quiz

For each of the following questions, circle the letter of the correct answer or answers. Remember, we may include more than one right answer for each question!

1. **WordPerfect formatting codes are...**

   A. Confusing — you need a secret decoder ring to decipher them.

   B. Visible in the Reveal Codes window.

   C. Formatting commands stored in your document.

   D. Useful in figuring out snafued documents.

   E. Better than chocolate.

2. **To display the Reveal Codes window...**

   A. Light a candle, dim the lights, and intone a special incantation.

   B. Press Alt+F3.

   C. Choose <u>V</u>iew⇨Reveal <u>C</u>odes.

   D. Click the right mouse button and choose Re<u>v</u>eal Codes from the Quick Menu that appears.

   E. Click and drag the black bar at the top or bottom of the scroll bar.

3. **To delete a formatting code...**

   A. Press Delete any time you think you're near one.

   B. Click and drag it out of the Reveal Codes window.

   C. With the Reveal Codes window open, press Delete or Backspace when the red cursor is immediately before or after the formatting code.

   D. Delete its partner.

   E. Yell that you would like it to leave . . . please.

4. **Mr. Parker is buying a gift for his...**

   A. Daughter.

   B. Niece.

   C. Granddaughter.

   D. Grandniece.

   E. No fair testing on content.

5. **You can tell which formatting codes are paired, because**

   A. The formatting codes gaze longingly at each other.

   B. Both formatting codes have the same name (for example, both say *Bold*).

   C. The formatting codes aren't rectangular in the Reveal Codes window: instead, they have pointed ends that point toward each other.

   D. The formatting codes are right next to each other.

   E. The first formatting code appears where formatting starts, and the second formatting code appears where it ends.

Unit 9 Exercise

on the CD

1. Open the document Flyer.101.WPD. It's a flyer about the Vermont Maple Works show at the fair, suitable for posting on bulletin boards.

2. Delete all of the Font and Font Size codes from the document. (The funnest way is to drag each formatting code out of the Reveal Codes window, making the formatting code vanish.)

3. Using the font and font size commands that you learned in Unit 8, format the flyer with the fonts and sizes of your choice.

   (**Hint:** If you want to center a line, put your cursor at the beginning of the line and press Shift+F7. You learn this officially in Unit 10, but we thought we'd sneak it in here.)

4. Save the flyer.

5. (Optional) Print the newly formatted flyer.

Formatting Lines and Paragraphs

Objectives for This Unit

- ✓ Setting spacing between lines and paragraphs
- ✓ Setting margins
- ✓ Indenting paragraphs
- ✓ Left-, right-, and center-justifying text
- ✓ Setting tab stops

Prerequisites

- ▶ Opening documents (Lesson 2-2)
- ▶ Selecting text (Lesson 5-1)
- ▶ Using WordPerfect codes (Unit 9)

on the CD

- ▶ Press Release.101.WPD
- ▶ Big Sale.101.WPD
- ▶ Big Sale2.101.WPD

This unit covers how to format your lines and paragraphs, how to make tables using tabs, and how to change the position of text on the page.

For most of the topics in this unit, it's useful to see the ruler, as shown Figure 10-1. The ruler sits below the Property bar (which is below the toolbar, which is below the menu bar). WordPerfect may not display the ruler — you may have to ask for it by choosing View⇨Ruler or by pressing Alt+Shift+F3. The ruler shows you the tabs and margins that are in effect at the point where your cursor is in your document. Because you haven't learned how to change tabs and margins yet, the same settings should apply throughout the document. If you get tired of having the ruler fill valuable typing space, use the View⇨Ruler command to close the ruler, just as you did to open it.

The ruler shows you tabs and margins. Using your mouse and the ruler, you can change tab and margin settings. As with everything else in WordPerfect, you have more than one way to change these: You can change tabs and margin settings by using commands and dialog boxes, too.

Press Alt+Shift+F3 to show ruler or make it disappear

The ruler shows tabs and margins

Figure 10-1: The ruler rules the world of tabs and margins.

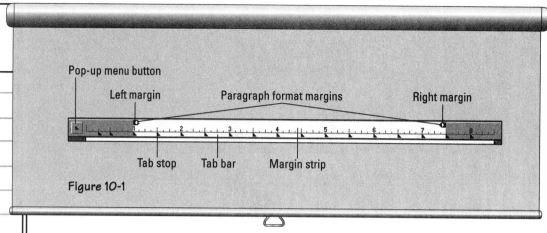

Pop-up menu button

Left margin   Paragraph format margins   Right margin

Tab stop   Tab bar   Margin strip

Figure 10-1

The ruler is divided into thirds: The topmost part is the margin strip, the middle part is the actual ruler, and the bottom part is the tab bar.

on the test

> ◆ **The margin strip:** That's the top part of the ruler. The dark, outside markers show you your document's *left and right margins*. Look at them before you load a document. They're probably set at 1 inch and 7.5 inches. The tiny black triangles just inside the margin markers on the margin strip show the *paragraph format margins*, that is, the margins for the paragraph that you're working on.

> ◆ **The ruler:** Marks off the page in eighths of an inch.

> ◆ **The tab bar:** Shows *tab stops* with differently shaped triangles. A tab stop is where the cursor goes when you press the Tab key. Tabs allow you to align text vertically on the page. The triangles that appear on the ruler in Figure 10-1 show the positions of normal tab stops — every half inch. Other types of triangles show where right tabs, decimal tabs, and other types of tab stops appear. Don't worry: You find out more about tabs and tab stops later in this unit.

Now that you are familiar with the ruler, you can fool around with formatting lines and paragraphs, starting with setting the spacing between lines.

Lesson 10-1   Setting Spacing between Lines and Paragraphs

If you write for a teacher or an editor, you probably have to double-space your text to leave space for extra comments and corrections — not that you ever make a mistake. The Line Spacing dialog box enables you to change line spacing. To open the dialog box, choose Format⏎Line⏎Spacing from the menu.

heads up

Pay attention to where your cursor is when you change the line spacing in a document. WordPerfect inserts a Spacing code at the cursor, and that affects all the text that comes after it. If you want to change the line spacing for a section of text rather than the whole document, you can select text before

---

ruler marks off page in eighths of an inch

Display the Line Spacing dialog box by choosing Format →Line→Spacing changing the line spacing. WordPerfect changes the line space only for the text you selected by inserting Spacing codes (more of those secret codes we talked about in Unit 9) before and after the selected text.

on the test

Here's the best way to set line spacing: Put a Spacing code at the top of the document that applies to most of the text in the document. For paragraphs that need different spacing, select them and change their spacing. In fact, this works for nearly any kind of formatting, not just line spacing.

Using the Line Spacing dialog box

on the CD

For this exercise, you'll use Press Release.101.WPD, as shown in Figure 10-2.

Press releases are often formatted using double-spaced lines. You can change line spacing in Press Release.101.WPD to double spacing by using the Line Spacing dialog box. Open the document now.

1 Place the cursor at the top of the first paragraph of the press release — the one that starts *Have you ever . . .*

You don't need to double-space the title, just the body of the document. You can also select the text you want to double-space.

2 Display the Line Spacing dialog box by choosing For̲mat⇨Li̲ne⇨S̲pacing from the menu.

WordPerfect displays the Line Spacing dialog box in Figure 10-3.

3 Change the value in the S̲pacing box to *2.*

The easiest way is to type the new value. The contents of the S̲pacing box are already selected, so anything you type replaces the current contents. You can also use the arrows to change the value.

extra credit

The value in the S̲pacing box is not limited to integers (1 for single spacing, 2 for double, and so on). You can use decimals. If you use a value of 1.5 in the S̲pacing box, for instance, each line is followed by half a line of white space.

4 Click OK.

The dialog box goes away, and the line spacing of the selected text changes. Notice that there are large white spaces (three lines' worth) between paragraphs. Those three lines' worth of blank space come from double spacing the Enter you typed at the end of the paragraph (that's one), and the Enter you typed on the blank line between the paragraphs (that's two more, one from the Enter itself, one from the double spacing you just turned on).

5 Save your changes and close the document.

Setting the format for your paragraphs

If you always indent the beginning of each paragraph and put an extra line between paragraphs, WordPerfect can do this work for you. Rather than pressing Tab at the beginning of each paragraph and pressing Enter an extra time at the end of each paragraph, you can tell WordPerfect how you like your paragraphs formatted. Then all you have to do is press Enter once at the end of each paragraph.

Notes:

paragraph
formatting saves
keystrokes

Figure 10-2: You'll learn how to apply double spacing to this press release.

Figure 10-3: The Line Spacing dialog box.

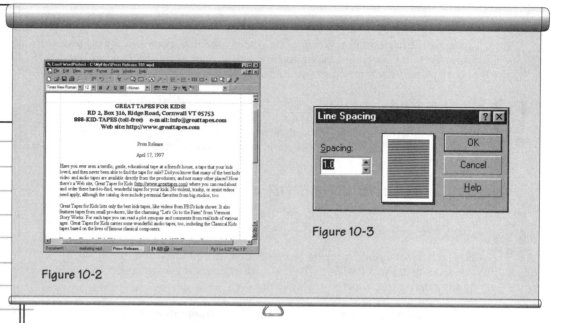

Figure 10-2

Figure 10-3

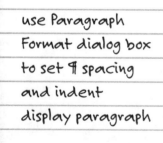

use Paragraph
Format dialog box
to set ¶ spacing
and indent
display paragraph

Take a look at the Paragraph Format dialog box, where you tell WordPerfect how you want paragraphs to look. To display the Paragraph Format dialog box, choose Format⇨Paragraph⇨Format from the menu bar (sounds redundant to us). Figure 10-4 shows the Paragraph Format dialog box.

on the CD

Open Big Sale.101.WPD. (You can see it in Figure 10-5.) (If you're still looking at the Paragraph Format dialog box, click on the Cancel button to make it go away.) Notice that the text looks all run together — that's because there's only one carriage return at the end of each paragraph (you can see them in the document by choosing View⇨Show ¶). Rather than adding Enters to separate the paragraphs, you can format the paragraphs in Big Sale.101.WPD to leave an extra line between paragraphs.

1 Move the cursor to the beginning of the first paragraph of the document, which is where you want the new formatting commands to begin.

If you make changes in the Paragraph Format dialog box settings with the cursor halfway through the document, you affect all paragraphs after the cursor.

2 Display the Paragraph Format dialog box by choosing Format⇨Paragraph⇨Format from the menu bar.

The Paragraph Format dialog box has four options. Refer to Figure 10-4 to look at this dialog box. You may want to use the first and last options — First line indent and Spacing between paragraphs — to format all the paragraphs in a document. To do this, move your cursor to the top of the document and then display this dialog box and change its settings. In this document you only change the Spacing between paragraphs.

extra credit

Although they can apply to the whole document, the two margin adjustment settings are more often used for indenting one or more paragraphs — for example, for a quote — in the middle of a document.

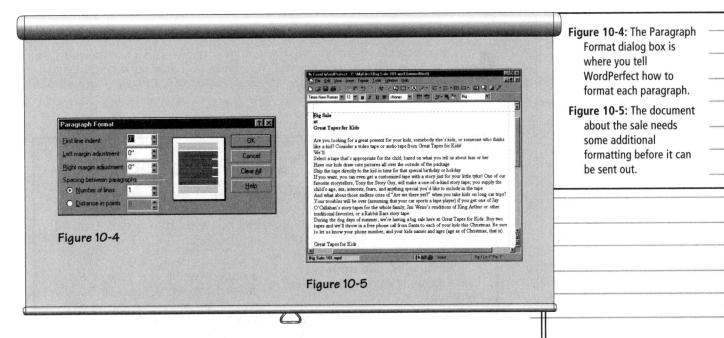

Figure 10-4

Figure 10-5

Figure 10-4: The Paragraph Format dialog box is where you tell WordPerfect how to format each paragraph.

Figure 10-5: The document about the sale needs some additional formatting before it can be sent out.

3 **Change the Number of lines setting to 2.**

This setting tells WordPerfect to double-space paragraphs (not the lines within paragraphs). A setting of two leaves an extra line between paragraphs (a value of 1.5 would leave half a blank line between paragraphs).

heads up

WordPerfect uses both the Number of lines option and the line spacing option when it decides how much space to leave between paragraphs. Think of it as if you're telling WordPerfect how many Enters you want between paragraphs. You type the first one, and it's as if WordPerfect types enough extra ones to make up the number you want: one additional one if you said you wanted two lines, two additional ones if you said you wanted three lines, and so on. Each invisible Enter that WordPerfect puts in adds whatever your line spacing is: one line if your text is single spaced, two lines if it's double spaced, and so on.

extra credit

Rather than trying to figure out the complexities of line and paragraph spacing, you may want to use the Distance in points setting. Remember that a point is ¹/₇₂ inch — fonts are measured in points, so check your font size to determine the distance in points to leave between paragraphs. (12 points is a good measure for a line of regular 10 point text; a good rule of thumb is to make the space between paragraphs a little bigger than your text point size.)

4 **Click OK.**

The dialog box goes away, and the paragraphs in the document are instantly more widely spaced.

5 **Press Ctrl+S to save your improvements to the document.**

The Paragraph Format dialog box enables you to tell WordPerfect how paragraphs will look. If you prefer to indent your paragraphs manually rather than use the Paragraph Format dialog box, make sure that you use the Tab key and not the spacebar. Using spaces marks you as a word processing newbie. Using tab stops enables you to make a change just once that affects the indentation of every paragraph. If you change the location of a tab stop, all text that includes that tab stop moves to the new tab stop location. Lesson 10-4 covers setting tab stops.

Open Paragraph
Format dialog box
by choosing
Format→
Paragraph→Format
from the menu bar

a point is 1/72
inch

Progress Check

If you can do the following, you've mastered this lesson:

❏ Change the line spacing of your whole document.

❏ Change the spacing of a few paragraphs.

❏ Change the spacing between paragraphs.

❏ Automatically indent the first line of each paragraph.

heads up

Remember to pay attention to the position of the cursor before formatting with the Paragraph Format dialog box. You format the rest of the document after the cursor if no text is selected. If text is selected, only that text is formatted with the new settings.

extra credit

Making a fancy first letter

A great way to jazz up the first paragraph of a document, or of each section of a document, is to make the first letter bigger. When the first letter of a paragraph is at least twice as big as the rest of the letters in the paragraph and takes up two or more lines, it is called a *drop cap*.

WordPerfect makes this fancy effect really easy: Move your cursor to the beginning of the paragraph where you want the drop cap, and choose Format➪Paragraph➪Drop Cap from the menu. WordPerfect creates a drop cap using the first letter of the paragraph.

You can also press Ctrl+Shift+C to create a drop cap. WordPerfect creates the drop cap and displays the Drop Cap Property bar, with buttons that let you change the way the drop cap looks. Click anywhere in the document, except on the drop cap, to see the familiar Text Property bar.

Lesson 10-2   Setting Margins

The left and right margin settings tell WordPerfect how much white space to leave along the sides of the paper. If you're artistic, you probably think that margins nicely frame your erudite text. Another good reason to use margins is that most printers can never manage to print close to the edge of the paper. Of course if you're writing a term paper, you probably want it to look longer than it would without margins. Whatever your reason for using margins, you'll find that WordPerfect is usually set to leave an inch on each side of the page unless you tell it otherwise.

The ruler tells you where your left and right margins are at the cursor position in the document. Using the ruler is one of the three ways to change left and right margins. You can also

▶ Click and drag the margin guidelines (the gray dotted lines in the typing area).

▶ Click and drag the margin marker on the margin strip.

▶ Use the Margins dialog box.

When you use the ruler or the Margins dialog box to change margins, a margin code is inserted where the cursor is and affects the rest of the document. If the cursor is at the top of the document, margins are changed for the whole document, but if you change the margins when the cursor is in the middle of the document, you change the margins from that point on. You can also select text before you change margins to change them for just the selected text.

When you use guidelines to change margins, the margins change at the point in the document where you click and drag the guideline.

Using guidelines to change margins

If you're a mouse aficionado, or if you're trying to fit a precise amount of text on a line, you may prefer to change left and right margins by using the dotted blue guidelines.

on the CD

Go ahead and change the margins for Big Sale.101.WPD. Open the document if it's not already open. If you didn't do the second exercise in Lesson 10-1, open Big Sale2.101.WPD to see a version of the document with tasteful paragraph spacing.

Following is how to change the margins by using the mouse and the guidelines (sounds kind of like the Prince and the Pauper):

1 **Move the pointer, not the cursor, to the first line of the document.**

2 **Move your mouse to the guidelines so that the pointer turns into a double-headed arrow with a vertical bar through the center.**

This transformation is how the mouse indicates that it's ready to click and drag the guidelines to change the margins.

If you don't see the dotted blue guidelines, choose View⇨Guidelines and make sure all the boxes on the Guidelines dialog box have checks in them. This means that they are turned on.

heads up

Make sure that you are next to the first line of the document, or even above that, in the top margin area on the vertical guideline that designates the left margin. The margin will change starting from where you drag the guideline.

3 **Click and hold down the mouse button, and move the margin — indicated by the number in the yellow box that pops up — to 1.25 inches.**

4 **Release the mouse button when the margin position is correct.**

WordPerfect moves the text around to fit within the new margins.

5 **Repeat Steps 2–4 to change the right margin to 1.25 inches.**

Again, make sure you drag the guideline at the top of the document.

Using guidelines is perhaps the easiest way to change margins. This method is useful when you're eyeballing the margins, but it's not so convenient when you know to the tenth of an inch how wide the margins should be.

Notes:

++
click and drag a guideline when you see this pointer to change margins

Notes:

Format—>Margins
to set all margins

F7 indents
paragraphs

Using the Page Margins tab of the Page Setup dialog box

Another way to change margins is to use the Page Margins tab of the Page Setup dialog box, as shown in Figure 10-6. Before displaying the dialog box, put the cursor where you want the new margins to begin. To display the dialog box:

- ◆ Choose Format⇨Margins from the menu bar.
- ◆ Press Ctrl+F8.
- ◆ Double-click the margin strip of the ruler.
- ◆ Right-click the ruler or in the left margin, and choose Margins from the QuickMenu that appears.

To change the margins, change the values in the dialog box and click OK. WordPerfect inserts a margin code in the document.

Indenting paragraphs

The easiest way to indent a paragraph is to use the F7 function key, which indents the paragraph one tab stop.

on the CD

The quote in Big Sale.101.WPD should be indented. Follow these steps:

1 **Put your cursor at the very beginning of the paragraph that you want to indent.**

The quote is the second to last paragraph in the document.

2 **Press F7.**

Alternatively, you can choose Format⇨Paragraph⇨Indent from the menu bar, but pressing F7 is so much easier.

WordPerfect indents the paragraph one tab stop. This format looks great for quotations and other material that needs to be set off from the rest of the text.

3 **Save and close the Big Sale.101.WPD document.**

Here's a rundown of the different ways you can indent a paragraph:

- ◆ Press F7 or choose Format⇨Paragraph⇨Indent.
- ◆ If you want to indent the paragraph from both the left and right margins (the traditional way of indenting a quotation), press Ctrl+Shift+F7 or choose Format⇨Paragraph⇨Double Indent.
- ◆ For a hanging indent, in which the first line of the paragraph *is not* indented but the rest of the paragraph *is*, press Ctrl+F7, or choose Format⇨Paragraph⇨Hanging Indent.

extra credit

An alternate way to indent a paragraph is to use the margin adjustment options on the Paragraph Format dialog box to change the margins for a selected paragraph or paragraphs.

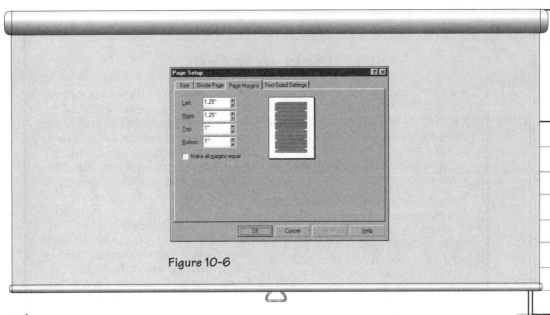

Figure 10-6

Figure 10-6: The Page
Margins tab of the Page
Setup dialog box lets you
set all four margins and
shows you a cute picture
of your page.

extra credit

Make it fit

If making a document a particular size is your problem, WordPerfect has the feature for you. The WordPerfect Make it Fit feature shrinks or expands margins, font size, and line spacing so that a document fits on the number of pages that you specify. To use it, choose Format⇨Make It Fit. Use the dialog box to tell WordPerfect how many filled pages you want and what settings it can change to get the document to that size, choosing any or all of the following: margins, line spacing, and font size. Click Make It Fit, and WordPerfect goes to work. Technically, you can use this feature to expand your seven-page essay into the ten pages required by old Professor Curmudgeon, but if you ask us, we think he'll probably notice that each page has a lot of white space on it. If you change your mind, choose Edit⇨Undo to return your document to its old look.

✓ **Progress Check**

If you can do the following, you've mastered this lesson:

❏ Change the margins of the whole document.

❏ Change the margins for part of a document.

❏ Indent a paragraph.

Centering and Right-Aligning Text   Lesson 10-3

So far, everything you've typed has been *left justified.* Justification has nothing to do with how well you make your argument — it has to do with how each line in a paragraph lies between the margins. Left justification means that the beginning of each line of text starts at the left margin and the right side of the text has an uneven edge (unless you have the necessary poetic talent combined with technical understanding of proportionally spaced fonts to make every line the same length). This method of formatting is also called *ragged right.*

on the test

WordPerfect gives you five ways to place each paragraph on the page between the margins: left justified, right justified, centered, full justified, and all justified:

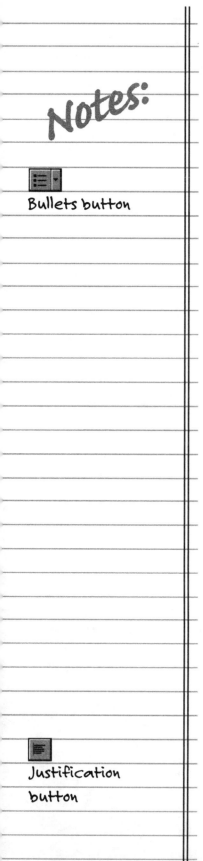

Notes:

Bullets button

Justification
button

extra credit

Making bullets

Bang! I shot your paragraph! In case you're having trouble connecting the name (bullets) with the face (what they do to your paragraph), bullets are those cute symbols that appear in front of each item in a list when you decide you don't want the list numbered.

The automatic way to put a bullet in front of a paragraph or a number of selected paragraphs is to click the Bullets button on the toolbar. You can choose the character you want to use as a bullet by clicking the down arrow on the Bullets button and selecting a bullet shape from the drop-down list. If you want to indent the paragraph and the bullet itself, press F7 when the cursor is to the left of the bullet.

To add a bullet using the manual method, format the paragraph with a hanging indent by moving the cursor to the beginning of the paragraph and pressing Ctrl+F7. Then type an asterisk and press Tab so that the asterisk is at the left margin and the rest of the paragraph is indented. If you don't like using an asterisk, you can find lots of other cool characters by pressing Ctrl+W to displays the WordPerfect Characters dialog box. You can see different sets of characters by changing the Set setting near the top of the dialog box. Insert a character by clicking it and then clicking the Insert and Close button.

- **Left justified:** The most common way to align text. It means that the left side of the text lines up against the left margin, and the right side is ragged (uneven).

- **Right justified:** The right side of the text lines up against the right margin. The left edge of the text is uneven.

- **Centered:** The text is centered between the left and right margins.

- **Full justified:** The text has extra spaces inserted so that each line starts at the left margin and continues all the way over to the right margin (except the last line of the paragraph, which is only justified on the left side). The extra spaces are tiny, and WordPerfect sticks them in evenly across the line, so you don't (usually) notice that they're there.

- **All justified:** The text is the same as full justified, but the last line is justified, too.

As with most formatting commands in WordPerfect, WordPerfect cares where your cursor is when you change the justification. If no text is selected, WordPerfect inserts another one of its secret codes, a *Just* code this time, where your cursor is, and the code affects the text that comes after it. If you select text, WordPerfect inserts Just codes at the beginning and the end of the text so that the justification affects only the selected text. **One caveat:** Justification works paragraph by paragraph, so if you select one sentence in a paragraph and center it, WordPerfect centers the whole paragraph.

To justify text, use the Justification button on the Property bar or the Format⇔Justification command.

on the CD

To try out justification, center the heading of the Big Sale document and make all the paragraphs full justified. Feel free to try out all the other kinds of justification, too.

1 **Select the first three lines of the document.**

The title of the document would look better centered.

2 **Click the Justification button to display the drop-down list.**

3 **Choose Center from the list.**

The three lines are now centered on the page.

4 **Put your cursor at the beginning of the first paragraph. Be sure that it is below the centered lines at the top of the document.**

5 **After your cursor is in place, click the Justification button on the Property bar and select Full from the drop-down menu.**

WordPerfect adds lots of tiny spaces to the text of your letter so that all the lines are the same length. Pretty clever, huh? (You see the difference more clearly at the bottom of the document.)

6 **Save and close the document.**

The easiest way to change the justification of a paragraph is to use the Justification button on the Property bar while your cursor is in the paragraph that you want to justify. If you select a paragraph first, WordPerfect turns the new justification on at the beginning of the paragraph and returns to the original justification for the next paragraphs.

Of course, WordPerfect has other ways to start full justification: you can choose Format⇨Justification⇨Full from the menu or press Ctrl+J (Ctrl+L left justifies, Ctrl+R right justifies, and Ctrl+E centers a paragraph).

You can change justification for part of a paragraph, but you need to use a different command. Put the cursor where you want the justification to change, and choose Format⇨Line⇨Center or Format⇨Line⇨Flush Right from the menu. This changes the justification of the text in the paragraph after the cursor.

☑ **Progress Check**

If you can do the following, you've mastered this lesson:

❑ Center headings.

❑ Change the justification of text in a paragraph.

Ctrl+J full-justifies
Ctrl+L left-justifies
Ctrl+R right-justifies
Ctrl+E centers

Setting Tab Stops

Lesson 10-4

So what is a *tab stop,* and how does it differ from, a bus stop? Well, because you brought it up, we can tell you that they do have similarities: A bus stop is a place where a bus stops when you stand there, and a tab stop is a place where your cursor stops when you press the Tab key. You can put as many tab stops along the route as you want. Tab stops are a matter of convenience, and are one way to line up text vertically. Another way is the table feature, which, though a little more complicated, often makes it easier to make your text look exactly the way you want it. The table feature is described in Unit 12.

heads up

Using spaces to put text in the same position on different lines just won't cut it — it marks you as an amateur, and besides, lining your columns up when you're using proportionally spaced fonts (where each letter takes up a different amount of space) is almost impossible.

Notes:

WordPerfect usually starts with a tab stop every half inch. How can you tell? Because that's what those little triangles are on the ruler. (What, you can't see the ruler? Choose the View⇨Ruler command.) To be more precise, those little triangles are *left tab stops*, just one of the many varieties of tab stops that WordPerfect has to offer.

WordPerfect has four types of tab stops, as you see in Table 10-1: left, right, center, and decimal. You can also tell WordPerfect to create *dot leaders* for a tab stop — that is, a row of dots leading up to the text at that tab stop.

Table 10-1	Types of Tab Stops	
Type	**What It Looks Like**	**What It Does**
Left	◣	Text starts after the tab stop (this one works the way tab stops on a typewriter do).
Center	▲	What you type is centered on the tab stop.
Right	◢	Text is right-aligned with the tab stop, so when you tab to a right tab stop and start typing, the text moves backward across the page, and the last letter you type is flush right against the position of the tab stop.
Decimal	▲	Useful for a column of numbers; decimal points are aligned with the tab stop.

All the types of tab stops described in Table 10-1 are also available with *dot leaders,* meaning that a line of dots leads up to the tabbed text. The symbols for dotted tabs are identical to the regular symbol, but have dots added. Right-click the tab bar to see a quick menu that shows all the tab symbols.

Figure 10-7 shows an example of each kind of tab stop:

- ◗ The Name column shows the effect you get with a left tab stop.
- ◗ The Address column is centered around a center tab stop.
- ◗ The Grade column is aligned with a right tab stop.
- ◗ The Amount Owed column is aligned with a decimal tab stop. Notice that the decimals all line up, but the title, which is all text and doesn't have a decimal, is right-aligned with the tab stop.

heads up

Notice also the funny symbol in the left margin. This symbol, the tab set icon, tells you that tab stops have been changed at this point in the document. If you click the symbol, you see a tab bar across the document that you can use to change tab stops.

Tab set icon

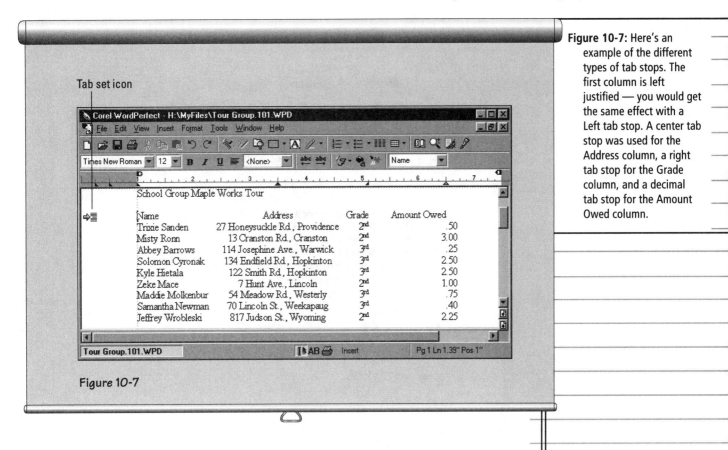

Figure 10-7

The ruler shows the tab stops that apply at the point in the document where your cursor is. Different parts of a document can have different tab stops, especially if you use tab stops to make tables. When you change even just one tab stop, WordPerfect puts a *Tab Set* code into your document that contains the position of all the tab stops that are defined at that point. Always position your cursor or select text before setting tab stops.

on the test

If you want to change tab stops for the whole document, put the cursor at the top of the document and change the tab stops. WordPerfect inserts a Tab Set code that affects all the text after the code. If you're changing tab stops for only a portion of the document and you'll want your old tab stops back eventually, select that portion of the document and change the tab stops. WordPerfect inserts two Tab Set codes: one at the beginning of the selected text to change tab stops, and one at the end to change them back.

Changing tab stops

As usual, WordPerfect gives you more than one way to change tab stop settings: you can use the Tab Set dialog box or the tab bar on the ruler (the tab bar is labeled in Figure 10-8). The Tab Set dialog box method may scare you off, so stick with the ruler method, which is easy.

put cursor before text that tab stops will apply to, or select text

Figure 10-8: This is the way documents you work on in this lesson will look after you complete Step 1.

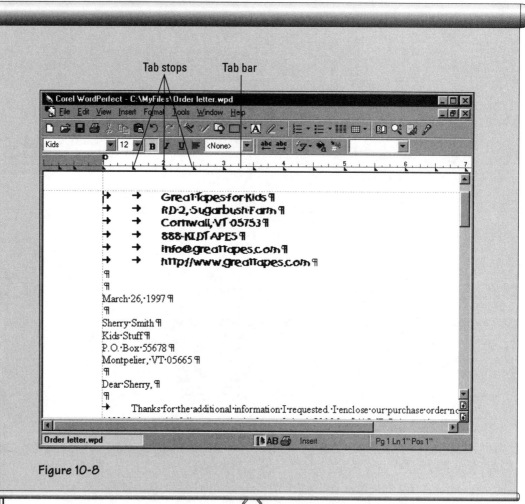

Figure 10-8

Notes:

If you press the Tab key, WordPerfect puts a *Tab* code in your text, and the next text you type appears at the next tab stop across the line. If you change the positions of the tab stops after you've typed something, the text moves to match. To move a tab stop, position the cursor before the text you want to affect; then click and drag the tab stop on the tab bar.

As you change tab stops you may find that you have some extra ones that you want to delete. The easiest way to delete a tab stop is to position the cursor before the text where the tabs are used, click on the tab stop you want to delete, and drag the tab stop anywhere off of the tab bar. You can delete all tab stops by right-clicking the tab bar and choosing Clear All Tabs from the QuickMenu.

heads up

Here are some general rules for making sure you put the Tab Set codes in the place you want them:

▶ If you want to affect the whole document, press Ctrl+Home to move to the beginning of the document before you change any tab stops.

▶ To affect part of the document, first select the text and then change the tab stops.

▶ If you're changing an existing tab stop setting, first click the Tab Set icon in the margin and then work with the tab stops on the tab strip that appears. The tab strip is a copy of the bottom part of the ruler, but it's snuggled right up against your text, making it easier to see exactly where your changes will begin affecting your text. In this case, you're changing the existing Tab Set code, so you don't have to worry about the position of the cursor.

on the CD

For this exercise you'll use Order Letter.101.WPD. Go ahead and open it now. This document is a letter, but the tab stops are in the wrong place. In this exercise, you'll check out the tab stops that currently exist and edit them so that the document has the more traditional format for a letter.

1 Choose View⇨Show ¶ from the menu.

Showing ¶ also shows tabs and spaces, which is a good way to see the simple formatting in your document without having to deal with codes.

2 Notice the tabs in the document.

Two tab stops are before the return address, the closing, and the signature. Each paragraph starts with just one tab. In the rest of the steps, you'll change the document so that the second tab stop is halfway across the page, and you'll decrease the paragraph indentation.

3 Move the cursor to the top of the document by pressing Ctrl+Home.

This is very important, because the new tab stop settings only affect the text after the cursor, and you want to make sure they affect the whole document.

4 Use the scroll bar to scroll down so you can see the body of the document.

You use the scroll bar because clicking the down button on the scroll bar does not move the cursor. (If you were to ignore this vitally important instruction, you would find yourself moving the cursor and changing the place where your new tabs go into effect.)

5 Click and drag the tab stop at 1.5" to 1.25".

As you drag the tab stop, you see a dotted vertical line, indicating where the tab stop is in the document, and a pop-up yellow box telling you the position of the tab stop in inches.

After you release the mouse button, the indentation of the paragraphs in the body of the letter decreases. The text that had two tabs in front of it stays in the same position. A tab set icon is inserted in the left margin — you may need to scroll left with the horizontal scrollbar to see it. Alternatively, you can zoom the document to Page Width to see the icon in the margin.

drag tab stops left or right on tab bar to change

6 Click the Tab Set icon in the left margin.

You now see a tab strip across the top of the document. Now that you've created new tab stop settings, you want to edit those settings using the tab strip rather than worry about the position of the cursor, which you have to do when you work with the ruler.

7 Delete the tab stop at 2.0 by clicking and dragging it off the tab bar into the document.

When you drag the tab stop off the tab bar, it turns into an icon with a trash can, indicating that you're deleting it.

drag tab stops off tab bar to delete

The text with two tabs in front of it jumps over .5", to where the second tab stop is.

8 Delete the tab stops at 2.5", 3.0", 3.5", and 4.0".

Use the same method — click and drag the tab stops off the tab bar.

The text with two tabs in front of it now starts 4.5" from the left edge of the paper.

9 Move the date to the correct position by putting the cursor in front of it and pressing Tab twice.

The date moves over to the second tab stop — it is now lined up with the return address.

10 Close and save the document.

Setting tabs

Setting tab stops is easy — just click the tab bar part of the ruler. The hard part is remembering to put your cursor *before* the text you want to format before setting your tab stops. If you want to have the same tab stops for your whole document, move your cursor to the top of the document whenever you work with tab stops. If you want to add a tab stop after you've made some changes to tab stop settings, make sure to first click the tab set icon, and then create the new tab stop on the tab strip that appears.

Here's how to make a new tab stop:

1 Move the cursor to the point where you want to insert the new Tabs. If you want to add a tab stop to an existing set of tabs, click the Tab Set icon in the left margin to display the tab strip for those tabs.

2 Right-click the tab strip that you are using to display the tab QuickMenu.

3 Click the type of tab stop you want to create.

4 Click the tab strip where you want to create the new tab stop.

5 If necessary, click the Tab Set icon again to remove the tab strip from the screen.

To change the type of a tab stop, use the QuickMenu to change the type of tab stop you're creating. Then click the tab stop on the tab bar whose type you wish to change.

heads up

If your tabs aren't working like you think they should (for instance, decimals aren't lining up at the decimal tab stop), use your newfound knowledge of the WordPerfect secret codes from Unit 9 and Reveal Codes to see if WordPerfect has replaced Tab codes with Indent codes. (WordPerfect does this sometimes; sometimes it's doing you a favor, and sometimes it's a pain in the neck.) If it has, delete the Indent code in the Reveal Codes window and press Tab again.

You can also change the settings of a tab stop by double clicking it — the Tab Set dialog box appears where you see all the settings for the tab stop that you double-clicked. You can change the tab stop by changing settings on the Tab Set dialog box and clicking OK.

Unit 10 Quiz

For each of the following questions, circle the letter of the correct answer or answers. Remember, there may be more than one right answer for each question!

1. **The margin strip of the ruler is…**

   A. The white part of the ruler.

   B. The upper third of the ruler.

   C. The part of the ruler that shows you where your left and right margins are set.

   D. The part of the ruler that you can use to change your left and right margins.

   E. The sleazy, marginal part of town where the strip joints are.

2. **Before you change margins, tab stops, or spacing in your document…**

   A. Give a small prayer to the deity of your choice (and save the document because deities help those who help themselves).

   B. Put your cursor at the very end of the document so that if you make a mistake, it won't mess anything up.

   C. Put the cursor just before the part of the document that you want to format, or click the tab set icon before the part of the document that you want to format.

   D. Select the part of the document that you want to format.

   E. Ah, to heck with it. No one will ever read it anyway.

3. **Which button is this?**

   A. Three Sideways Exclamation Points.

   B. Slice and Dice Text.

   C. Bullets.

   D. Intercom.

   E. Decimal Align.

4. **Right justification means…**

   A. Proving that you're right.

   B. Being a good conservative orator.

   C. Spacing words across the line the right way.

   D. Moving lines of text to the right so that they all end at the right margin.

   E. The same thing as *ragged left.*

5. **To make a tab stop...**

   A. Type code=tab stop.

   B. Click the tab bar part of the ruler.

   C. Choose Format⇨Line⇨Tab Set from the menu bar, enter the position and type of the tab stop, click the Set button, and click OK.

   D. Right-click the tab bar and choose Tab Set from the QuickMenu that appears.

   E. Yell, "Stop, tab!"

6. **In *Peter Pan,* the three children who travel to Never-Never-land are named...**

   A. Wendy, John, and Michael.

   B. Huey, Dewey, and Louie.

   C. Winken, Blinken, and Nod.

   D. Aladdin, Belle, and Ariel.

   E. Larry, Moe, and Curly.

Unit 10 Exercise

1. Open the document Marketing.101.WPD.

2. Set the left and right margins 1.5 inches in from the edges of the paper.

3. Change the paragraph formatting to leave an extra line between paragraphs and to indent each paragraph half an inch.

4. Center the title.

5. Set the justification for the entire document to full justification.

6. Format the first paragraph so that it is indented an additional half-inch from both margins.

7. Save the document.

Formatting Pages

Objectives for This Unit

✓ Centering text on a page

✓ Numbering pages

✓ Adding headers and footers to your documents

✓ Controlling where page breaks occur

▶ GTK Catalog
.101.WPD

▶ GTK Catalog2
.101.WPD

▶ GTK Catalog3
.101.WPD

The other units in Part III deal with character, line, and paragraph formatting. This unit steps back to look at the larger picture: formatting entire pages and documents.

When a document gets longer than one page, you'll want to tell WordPerfect to leave nice-looking margins at the tops and bottoms of pages, number your pages, or even put titles, dates, or other information at the top and bottom of each page. All of this is called *page formatting*.

on the test

To format pages, you use these commands:

- ▶ File⇨Page Setup. The Page Setup dialog box has settings where you can tell WordPerfect what size paper you're using, set your whole document up as having columns, and set margins for you whole document, among other things.

- ▶ Format⇨Keep Text Together. Here's where you tell WordPerfect where not to insert page breaks.

- ▶ Format⇨Margins. Use this command (or any of the other methods you used in the last unit) to set the top and bottom margins for each page.

Notes:

♦ Format➪Page➪Numbering. Tell WordPerfect to add numbers to your pages.

♦ Insert➪Header/Footer. Tell WordPerfect to include text at the top and bottom of each page.

In this unit, you'll review how to set top and bottom margins as well as learn how to center text on a page, which you may want to do with a title page or a table. You'll also learn how to number your pages and add headers and footers to your document. In the final lesson, you'll learn how to tell WordPerfect not to put page breaks where they'll be awkward — otherwise known as *bad breaks.*

heads up

Most of the commands described in this unit affect the entire document. For example, you usually want the same top and bottom margins for each page of a document. Like other WordPerfect formatting commands, these commands insert invisible WordPerfect codes into your document at the point where your cursor is located. To ensure that the formatting codes affect the entire document, be sure to move your cursor to the top of the document before you use each command or be conscious of putting the cursor before the part of the text that you want to format.

Lesson 11-1   Controlling Your Top and Bottom Margins

In addition to setting top and bottom margins, this lesson shows you how to center text vertically on the page.

Setting top and bottom margins

If you think that you might already know how to set top and bottom margins, you're probably right. You learned how to set margins in Lesson 10-2, when you set the left and right margins for your document. But for the sake of completeness (after all, this is the unit on formatting pages), we'll quickly go over setting margins here, as well as tell you how to center text vertically on a page.

You can change the margins in lots of ways. Pick your favorite:

Format→Margins or Ctrl+F8 to set top and bottom margins

♦ Choose Format➪Margins from the menu bar.

♦ Press Ctrl+F8.

♦ Double-click the margins strip of the ruler (see Lesson 10-2) to display the Page Margins tab of the Page Setup dialog box.

♦ Click and drag the dotted gray guidelines.

Centering text vertically on the page

What if you want to create a title page with its information centered vertically on the paper? Or you're writing a report in which Table 3 occupies a page by itself? The table might look better with equal amounts of white space above and below it.

You could press Enter at the top of the page to insert a bunch of carriage returns and center the text by eye, but WordPerfect can center text vertically and precisely on a page for you. Using the WordPerfect command to center text on a page is a better idea than using carriage returns because the WordPerfect center page command carefully leaves the same amount of space above and below the text on the page. Even if you change the size of the font or change another type of formatting, WordPerfect keeps the same amount of space above and below your text to keep it centered.

on the CD

In this unit, you'll edit the GTK Catalog.101.WPD document, a catalog to be sent to prospective buyers. The document consists of front material — a table of contents, information about Great Tapes for Kids — and then the actual catalog of products sold by GTK. The document needs lots of formatting. The beginning of GTK Catalog.101.WPD is shown in Figure 11-1.

The first page of the GTK Catalog.101.WPD document is a title page that may look better if the information is centered vertically on the page. Follow these steps:

1 **Open GTK Catalog.101.WPD and place your cursor on the page to be centered.**

Otherwise, you'll end up centering the wrong page! When you give the command to center a page, WordPerfect inserts a code at the top of the current page (the one the cursor is on).

2 **Choose Format⇨Page⇨Center from the menu bar.**

The Center Page(s) dialog box appears, as shown in Figure 11-2.

3 **If it's not already selected, click the Current page radio button to center only the current page.**

If you later decide that you don't want the page centered, display the dialog box again and change the choice to Turn Centering Off.

on the test

4 **Click OK.**

WordPerfect inserts the centering code, and the text on the page moves down to the center. If you're in Page view, the text may have seemed to disappear, but it didn't; it just moved further down the page. You may want to use Two Page view or zoom to Full Page to see the formatting better (use the View menu or the Zoom button on the toolbar).

5 **Press Ctrl+S or click the Save icon on the toolbar to save the GTK Catalog.101.WPD document.**

Zoom button

Figure 11-1: The GTK Catalog.101.WPD document may look a little familiar.

Figure 11-2: How would you like your page centered?

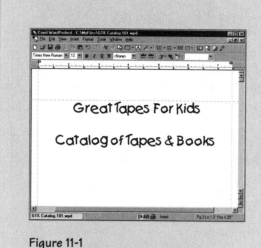

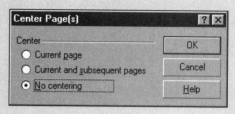

Figure 11-2

Figure 11-1

 **Progress Check**

If you can do the following, you've mastered this lesson:

❏ Set top and bottom margins.

❏ Center a title or table on a page vertically.

extra credit

Telling WordPerfect how big your paper is

If you always print on 8½-x-11-inch paper in portrait orientation, you never need to set the page size, because that's the kind of paper that WordPerfect is set up to deal with. If you want to print in landscape mode (sideways), or on a different size of paper, follow these steps:

1. **Press Ctrl+Home to move your cursor to the beginning of the document.**

   You'll be inserting a WordPerfect formatting code that should go before the text you want it to affect.

2. **Choose Format⇨Page⇨Page Setup or File⇨Page Setup from the menu bar.**

   WordPerfect displays the Page Setup dialog box, which includes a list containing Page information. This list differs depending on what sizes of paper your printer can cope with.

3. **Click the Size tab.**

   The Size tab has options for Page information and orientation (whether the page will print sideways or straight).

4. **Move the highlight to the Page information entry that describes the paper that you want to use.**

   When you choose a Page Definition, the Orientation box shows a diagram of how the document will look.

5. **Click the OK button.**

   WordPerfect inserts a *Paper Sz/Typ* code that specifies the paper size and orientation (see Unit 10 for information about codes).

If you can't find the paper definition you need on the list, click the New button to display the New Page Size dialog box where you can create a new definition.

Numbering Pages Lesson 11-2

Whenever you create a document that's more than a couple of pages long, numbering the pages is a good idea. Don't you hate it when someone gives you a long report to read that has no page numbers, and you drop the pages on the floor? Without page numbers, getting your pages back in order is a real chore.

heads up

Word-processing newbies may get the urge to type a number at the bottom of each page. Don't do it! This mistake will cause you grief if you add a sentence to the first page of your document and cause the page number at the bottom of page 1 to slide to the top of page 2 (or worse — to follow the first few lines on page 2), and so on, for the rest of the document. And, if you should decide to change the font or font size, don't even try to figure out what your document will look like and where your typed-in page number will end up!

Instead, ask WordPerfect to put the page numbers on for you. Believe us, automated page numbering is much less complicated than spending your life moving page numbers around!

WordPerfect has — you'll never believe this — two different ways to number pages. The first way is to use the Format➪Page➪Numbering command, which is perfect when all you care about is getting numbers on the page. The alternative is the Insert➪Header/Footer command, which enables you to add page numbers to headers and footers. The Header/Footer command is ideal when you want to include not only page numbers but also a title, date, or other information at the top or bottom of each page.

This lesson describes how to create just plain page numbers using Format➪Page➪Numbering command. You'll find out how to make fancier headers and footers that may or may not include page numbers by using the Header/Footer command in Lesson 11-3.

By the way, it doesn't matter *where* on the page your cursor is when you give a page numbering command. When you tell it to start numbering pages, WordPerfect is clever enough to put a page numbering code at the top of the current page. That way, page numbering starts on the page the cursor is on when you give the page numbering command.

We'll guide you through putting page numbers in the GTK Catalog.101.WPD document. You'll start by putting ordinary page numbers on every page. But after you're finished, the introduction will be numbered separately from the body of the proposal, the numbering style will be different in each part (introduction and body), the numbering will start over for the body of the catalog, and the cover page won't have a page number on it. Ready to start with the simple stuff?

Putting numbers on your pages

When all you want is page numbers, this is the way to do it:

on the CD

1 If you don't have GTK Catalog.101.WPD open, open it now.

Refer to Figure 11-1 for a picture of the document.

2 Put your cursor anywhere on the second page.

The title page doesn't need a page number.

3 Choose Format⇨Page⇨Numbering from the menu bar.

WordPerfect displays the Select Page Numbering Format dialog box, shown in Figure 11-3.

4 Use the Position setting to tell WordPerfect where to print the page numbers. Make sure that it is set to Bottom Center.

Our favorite setting is Bottom Center or Bottom Right, but you may certainly choose something else (far be it from us to squelch your creativity).

5 Check the Page numbering format. The selected format should look like a plain 2.

You have lots of choices here, but keeping things simple is often a good idea. You may want to scroll through the options, though, just to see what's there.

6 Click OK to exit the Select Page Numbering Format dialog box and add page numbers to the document.

Now page numbers appear at the bottom of each page. (The numbers don't appear in Draft view, so switch to Page view or Two Page view to see them if you don't see them.)

heads up

Page numbers start on the page where the page numbering code is, but the number printed on that page is the actual page number. So if you insert a page numbering code on the second page of the document, the page number that appears on that page is *2*. In a later exercise, you'll learn how to change the page number that WordPerfect starts on.

After you tell WordPerfect in the Select Page Numbering Format dialog box that you want a position for page numbers, WordPerfect enters a Pg Num Pos code into your document. That code tells WordPerfect that you want numbers on the page that the code is on and all the pages after that — even ones you haven't written yet.

Tip: If you set the Position setting in the Select Page Numbering Format dialog box to on of the Alternating settings (Top Outside Alternating, Top Inside Alternating, Bottom Outside Alternating, or Bottom Inside Alternating), WordPerfect puts the page numbers on a different side for odd- and even-numbered pages. When you print the documents on two sides of the paper, the page numbers are in the outside or inside corners of the pages — very professional! (Whether or not the text lives up to the format is up to you.)

extra credit

You can change the font used for the page numbers, making it bigger, smaller, bold, or italic. Click the Font button in the Select Page Numbering Format dialog box. If you don't change the font, WordPerfect uses the document's default font (refer to Lesson 8-2), which usually looks just fine.

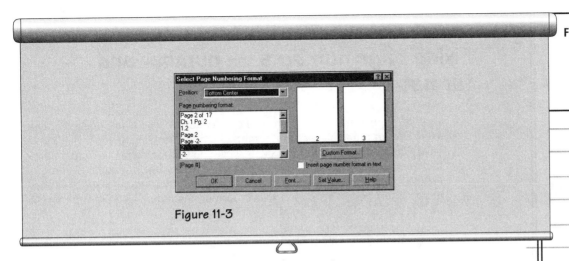

Figure 11-3

Figure 11-3: When all you want is just plain page numbers, use the Select Page Numbering Format dialog box.

Using Roman page numbers

Introductory material is often numbered with small Roman numerals. Here's how to do it for the GTK Catalog document.

1 Move your cursor to the second page of the document (that's where you put the page numbering code).

2 Reveal codes by pressing Alt+F3.

3 Find the Pg Num Pos code.

This is the code that you put into the document when you used the Select Page Numbering Format dialog box in the last exercise.

extra credit

If you have trouble finding the Pg Num Pos code, you can try using the Find and Replace Text dialog box to look for it. Press F2, choose Match⇨Codes from the dialog box menu, find the Pg Num Pos code in the list of codes, Insert it into the Find box, and click Find Prev. You'll still need to have the Reveal Codes window open. This isn't a way to avoid having to look at codes!

4 Double-click the Pg Num Pos code.

The Select Page Numbering Format dialog box appears.

5 Scroll down the Page numbering format setting to find the plain old, small Roman numeral — it looks like ii.

For the beginning pages of a long document, lowercase Roman numerals are traditional, so that's what we recommend choosing.

6 Click OK to leave the Select Page Numbering Format dialog box with a sigh of relief.

Now WordPerfect puts lowercase Roman numerals at the bottom of each page.

Editing an existing code avoids having two competing codes in the document. The Page numbering format setting on the Select Page Numbering Format dialog box enables you to change your page numbers to Roman numerals or to letters.

Fixing page numbers — number and format

Look through at the page numbers of the document. The whole document has small Roman numerals for page numbers — not surprising, because that's what you ordered, but it's not exactly what you want, either. Page 5 starts the body of the catalog, and ideally the number on that page should be *1*. Fortunately, fixing the page number isn't hard — you'll insert another page numbering code that tells WordPerfect to start numbering in regular Arabic numbers on this page starting with the number *1*.

1 Move your cursor anywhere on page 5.

This is the first page of the body of the catalog. You can get to page 5 by using Go To — double-click the last part of the status bar or press Ctrl+G — then type 5 and press enter. Voilà! Page 5.

2 Display the Select Page Numbering Format dialog box.

Same old same old. Choose Format⇨Page⇨Numbering from the menu.

3 Now change the Page numbering format to regular old Arabic numbers — choose 5.

That selection changes the way the number looks (Arabic instead of Roman numerals), but you still want to change the value of the number on this page.

heads up

4 Click the Set Value button on the Select Page Numbering Format dialog box.

This displays the Values dialog box. Don't we often wish that our friends and family had one of these so that we could set *their* values! This dialog box is available for your viewing pleasure in Figure 11-4. Fortunately, you don't need to worry about the tabs at the top of the dialog box — the settings you need are already displayed (on the Page tab).The other tabs are for very long documents, so you get to ignore them completely.

5 Change the Set page number setting to one and check that the radio buttons are set to Always keep number the same.

Because you are on the first page of the body of the document, you want the page numbers to start at 1 on this page, even if more pages are added to the front matter (as they say in the publishing biz) — that is, the title and the table of contents of the GTK Catalog. The other setting, Let number change as pages are added or deleted, lets you skip a page number so that you can add material that you may not be able to put in a WordPerfect document, such as a table or figure, although these days, you can put just about anything in a WordPerfect document.

6 Click OK on the Values dialog box and OK on the Select Page Numbering Format dialog box.

You're back to your document. Scroll down to the bottom of the page and have a look at the page numbers and see if they look like they should.

If your page numbers aren't behaving like you want them to, give the Format⇨ Page Numbering⇨Select command again on the page where the numbering should be different and then change the settings to insert a new code.

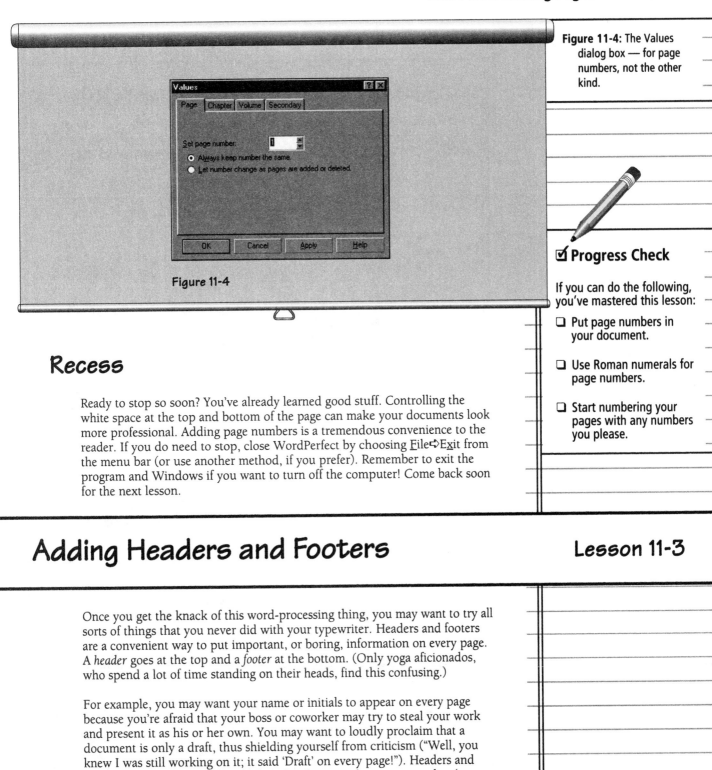

Figure 11-4: The Values dialog box — for page numbers, not the other kind.

Values

Page | Chapter | Volume | Secondary

Set page number: 1

○ Always keep number the same.
○ Let number change as pages are added or deleted.

OK | Cancel | Apply | Help

Figure 11-4

Recess

Ready to stop so soon? You've already learned good stuff. Controlling the white space at the top and bottom of the page can make your documents look more professional. Adding page numbers is a tremendous convenience to the reader. If you do need to stop, close WordPerfect by choosing File⇨Exit from the menu bar (or use another method, if you prefer). Remember to exit the program and Windows if you want to turn off the computer! Come back soon for the next lesson.

☑ **Progress Check**

If you can do the following, you've mastered this lesson:

❑ Put page numbers in your document.

❑ Use Roman numerals for page numbers.

❑ Start numbering your pages with any numbers you please.

Adding Headers and Footers   Lesson 11-3

Once you get the knack of this word-processing thing, you may want to try all sorts of things that you never did with your typewriter. Headers and footers are a convenient way to put important, or boring, information on every page. A *header* goes at the top and a *footer* at the bottom. (Only yoga aficionados, who spend a lot of time standing on their heads, find this confusing.)

For example, you may want your name or initials to appear on every page because you're afraid that your boss or coworker may try to steal your work and present it as his or her own. You may want to loudly proclaim that a document is only a draft, thus shielding yourself from criticism ("Well, you knew I was still working on it; it said 'Draft' on every page!"). Headers and footers can contain not only text but also the time, date, page number (yes, this is the other way to number pages), and even graphics.

Notes:

extra credit

A picture is worth a thousand words

You can add pictures to your document by creating a graphics box. You need to have a picture to add, of course, in the form of a graphics file. Collections of pictures sold with the intention that they'll be included in documents are called clip art, left over from the days when you needed a pair of scissors to use them. WordPerfect comes with a bunch of sample pictures, and you can buy graphics files, too, or find them on the Internet.

Here's how to display a picture in your document:

1. **Move your cursor where you want the picture to appear.**

2. **Create an image box by choosing Insert⇨Graphics⇨ Clipart (to insert a graphic that came with WordPerfect) or Insert⇨Graphics⇨From File (to insert a graphic whose name and location you know).**

 You can also insert the WordPerfect Clipart by clicking the Clipart button on the toolbar.

When you choose to insert Clipart, you see the Scrapbook window. To insert an image, drag it from the Scrapbook window into the WordPerfect window, or copy it using Ctrl+C to copy from the Scrapbook, and Ctrl+V to paste it into your document.

When WordPerfect was installed on your computer, it probably copied some of its Clipart to your computer's disk drive. But

WordPerfect comes with too much Clipart to have clogging up your hard drive. That Clipart remains on the WordPerfect CD. To use it, put that CD into your CD-ROM drive and click the CD Clipart tab in the Scrapbook window. Double-click a folder (each folder is a category of Clipart) to see the actual Clipart. To return to the categories, click the Up One Level button near the top right corner of the Scrapbook window. Close the Scrapbook when you're done with it.

When you choose to insert a graphic from a file, you see the Insert Image dialog box. Navigate your way to the file so that the name of the file appears in the File name box; then click the Insert button.

WordPerfect does three things: 1) It creates what is called a "graphics box" (the WordPerfect container for the graphic); 2) It puts the contents of the file you selected in that box; and 3) It selects the graphics box, surrounding it with eight little black squares called "handles." You can select the box yourself (if you're been working elsewhere in your document for instance) by clicking on the graphic.

When a graphics box is selected, the Property bar changes to display tools used for editing graphics. You can also edit a box by right-clicking it and using the QuickMenu options. Use either of these methods to add a caption, border, or other fancy stuff. To move a graphics box, select it (so that little boxes appear around its edges) and drag it where you want it. Delete the box by selecting it and pressing the Delete key.

on the test

Tip: Being in Page view when you're working with headers and footers helps — you can't see them in Draft view except when you're creating or editing them. As you may recall, Page view (which is probably what you're in anyway) displays what will be printed, including the header at the top of each page and the footer at the bottom. If you prefer Draft view (as we often do), stick with that and remember that headers and footers don't appear on the screen.

Use Page view when working with headers and footers

WordPerfect lets you have up to two different headers and footers at a time in a document. For example, you can have different headers (Header A and Header B) and footers (Footer A and Footer B) for even- and odd-numbered pages. For another section of a document, you might want *different* headers and footers, one set for even pages and one set for odd pages. Mostly we have just one header or footer at a time (forget the odd and even thing), so you can stick with using Header A and Footer A and reuse them when you want a different header for a different set of pages. You can also have both headers and/or footers on the same page — but they appear in the same space at the top of the page, so you need to be careful that the text of one doesn't overlap the text of the other.

Creating a header or footer

on the CD

How about adding headers to the GTK Catalog.101.WPD document? The header you'll create will include the title of the document and the date. You don't need to include a page number in your headers because you already defined page numbers for the document in Lesson 11-2. If you didn't define page numbers, open GTK Catalog2.101.WPD, which includes defined page numbers.

To put a header or footer in your document, follow these steps:

1 **Move your cursor to the top of the first page on which you want the header or footer to appear. For the catalog that you're editing, move to page 2.**

That is, the real page 2 — the second page of the document. The real page 2 contains the first page of the table of contents.

2 **Choose Insert⇨Header/Footer from the menu.**

The Headers/Footers dialog box appears, as shown in Figure 11-5.

3 **Choose the header or footer that you'll create — in this case, Header A.**

If you want something to appear at the top of the page, choose Header A (wiseacres can choose Header B; it comes out the same), and if you want something at the bottom, choose Footer A (same goes for Footer B as for Header B). If you plan to use only one header or footer at a time for the document, stick with Header A or Footer A.

4 **Click the Create button in the Headers/Footers dialog box.**

The cursor appears in a box outlined by guidelines at the very top of the page. The Property bar changes a little to display tools for working with headers and footers. Figure 11-6 shows the WordPerfect window as it appears after you've given the command to create a header. Your cursor appears where the header will appear on the page (if you're in Page view).

5 **Type the text of your header or footer,** Great Tapes for Kids Catalog.

You can control how your text looks in all the usual ways — changing font size, text style, and so on. If you want more than one line in the header or footer, feel free to use the Enter key to start a new line.

Format→Header/ Footer to create or edit header or footer

Figure 11-5: WordPerfect lets you create two different headers and two different footers.

Figure 11-6: Your WordPerfect window looks like this when it's ready for you to type a header.

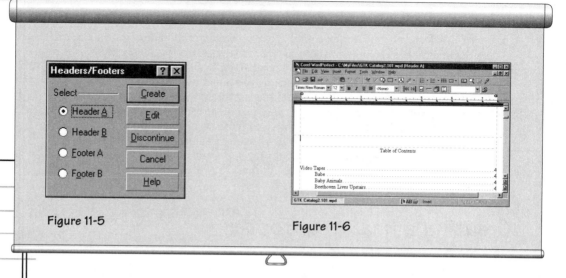

Figure 11-5

Figure 11-6

Ctrl+Shift+D inserts code for current date (changes every day)

Ctrl+D inserts today's date (doesn't change)

Close button

Page Numbering button

6 Press Alt+F7 to get ready to type text to appear at the right margin.

It's the old flush-right command. You can also choose Format⇨Line⇨Flush Right from the menu bar.

7 To insert the date, press Ctrl+Shift+D.

WordPerfect inserts a Date code that always shows the current date. If you open this document tomorrow, WordPerfect updates the code to show tomorrow's date.

If you want to insert today's date as text so that the date is *not* automatically updated, choose the command Insert⇨Date⇨Date Text instead, or Ctrl+D.

To change the date format, choose Insert⇨Date/Time.

8 Click the Close button on the Header/Footer Property bar after you're done editing your header or footer.

WordPerfect inserts a code where the cursor is: a Header A, Header B, Footer A or Footer B code. Move forward in the document. You see the same header on every page starting with page 2.

To put a header or footer in your document, choose the Insert⇨Header/Footer command, format the header, and click the Close button on the Header/Footer Property bar. The header or footer appears on every page of the document, starting with the page on which you defined it. To display the Header/Footer Property bar again, or to edit the header, click the header at the top of any page on which it appears.

on the test

Remember that you can use headers and footers to add page numbers. To put a page number in your header or footer, click the Page Numbering button on the Header/Footer Property bar and choose Page Number.

Suppressing headers and footers on the first page

on the test

Suppressing headers and footers on the first page of a document is standard. *Suppressing* them means that they don't appear, and this is often done because the first page of a document already has all the information that is in the header or footer. The header and footer may just clutter up the initial presentation of a document.

on the CD

In the GTK Catalog.101.WPD document that you've been slaving over for the last few lessons, you created a header starting on page 2. Now you decide to suppress the header on the page that begins the actual catalog.

1 **Move your cursor to the page on which you don't want the header or footer to appear. In this case, it's page 5.**

You can suppress headers and footers on any page — just move your cursor there. Be aware, though, that the Suppress code that you're about to insert may end up on a different page if you insert or delete text, so it's a good idea to put the code near the text that will always be on the page that shouldn't have headers and footers — that's usually the title.

2 **Choose Format➪Page➪Suppress from the menu.**

The Suppress dialog box appears, as shown in Figure 11-7, with suppression options (something that some governments seem to have easy access to).

3 **Choose what to suppress by clicking it to put an check mark in the box. The header that you created is Header A, so click Header A.**

If you want no headers or footers, and you've embedded the page number in one or the other but would still like a page number, notice that you can choose that option at the bottom of the dialog box.

4 **Click OK to close the dialog box.**

The header and footer disappears from this page but still appears on other pages.

5 **Save GTK Catalog.101.WPD by pressing Ctrl+S.**

If your dog kicks your computer's plug out of the wall right now, you'll lose all the work that you've done on this document. Why risk it, even if you don't have a dog? Save early and often!

The Format➪Page➪Suppress command enables you to skip printing headers and footers on specific pages.

Notes:

Format→Page→ Suppress to skip printing header or footer on current page

Figure 11-7: This dialog box lets you suppress what you've gone to great pains to create.

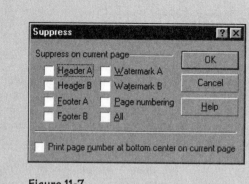

Figure 11-7

Horizontal Line button

Header/Footer Placement button

Dressing up your headers and footers

You can use all of WordPerfect's formatting commands to format the text of your headers and footers. Here are formatting tips:

- To make a three-part header or footer with some text left justified, some centered, and some right justified, type the first part of the header, use Shift+F7 to center the next part, press Alt+F7, and type the right justified part.

- If you want a horizontal line in your header — perhaps to separate the text of the header from the text in the document — click the Horizontal Line button on the Property bar. This gives you a basic single horizontal line. If you're interested in getting fancier, check out your options by selecting the line (clicking on it) and using the tools that appear on the Property bar.

You can also double-click the line to display the Edit Graphics Line dialog box.

- If you want the header or footer to appear on only odd or even pages, use the Header/Footer Placement button on the Header/Footer Property bar to specify Odd Pages, Even Pages, or Every Page. If you print a header on even pages, you'll probably want to define another header to print on just odd pages.

To discontinue a header or footer so that it doesn't appear past a certain page, go to the first page that the header or footer should *not* appear on, display the Header/Footer dialog box, choose the header or footer you want to discontinue, and click the Discontinue button. From that point forward in your document, the header or footer is gone, gone, gone.

extra credit

Creating footnotes and endnotes

A footnote or endnote is a number in the text and a reference or annotation to which that number refers. The only difference between a footnote and an endnote is that footnotes appear at the bottom of the page that contains the reference; endnotes appear at the end of a document.

WordPerfect makes footnotes and endnotes easy to use — it numbers them for you automatically so that when you add a note to the text, WordPerfect juggles the numbers to make them appear in order with the correct reference. For footnotes, it also figures out how much space is needed at the bottom of each page for the footnotes on that page.

Not everyone needs to use footnotes or endnotes — if you need to use them, you know it, so here's how to do it:

1. **Put your cursor where the footnote or endnote number should appear.**

   Usually, you place the cursor after the period ending the sentence that contains the reference.

2. **Choose Insert⇨Footnote/Endnote.**

   You see the Footnote/Endnote dialog box.

3. **Choose Footnote or Endnote and click Create.**

Usually, you don't need to change the number.

WordPerfect displays a footnote or endnote typing area. The cursor appears after the footnote or endnote number and the Property bar changes to include some buttons specific to footnotes and endnotes.

4. **Type the reference or annotation.**

   Don't change the reference number, because keeping footnotes in the correct order is one of the things that WordPerfect does best.

5. **Click the Close button on the Property bar.**

   WordPerfect returns you to your regular text.

If you're in Page view, footnotes appear at the bottom of the page and move to a new page if the footnote number moves — maybe because of added text. If you move the block of text with the reference number in it, WordPerfect changes the number, if needed, and keeps the references in the right order.

To edit a footnote or endnote, click the text in the note (you need to be in Page view). Click the Next or Previous button to go to the next or previous note. To delete a footnote or endnote, delete the reference number in the text.

Notes:

☑ **Progress Check**

If you can do the following, you've mastered this lesson:

❑ Put headers and footers in your document.

❑ Include today's date in a header or footer.

❑ Omit the header or footer for a certain page.

Avoiding Bad (Page) Breaks

Lesson 11-4

When you want to end one page and start another, insert a hard page break code by pressing Ctrl+Enter. In general, though, you should let WordPerfect choose where to put page breaks.

bad break = page
break in lousy-
looking place

But what about when WordPerfect inserts a page break in a place that looks just terrible, like between a heading and the first paragraph of the section that follows the heading? Or in the middle of a table? When WordPerfect (or any word processor) inserts a page break in a silly-looking place, it's a *bad break*. This lesson is about avoiding bad breaks.

on the test

Luckily, you can avoid bad breaks in your documents by telling WordPerfect about sections of your document that should not be broken into separate pages. WordPerfect has an unusually appropriate name for the dialog box that enables you to tell WordPerfect where *not* to put page breaks — it's called the Keep Text Together dialog box.

on the CD

You'll learn to avoid two kinds of bad breaks:

- A page break that occurs after the first line of a paragraph (the lone line is called an *orphan*) or before the last line (the lone line is called a *widow*) — leaving one line of a paragraph all by itself at the top or bottom of a page is bad form.

- A page break that occurs right after a heading so that the heading is sitting by itself at the bottom of the page while the text that goes with it appears on the next page.

You can avoid both of these problems by using the Keep Text Together dialog box, which you display by choosing Format⇨Page⇨Keep Text Together from the menu bar.

Format→Page→
Keep Text Together
to control bad
breaks

heads up

Try not to use a hard page break (Ctrl+Enter) to avoid a bad break. Hard page breaks can cause trouble later if you're still editing your document and the position of the page break changes. Use the Keep Text Together dialog box instead.

Preventing widows and orphans

on the test

Widows and *orphans* are single lines that get separated from the rest of the paragraph that they belong to. Think of each line in a paragraph as a family. Keep families together in the following way:

on the CD

1 **If it's not already open, open the GTK Catalog.101.WPD document, which you'll edit during this lesson. If you haven't done the previous lessons in this unit, open GTK Catalog3.101.WPD.**

2 **Move the cursor to the beginning of the document by pressing Ctrl+Home.**

As always, WordPerfect inserts a code that affects only the text after it. Insert the code at the tippy-top of the document so that widows and orphans are prevented throughout the document.

3 **Choose Format⇨Keep Text Together from the Menu bar.**

WordPerfect displays the aptly named Keep Text Together dialog box, as shown in Figure 11-8.

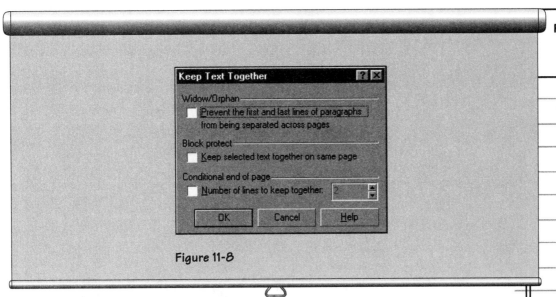

Figure 11-8

4 **Click the box next to Prevent the first and last lines of paragraphs from being separated across pages.**

A check mark now appears in the box.

5 **Click OK to leave the dialog box.**

WordPerfect inserts a *Wid/Orph:On* code where your cursor was when you started this command. Aren't you glad you don't have to remember the codes?

Use the Keep Text Together dialog box to prevent the first and last lines of paragraphs from being separated across pages — otherwise known as preventing widows and orphans.

Keeping text together

You may want to keep blocks of text together. For example, tables look terrible with a page break in the middle. WordPerfect has just the thing for these occasions: it's called Block Protect. When you have a chunk of text that you want to keep on one page, you can select the text and tell WordPerfect to *protect the block* — that is, avoid inserting a page break within the block.

In GTK Catalog.101.WPD, the Books part of the Table of Contents has a page break in the middle of it. Protect the Books block so that all the books appear on the same page.

1 **Select the text that should appear together on the page: all of the book titles, including the heading.**

2 **Display the Keep Text Together dialog box by choosing Format⇨Keep Text Together from the menu.**

Refer to Figure 11-8 for a look at the Keep Text Together dialog box. The middle section of the dialog box is called Block protect, and enables you to tell WordPerfect to keep selected text all on the same page (it protects the selected block of text).

3 **Click the box next to <u>K</u>eep selected text together on same page so that a check mark appears in the box.**

4 **Click OK to leave the Keep Text Together dialog box.**

Word Perfect inserts *Block Pro* codes at the beginning and the end of the selected text and moves the page break so that it occurs before the selected text.

Remember to use the WordPerfect Block Protect feature whenever you need to tell WordPerfect to keep selected text all on one page.

Keeping heads with bodies

You've learned how to keep families together; read on to find out how to keep sections from getting decapitated. Specifically, you'll learn how to keep a heading with at least part of the text that follows. To perform this feat, you insert a *Condl EOP* (*Conditional End of Page*) code in your document, which says to WordPerfect, "If this line falls within x lines of the end of the page, take the whole kit and caboodle and put it on the next page." You get to determine how many lines x is.

on the CD

Unlike preventing widows and orphans, which can be done once for the entire document, you must tell WordPerfect each time that you want a heading to be kept with some of the next paragraph. If you want to get fancy, you can use styles (we talked about them in Unit 9); the style you use for your heading can contain a Conditional End of Page code that will skip text to the next page if you begin using the style within x lines of the end of the page. For simplicity's sake, learn to use Conditional End of Pages on this one paragraph in the GTK Catalog. With GTK Catalog.101.WPD open, follow these steps:

1 **Move your cursor to the beginning of a heading that is separated by a page break from the information that follows it.**

The Beethoven Lives Upstairs heading probably appears by itself at the bottom of the page numbered one.

If you can't find an orphaned heading, create one hitting the enter key a few times — just for this exercise though. Because you all have different printers, this exercise will work a little differently for everyone.

2 **Choose Fo<u>r</u>mat⇨<u>K</u>eep Text Together from the menu.**

WordPerfect displays the Keep Text Together dialog box, a familiar sight by now. Refer to Figure 11-8 if it's not.

3 **In the Conditional End of Page section of the dialog box, click the little box to the left of the label <u>N</u>umber of lines to keep together.**

A check mark appears in the box to tell WordPerfect that you're interested in inserting a Condl EOP code.

4 **Enter 3 in the box to the right of the <u>N</u>umber of lines to keep together the heading with the subheading and at least one line of the paragraph that follows.**

select text; then, in Keep Text Together dialog box, select the option to keep selected text together on same page

heading should always have 2+ lines of text after it on same page

This tells WordPerfect how many lines to keep together. Because the paragraphs in this document are formatted to leave extra space after each carriage return, you need to keep together only three lines: the heading, followed by the subheading, followed by at least one line of the paragraph. Because you already turned on the widows and orphans option, WordPerfect translates this into at least two lines of the paragraph.

5 Choose OK to leave the dialog box.

WordPerfect enters the Condl EOP code in your document, and the page break is moved if necessary.

6 Save the GTK Catalog.101.WPD document by pressing Ctrl+S.

A Conditional End of Page code is the best way to keep a heading with the text that follows.

on the CD

Have consideration for WordPerfect when you use the Keep Text Together features — WordPerfect has to put page breaks somewhere! If you insert too many Condl EOP codes, especially ones in which you type a large number for the number of lines to keep together, WordPerfect may have trouble figuring out where it *can* insert a page break! You may end up with large white spaces at the bottoms of pages.

The time saving way to keep headings with text is to first finish your document. You can then start at the top of the document, find where WordPerfect has left a heading hanging lonely at the end of a page, and insert a Condl EOP code.

Well done! You've learned how to spiff up your documents in a bunch of new ways, including setting top and bottom margins, numbering pages, creating headers and footers, and avoiding bad page breaks.

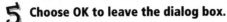

☑ Progress Check

If you can do the following, you've mastered this lesson:

❑ Prevent widows and orphans, and achieve other worthy social goals.

❑ Keep a block of text together on a page.

❑ Keep a heading with text that follows.

Unit 11 Quiz

Notes:

For each of the following questions, circle the letter of the correct answer or answers. Remember, there may be more than one right answer for each question!

1. **To display the Margins dialog box, you can . . .**

   A. Choose Format⇨Margins from the Menu bar.

   B. Press the Margins key on the keyboard (if you can find it).

   C. Press Ctrl+F8.

   D. Hold down the Ctrl, Alt, and Shift keys while typing the word *margin*.

   E. Double-click the margins strip of the Ruler.

2. **A header is . . .**

   A. A soccer play.

   B. A yoga posture.

   C. Something that appears at the top of every page of a document.

   D. A section title.

   E. Something that appears at the bottom of odd pages of a document.

3. **Block protect . . .**

   A. Is something that your neighborhood watch does.

   B. Is frequently seen in nursery schools and play groups.

   C. Keeps a block of text together on a page.

   D. Is what to use when you don't want a page break in the middle of a table.

   E. Is performed using the Format⇨Keep Text Together command.

4. **In this unit you learned . . .**

   A. How to use letters instead of page numbers.

   B. How to put page numbers on only odd numbered pages.

   C. How to suppress page numbers on a particular page.

   D. How to change the value of the printed page number.

   E. How to change the font the page number is printed in.

5. **Which of the following are *not* positions in which WordPerfect can place page numbers:**

   A. Bottom Center.

   B. Alternating Top.

   C. No Page Numbering.

   D. Third Base.

   E. Shortstop.

Unit 11 Exercise

1. Type a title page for your next novel, the one about how a secret agent single-handedly averts World War III. Include the title of the novel, your name, and the name of the publisher.

2. Insert a page break after the title page.

3. On page 2, type the copyright information. Indicate that this is the sixth printing of your book because the first five printings sold out. Thank your mother, father, and cat for helping you write the book. Also thank the authors of *Dummies 101: WordPerfect 8 For Windows* for helping you learn to use WordPerfect.

4. Center the title page vertically.

5. Start numbering the pages on page 2.

6. Save the document as Novel.WPD.

7. (Optional) Insert a page break after page 2 and write an entire novel (or make it a short story, if you're a little short on time). Make sure that page numbers appear on each page.

8. (Optional) Save and print the novel, hire a literary agent, and submit the novel to a publisher.

Part III Review

Unit 8 Summary

▶ **Formatting characters:** To make characters bold, italic, or underlined, select the text to be formatted and click on the Bold, Italic, or Underline button on the toolbar. Alternatively, use the keystrokes Ctrl+B, Ctrl+I, or Ctrl+U.

▶ **Formatting text:** To format text that is about to be written, click on the appropriate button or press the corresponding keys — then as you type, the text will be formatted.

▶ **Changing fonts:** Change the font of selected text by selecting the text, clicking on the Font Face button on the toolbar and choosing a new font. Change the font for the rest of the document by using the same steps with no text selected.

▶ **QuickFonts:** Use the QuickFonts button to change the font of selected text to a recently used font.

▶ **Changing type size:** Change the type size by clicking on the Font Size button on the toolbar — when text is selected, the size of the selected text changes; when no text is selected, the size of the type changes for the rest of the document.

▶ **Identifying font and font size:** The Font Face and Font Size buttons show the name and size of text where the cursor is.

▶ **Changing the initial font:** Change the initial font of a document by choosing Format⇨Document⇨Initial Font and changing the font in the Document Initial Font dialog box.

▶ **Changing capitalization:** Change the capitalization of text that you've already typed by selecting the text and choosing Edit⇨Convert Case from the menu.

▶ **Copy character formatting:** Copy character formatting by selecting some formatted text, clicking on the QuickFormat button on the toolbar, choosing Characters or Headings, and selecting the text that you want to format in the same way.

Unit 9 Summary

▶ **Revealing codes:** Reveal codes by pressing Alt+F3 or choosing View⇨Reveal Codes from the menu bar. Make the Reveal Codes window go away by using the same technique.

▶ **Deleting a code:** Delete a code by putting the cursor (the red block in the Reveal Codes window) next to the code and pressing Delete or Backspace. Alternatively, click on the code and drag it out of the Reveal Codes window. When the Reveal Codes window isn't visible, you can't delete codes.

▶ **Expanding a code:** Expand a code to see more details about it by putting the cursor immediately to its left.

▶ **Changing code settings:** Change the settings in a code by double-clicking on it to display the appropriate dialog box. Change the settings in the dialog box and make the code changes also.

Part III Review

Unit 10 Summary

▶ **Changing line spacing:** Double-space (or otherwise change the spacing between lines) by using the Line Spacing dialog box — display it by choosing Format⇨Line⇨Spacing.

▶ **Displaying the ruler:** Display the ruler by pressing Alt+Shift+F3 or by choosing View⇨Ruler from the menu bar.

▶ **Formatting paragraphs:** Use the Paragraph Format dialog box to set paragraph formatting for the whole document. Display the dialog box by choosing Format⇨Paragraph⇨Format from the menu bar.

▶ **Setting margins:** Set margins in the Margins dialog box — display it by choosing Format⇨Margins, or by pressing Ctrl+F8, or by clicking and dragging the dotted gray guidelines — but make sure that the cursor is where the new margins should begin!

▶ **Indenting paragraphs:** Indent paragraphs by putting the cursor at the beginning of the paragraph to be indented and pressing F7 (indent), Ctrl+F7 (hanging indent), or Ctrl+Shift+F7 (double indent).

▶ **Justifying text:** Justify text in the paragraph the cursor is in (or selected paragraphs) by clicking on the Justification button on the Property bar.

▶ **Setting tab stops:** Set tab stops by clicking on the tab strip of the ruler. Delete a tab stop by dragging the tab stop off the tab strip.

Unit 11 Summary

▶ **Centering text:** Center text on a page by choosing Format⇨Page⇨Center from the menu bar.

▶ **Numbering pages:** Number pages by choosing the Format⇨Page Numbering⇨Numbering from the menu bar or by putting a page number in a header or footer by using the Number button on the Header/Footer bar.

▶ **Adding headers and footers:** Add headers and footers by choosing the Format⇨Header/Footer command.

▶ **Controlling page breaks:** Control page breaks by making use of the Keep Text Together dialog box — display it by choosing Format⇨Page⇨Keep Text Together from the menu.

Part III Test

The questions on this test cover all of the material presented in Parts I, II, and III, Units 1-12.

True False

T   F   1. There are at least three different ways to make text bold, italic, or underlined.

T   F   2. If text is bold, it's impossible to make it underlined, too.

T   F   3. The word *it's* is spelled wrong in this sentence: "WordPerfect is great but it's manual is not so hot."

T   F   4. If you hit the Caps Lock key by mistake, the only way the fix the text you wrote is to retype it correctly.

T   F   5. Fonts only come in one size.

T   F   6. Double-clicking on a code is a really cool way to change the settings.

T   F   7. The best line in *Star Wars* is when Hans Solo tells Princess Leia that he loves her and she says, "I know."

T   F   8. Codes always look the same, no matter where the cursor is.

T   F   9. The best way to double-space a document is to type it and then go back and hit Enter twice at the end of every line.

T   F   10. The best way to add page numbers is to type each page number at the bottom of each page.

Multiple Choice

For each of the following questions, circle the correct answer or answers. Remember, there may be more than one right answer for each question!

11. Add page numbers to a document by:

A. Adding them to a header or footer.

B. Typing them at the bottom of each page.

C. Printing the document and then handwriting the correct number on each page.

D. Choosing Format⇨Page Numbering⇨Select from the menu bar.

E. Inserting a *Pg Num Pos* code at the point in the document where the page numbers should begin.

12. Which of the following movies was Susan Sarandon not in?

A. *Little Women.*

B. *The Witches of Eastwick.*

C. *The Big Easy.*

D. *The Client.*

E. *The Rocky Horror Picture Show.*

Part III Test

13. **Which of the following can't you do with the Keep Text Together dialog box?**

    A. Prevent widows and orphans.

    B. Keep selected text on the same page.

    C. Keep a heading with at least some of the section that follows it.

    D. Insert a page break after the title page.

    E. Keep a designated number of lines together on the same page.

14. **Which of the following colors do not appear in the Reveal Codes window?**

    A. Black.

    B. Yellow.

    C. White.

    D. Gray.

    E. Red.

15. **Which of the following makes your document seem shorter?**

    A. A larger font.

    B. Smaller margins.

    C. Changing line spacing to 2.2.

    D. Smaller paper.

    E. A bigger, longer title.

16. **Which of the following are enemies of the Federation?**

    A. The Borg.

    B. The Klingons.

    C. The Romulans.

    D. The Bajorans.

    E. The Vulcans.

17. **WordPerfect does *not* use a code to:**

    A. Change margins.

    B. Change font size.

    C. Center text on a page vertically.

    D. Center text on a page horizontally.

    E. Save a document.

18. **Which of the following cannot be done using a choice from the Format menu?**

    A. Change the font of selected text.

    B. Add a header or footer.

    C. Change margins.

    D. Indent a paragraph.

    E. Copy selected text.

Part III Test

Matching

19. **Match up the following buttons with the corresponding tasks:**

    A.

    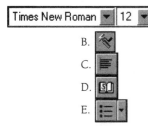

    B.

    C.

    D.

    E.

    1. Add bullets at the beginning of each paragraph.
    2. Change font.
    3. Check spelling.
    4. Copy formatting.
    5. Change the justification of the text.

20. **Match up the features with the part of the screen they appear on.**

    A. Tab stops.
    B. Codes.
    C. Redo button.
    D. Font Face button.
    E. Printer you're using.

    1. Property bar.
    2. Toolbar.
    3. Application Bar.
    4. Reveal Codes window.
    5. Ruler bar.

21. **Match up the following keyboard shortcuts with the corresponding tasks.**

    A. Alt+F3.
    B. F5.
    C. Ctrl+Z.
    D. F7.
    E. Ctrl+X.

    1. Go To.
    2. Undo.
    3. Reveal Codes.
    4. Cut.
    5. Indent.

22. **Match the following authors with their books:**

    A. J.R.R. Tolkien.
    B. Madeline L'Engle.
    C. David Brin.
    D. Ursula LeGuin.
    E. Anne McCaffrey.

    1. *The Ship Who Sang.*
    2. *Earth.*
    3. *The Dispossessed.*
    4. *A Wrinkle in Time.*
    5. *The Two Towers.*

Part III Lab Assignment

Create a flyer announcing a new line of videos from Great Tapes for Kids (or some other kind of event, if you like).

Step 1: Create the text

Load Sammy.101.WPD if you're a lazy typist — it has the basic text, unformatted. Or create your own text.

Step 2: Edit and Format

Center the text vertically on the page.

Center the lines on the page, as you think appropriate. Make at least one line all justified, so that it spreads from margin to margin.

Change font and font size and character formatting to make the most important text stick out and to make the flyer eye-catching.

Step 3: Save the document

Save the document with the name Invite.WPD.

Celebrate a line of new videos from
Great Tapes for Kids

Sammy the Studly Storyteller entrances
children and adults alike with his good looks
and mellifluous voice!

Get in your orders early
for these forthcoming videos:

Sammy the Studly Storyteller Flexes His Biceps

Sammy the Studly Storyteller Takes a Walk

Sammy the Studly Storyteller Does Sit-Ups

http://www.greattapes.com

Working with Advanced Features

Part IV

In this part . . .

WordPerfect has lots of advanced features that save you time and make your documents look great. Create your own newsletter using columns and tables and use the merge feature to send letters announcing your newsletter to hundreds of your closest friends. This part helps you start getting some of the real power out of WordPerfect's many capabilities.

Creating Multiple Column Documents and Tables

Objectives for This Unit

✓ Making newspaper-style, multiple-column documents

✓ Creating tables using the WordPerfect table feature

Prerequisites
▶ Using commands and dialog boxes (Unit 2)
▶ Starting a new page (Lesson 3-1)
▶ Understanding WordPerfect formatting codes (Lesson 9-1)
▶ Changing margins (Lesson 10-2)

on the CD
▶ Newsletter. 101.WPD
▶ Newsletter2. 101.WPD
▶ Chorus2. 101.WPD
▶ Guyana. 101.WPD

You have two ways to put text in vertical columns on the page: One is to use a table, and the other is to use columns. WordPerfect has a raft-load of features that help you create great-looking tables and multiple column documents. You'll get an introduction to these features in this unit. WordPerfect has a daunting number of table-related features, so we've selected just those commands, keys, and dialog boxes that we think you'll really find useful.

In general, columns align text vertically, and tables enable you to create text with both horizontal and vertical links. For example, a newsletter may be arrayed in columns, while text comparing two cars according to price and reliability would be easily set up in a table. There will be those of you, however, who are used to making tabbed tables. (You learned how to do those in Lesson 10-4.) We hope that you will experiment with the table feature, however, and learn that it's easier to use.

You array text in columns for different reasons. Deciding when to use tables and when to use columns can get confusing. We think that you'll find the table feature particularly useful — we use it for everything from resumes to timesheets. Columns are great for a newsletter layout, but we find that we don't use columns for much more than that.

use either table or columns feature for multiple columns

Notes:

on the test

Here's a way to decide whether you need columns or a table:

♦ If text flows from beginning to end and just happens to need to snake across the page, as in a newspaper or newsletter, use columns.

♦ For a multiple column list in the middle of regular text, use balanced newspaper columns to have WordPerfect automatically make each column the same width, or a table if each column of the list is a different category.

♦ If text has horizontal connections — for example, a title on the left is relevant across the row — use a table.

♦ If text appears in columns but one column is not related to the next — for example, one column heading is *Brownies* with text underneath, and one heading is *Butterscotch Bars* with text underneath — use a table.

♦ If a heading in one column needs to stay level with multiline text in another column — for example, a resume where one column lists dates and another lists specifics such as job title, responsibilities, and accomplishments — use a table.

In this unit, you'll learn how to put text into columns in various ways. You'll learn how to make a table with tabs, with the table feature, and how to make newspaper columns.

Lesson 12-1

Creating Newspaper Columns

You can create columns out of text either before or after you've written the text. You may find that it's easier to write, read, and edit if you begin without columns. What we're talking about here is something that looks like a newspaper or newsletter — flowing text that starts by going down one column and then continues in another column to the right of the first. If you're putting anything but flowing text into columns, you should probably be using the table feature. See Lesson 12-2 to learn about the table feature.

Columns come in four varieties:

newspaper columns:
text flows to
bottom of column
and then to top of
next column

♦ **Newspaper:** Text flows down the first column to the bottom of the page and then continues at the top of the next column.

♦ **Balanced newspaper:** Same as newspaper columns, but on the last page WordPerfect inserts column breaks to make all the columns about the same length.

♦ **Parallel:** Columns are grouped across the page in rows. The effect is much the same as a table.

♦ **Parallel with block protect:** Same as parallel columns, each row of columns is protected by block protect and will always appear without a page break. Refer to Lesson 11-4 for a description of block protect.

Figure 12-1 shows a diagram of newspaper and parallel columns.

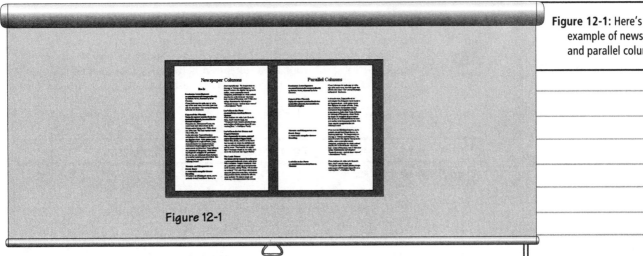

Figure 12-1

Figure 12-1: Here's an example of newspaper and parallel columns.

heads up

A table is usually more convenient than parallel columns. The idea of parallel columns is that paragraphs of text appear in a grid with rows and columns — each piece of text in one column is paired with a piece of text in the next column that must stay connected. The parallel column predated the table feature, and it's been left in WordPerfect mainly for people who already know how to use it. If you want rows and columns, you'll probably find the table feature easier to use.

The easiest way to create columns is to position the cursor where you want columns to begin or select the text you want to appear in columns. Then use the Columns button on the toolbar. Not coincidentally, it's right next to the Table QuickCreate button. The Columns button turns on columns starting where the cursor is. You can choose 2, 3, 4, or 5 columns. You can also choose Format⇨Columns from the menu to display the Columns dialog box — but don't bother. Use the Columns button on the toolbar for simplicity. You can always spruce up the columns later using the extra options that appear on the Columns dialog box. Creating columns inserts a *Col Def* code in your document, which defines columns and turns the columns feature on starting where the formatting code is.

Just because you have columns in your document doesn't mean your whole document has to be in columns, or that all the columns have to look the same. You can turn columns off by positioning the cursor where you want columns to end and clicking the Columns button on the toolbar and then choosing Columns Off from the drop-down menu. You can also choose Format⇨ Columns⇨Off from the menu to insert a *Col Def: Off* code in the document.

To change how your columns look, put the cursor in the columns of text, click the Columns button, and then choose Format from the drop-down menu that appears. You see the Columns dialog box, where you can change the type or number of columns, the space between columns, and the width of each column. You can also adjust the width of each column and the space between columns by clicking and dragging the column margins on the ruler.

Columns button

heads up

Moving your text around after you've put the text in columns can be tricky. That's why we suggest getting the text into final form before you put it into columns. See Table 12-1 for keystrokes that help you navigate when text is in columns. You may also find the Zoom feature useful so that you can see more of the document. Use the Zoom button on the far right of the toolbar or choose View➪Zoom from the menu bar.

Table 12-1	Moving Your Cursor Around in Columns
To Go Here . . .	**Press This**
Top of a column	Alt+Home
Last line of a column	Alt+End
Previous column	Alt+left arrow
Next column	Alt+right arrow

> *Alt key plus cursor movement keys to move around in columns*

Putting text into newspaper columns

on the CD

Start with the easy way to make columns: Use the Columns button on the toolbar. Take the text in Newsletter.101.WPD and make it look like a newsletter.

1 Open Newsletter.101.WPD.

Figure 12-2 shows the text of a *Great Tapes for Kids* newsletter. It would look more like a newsletter in two columns.

2 Put the cursor at the beginning of the line that reads *Welcome*.

heads up

Columns take effect starting where the cursor is, so make sure that your cursor is at beginning of the text that you want to appear in columns. In the document you're working on now, the text above this line makes up the masthead, which should stretch across the page.

3 Click the Columns button on the toolbar. Choose 2 Columns from the drop-down menu.

Poof! The text turns into two newspaper columns as shown in Figure 12-3. The text of the newsletter runs down to the bottom of the first page in the first column, continues to the top of the first page in the second column, continues to the first column of the second page, and so on. Notice that each column has its own margin guidelines — those guidelines can be clicked and dragged just like the margin guidelines.

> *click Columns button on toolbar to start using columns*

By far the easiest way to put text into newspaper columns is to use the Columns button on the toolbar. WordPerfect inserts a *Col Def* code in your document, which defines columns and turns them on starting where the code is.

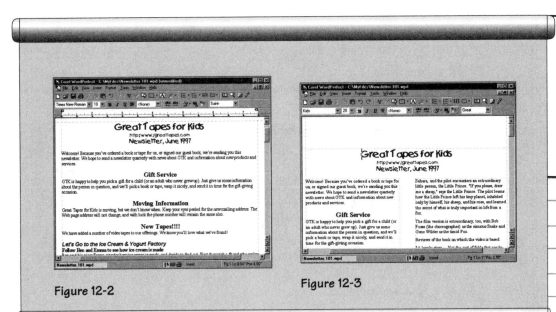

Figure 12-2: The Newsletter.101.WPD document would look more like a newsletter if you put the text in columns.

Figure 12-3: This is how the newsletter looks in two columns.

Figure 12-2

Figure 12-3

Notes:

Turning columns off

You may decide that you want part of your document in columns, but not all of it. WordPerfect can easily handle that. You just need to know how to tell WordPerfect what to do.

To put just part of your text in columns, you have a couple of choices:

▶ Turn columns on at the beginning of the text to be in columns (by defining columns, as in Lesson 12-1) and then to turn columns off at the end of the text (by choosing Off from the Columns button drop-down menu).

▶ Select the text that you want in columns and then define your columns.

Either way, WordPerfect puts a *Col Def* code at the beginning and the end of the text in columns. The formatting code at the beginning of the columns contains the definition for the columns, and the formatting code at the end of the columns is *Col Def: Off*.

Turning off columns by using a *Col Def* code is different from undoing the columns altogether. When you turn off columns, you tell WordPerfect that the text following the *Col Def: Off* code should not appear in multiple columns. If you want to forget about columns completely, the best way is to use the Reveal Codes window to find the formatting code that defines the columns and delete it. You can delete a formatting code by using the Delete key or by dragging the formatting code out of the Reveal Codes area.

on the CD

Currently, Newsletter.101.WPD is in columns from near the beginning of the document through the end. In this exercise, you'll turn off the columns before the contact information — that is, you'll add a *Col Def: Off* code.

1 Move your cursor to the beginning of the contact information at the end of the newsletter.

Because columns will be turned off starting where the cursor is, it is important to have the cursor in the right place. By turning columns off before this last section, the last section will not be formatted into two columns.

2 Click the Columns button on the toolbar and choose Discontinue from the drop-down menu.

WordPerfect inserts a Col Def: Off code into the text, turning off columns. The last section is, at this point, on the next page and not in columns. It's on page 3 because the first column reaches to the bottom of page 2.

3 Save the document.

If you don't want the text at the end of your document to appear in multiple columns, turn columns off by clicking the Columns button on the toolbar and choosing Discontinue from the drop-down menu. If you don't want the columns to fill the whole page from top to bottom, you can make them Balanced Newspaper, which you'll do in the next exercise.

Tip: When you're unsure whether or not text is formatted in columns, move the cursor in the text in question and see whether the ruler bar shows column margins.

Adjusting columns

Now you've made a document with multiple columns — cool! But what if you don't like the way the columns look? You can change the column definition — that is, the number of columns, type of columns, and space between the columns — by changing values in the Columns dialog box, as shown in Figure 12-4.

Display the Columns dialog box by

▶ Choosing Format⇨Columns from the menu

▶ Clicking the Columns button on the toolbar and choosing Format from the drop-down menu that appears

▶ Double-clicking the Col Def code in the Reveal Codes window

If you want to change the widths of your columns, you can make adjustments by using the guidelines or the ruler. Notice that each column has margins on the ruler bar. You can click and drag those the same way that you click and drag regular margins. In general, the click and drag method works best when you know how you want the columns to look.

on the test

If you want precisely equal columns, with the same space between each, or if you need to change the type of column, stick with the Columns dialog box — it's not that hard to use! Table 12-2 shows a list of the options in the Columns dialog box and what each setting does.

Margin notes:

click Columns button and choose Discontinue to turn columns off

Format→Columns to adjust column number, type, spacing, and widths

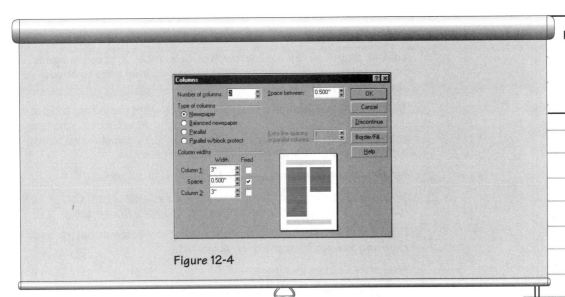

Figure 12-4

Notes:

Table 12-2	Columns Dialog Box Options
Option	**What It Does**
Number of columns	Sets the number of columns (use the up- and down-arrows). You can have up to 24 columns on a page.
Type of columns	Sets the type: Newspaper, Balanced newspaper, Parallel, or Parallel w/block protect.
Column widths	Sets the width of each column and space between columns; if the Fixed box is checked for a column or a margin between columns, the width stays constant, even if other space or column widths are changed. This is useful when you want to change some column widths by using the ruler bar and keep other column widths constant.
Space between	White space between columns, measured in inches or centimeters.
Extra line spacing in parallel columns	White space between rows, used only with parallel columns.

Adjust the column type in the Newsletter.101.WPD document so that the text is in Balanced newspaper columns rather than plain Newspaper columns. These columns leave room for the contact information at the bottom of the second page. If you didn't do Lesson 12-2, use Newsletter2.101.WPD for this exercise.

1 Look at page 2 of the newsletter. Notice that the first column goes to the bottom of the page, and the second column goes to about the middle of the page.

That's the definition of regular newspaper columns — the first column takes up the whole length of the page before text is put in the second column. When you change them to balanced newspaper columns, the text is moved around so that both columns will end at about the same place on the page.

2 Put the cursor somewhere in the text that is in columns.

As long as the cursor is in the column text, you will edit the original *Col Def* code when you display the Columns dialog box and make changes to it.

3 Display the Columns dialog box by clicking the Columns button and choosing Format from the drop-down list.

You see the Columns dialog box.

4 Change the Type of columns to Balanced newspaper.

5 Click OK.

6 Now look at the second page of the document. Can you tell that it's different?

7 Save and close the document.

☑ **Progress Check**

If you can do the following, you've mastered this lesson:

❑ Create text formatted in multiple columns.

❑ Change the type of columns used.

❑ Adjust the way columns look.

Ctrl+Enter to create column break when using multiple columns

extra credit

Controlling column breaks

You can control where WordPerfect inserts *column breaks* — where WordPerfect stops putting text in one column and switches to the next column. When you want to start a new column, insert a column break — another secret formatting code.

Wait! Column breaks and page breaks are closely connected. When all the columns on one page are full, WordPerfect puts text in the first column of the next page. In fact, you insert a column break the same way you insert a page break — by pressing Ctrl+Enter. You can also position the cursor and click the Columns button on the toolbar and choose New Column from the drop-down menu.

Here are some pointers for using column breaks:

♦ When using newspaper columns, keep an eye on the column breaks that you insert. If you edit the text in the columns so that one column gets longer or shorter, you may have to delete or move your column breaks to make your columns the right length. If you want perfectly even columns, you should set them up using the balanced newspaper column option to save yourself the bother of moving around column breaks. (You may not get perfectly balanced columns if you use any of the Keep Text Together options — like preventing widows and orphans — discussed in Unit 11.)

♦ When you insert a column break into balanced newspaper columns, WordPerfect begins a whole new block of balanced columns.

♦ When you use parallel columns, use column breaks to tell WordPerfect when to switch to the next column. Also use a column break to end the text in the rightmost column and begin putting text in the first column.

Recess

Working with columns can make you see double — or triple, if you're working with three columns. You may want to take a walk to clear your brain! If you need to exit WordPerfect, press Alt+F4 now, but be sure to save the work that you've done.

Using the Splendiferous Table Feature

Lesson 12-2

In Lesson 10-4, you learned about tab stops. You can create a table using tab stops, but the table feature offers you much more flexibility.

on the test

To make tables in which entries can be entire paragraphs or tables with lines between the rows or columns, consider using the Table command instead of tabs. You'll learn enough in the next lesson, we hope, to make you give up tabbed table-making forever!

For those of you coming straight from working on a typewriter, making a table the way this lesson shows you will be very different from what you're used to. On a typewriter, you need to have a very good idea of how the table will look, so that you can measure out columns and set tab stops. In WordPerfect, it's easy to make a "back-of-the-envelope" table and adjust it later to make it presentable. Adding or deleting rows or columns is a piece of cake, as is adjusting column widths. When you're creating a table for a fancy report or presentation, WordPerfect has a feature called Table SpeedFormat to help you spiff up your data with shading, fonts, and character formatting.

on the test

One reason that using the table feature is better any day than making a tabbed table is that you can change column widths without worrying about exactly where those pesky tab stop formatting codes are hiding. You can also add shading and lines that we wouldn't have a clue how to do with a tabbed table.

Here's a little terminology: A table is made up of *cells,* much like a spreadsheet. The first row is row 1, and the first column is column A. The cell in the third row of the first column is called A3, and so on. You know which cell you're in by looking at the first box on the status bar, which even names the table for you, starting with A. For example, if it says *TABLE A Cell A1,* you're in the first table in your document (Table A) in the first column of the first row (Cell A1).

A cell is like a tiny document: It holds as much as you put in it, and you are by no means limited to one line. In fact, a cell can contain several paragraphs of information, pictures, or whatever the spirit moves you to include.

It's easy to make a table. The toolbar has a key named Table QuickCreate. The button says *Tables* and it's just to the left of the Columns button. You can guess what it does! If you prefer, you can choose Insert⇨Table from the menu bar or press F12.

Notes:

table = grid of cells in rows and columns

Table QuickCreate button

Notes:

You move your cursor to another cell by pressing the Tab key. Your cursor moves to the right until there are no more cells, in which case it moves to the first cell on the next line. You can always use your mouse to position the cursor. Table 12-3 lists ways to move your cursor around in tables.

Table 12-3	Moving Around in a Table
To Move Here . . .	*Press This*
One cell to the right	Tab
One cell to the left	Shift+Tab
One cell down	Alt+down-arrow; down-arrow alone if the cell is only one line
One cell up	Alt+up arrow; up-arrow alone if the cell is only one line
First cell in row	Home, Home
Last cell in row	End, End

Format the contents of a table cell in the same way that you format regular text — you can make it centered or right justified, change the font, or make it bold or italic or underlined.

You format text by selecting the text or the cell or cells that the text is in. Selecting an entire row and column to format can be tricky. Move the pointer around the table until it turns into a big arrow and then:

- **To select a cell:** Click once when the pointer points left or up.
- **To select a column:** Double-click when the pointer points up.
- **To select a row:** Double-click when the pointer points left.
- **To select the whole table:** Triple-click when the pointer points left or up.
- **To select a number of contiguous cells:** Click and drag across the cells.

Tip: WordPerfect has a whole menu of commands about tables. Just right-click in the table to see them, or click the Table choice that appears in the Property bar when the cursor is in the table. If you need to do something that we don't cover here, take a look at those menu choices. Also notice that the Property bar changes to show new buttons relevant to using tables when the cursor is in a table — we refer to the Property bar you see when the cursor is in a table as the Table Property bar.

Creating a table

In this lesson, you'll create a table that looks like Figure 12-5.

1 **Begin a new document by closing any document you have open, or by clicking the New Blank Document button on the toolbar.**

You're going to do this one from scratch!

use formatting commands to format text in table cells

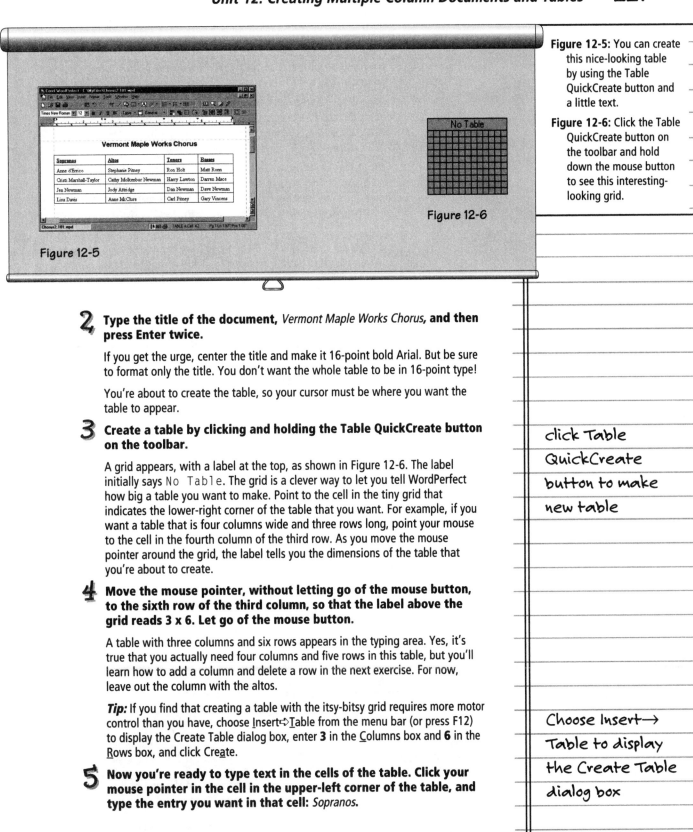

Figure 12-6

Figure 12-5: You can create this nice-looking table by using the Table QuickCreate button and a little text.

Figure 12-6: Click the Table QuickCreate button on the toolbar and hold down the mouse button to see this interesting-looking grid.

Figure 12-5

2 Type the title of the document, *Vermont Maple Works Chorus,* **and then press Enter twice.**

If you get the urge, center the title and make it 16-point bold Arial. But be sure to format only the title. You don't want the whole table to be in 16-point type!

You're about to create the table, so your cursor must be where you want the table to appear.

3 Create a table by clicking and holding the Table QuickCreate button on the toolbar.

A grid appears, with a label at the top, as shown in Figure 12-6. The label initially says No Table. The grid is a clever way to let you tell WordPerfect how big a table you want to make. Point to the cell in the tiny grid that indicates the lower-right corner of the table that you want. For example, if you want a table that is four columns wide and three rows long, point your mouse to the cell in the fourth column of the third row. As you move the mouse pointer around the grid, the label tells you the dimensions of the table that you're about to create.

4 Move the mouse pointer, without letting go of the mouse button, to the sixth row of the third column, so that the label above the grid reads 3 x 6. Let go of the mouse button.

A table with three columns and six rows appears in the typing area. Yes, it's true that you actually need four columns and five rows in this table, but you'll learn how to add a column and delete a row in the next exercise. For now, leave out the column with the altos.

Tip: If you find that creating a table with the itsy-bitsy grid requires more motor control than you have, choose Insert⇨Table from the menu bar (or press F12) to display the Create Table dialog box, enter **3** in the Columns box and **6** in the Rows box, and click Create.

5 Now you're ready to type text in the cells of the table. Click your mouse pointer in the cell in the upper-left corner of the table, and type the entry you want in that cell: *Sopranos.*

click Table
QuickCreate
button to make
new table

Choose Insert→
Table to display
the Create Table
dialog box

Notes:

6 **Press Tab to move from one cell to the next, filling in the rest of the cells in the table.**

Fill in your table to make it look like the one you saw in Figure 12-5, but leave out the column of altos (poor things!). Feel free to enter the names of your friends and relatives in place of the names of our friends and relatives in the figure. You should have one more row than you need.

7 **Adjust the column widths to make them only as wide as they need to be. Move the mouse pointer slowly near the vertical divider. When it turns into a vertical line with two horizontal arrows, click and drag the column divider where you want it.**

As soon as you click the mouse button, a vertical dotted line appears. Wherever you drop this dotted line is where the column border moves to. When you release the mouse button, the column divider jumps to its new position. If a column is too narrow for its contents, the text wraps onto a second line, and the row expands vertically to fit its contents. For example, what was a one-line cell becomes a two-line cell when you make the cell too narrow to fit its contents.

8 **Select the top row of the table — the headings *Sopranos, Tenors,* and *Basses* — and make them bold and underlined.**

Your document should look like Figure 12-7.

9 **Save your document as Chorus.WPD.**

Tip: If you don't have enough rows in your table, don't panic! Pressing Tab in the last cell of the table automagically adds another row to the table.

Deleting rows and columns

You can add and delete rows and columns in a table in two ways: with commands or with keystrokes. It's easier to use the QuickMenu commands (right-click in the table and choose Insert or Delete) than to remember the keystrokes, which are listed in Table 12-5. The QuickMenu commands are also available by clicking the Table button on the Table Property bar.

heads up

For some reason, WordPerfect assumes you'll add rows more than any of the other adding or deleting options: It includes a button on the Table Property bar for inserting rows in a table.

Insert row button

Table 12-5 Keystrokes to Add and Delete Rows and Columns

Press This Key . . .	To Do This
Alt+Insert	Insert a row before the cursor
Alt+Shift+Insert	Insert a row after the cursor
Tab	Add a row to the end of the table when the cursor is in the last cell
Alt+Delete	Delete the current row

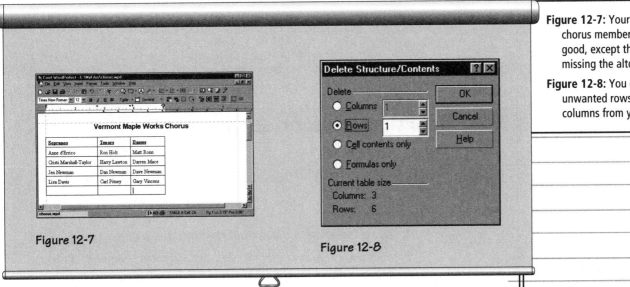

Figure 12-7: Your table of chorus members looks good, except that it's missing the altos!

Figure 12-8: You can delete unwanted rows or columns from your table.

Figure 12-7

Figure 12-8

Using the Chorus.WPD document that you just created, first delete the extra blank row in your table. If your version of Chorus.WPD didn't work out, you can open Chorus2.101.WPD instead.

1 Click the mouse pointer in any cell in the last row of the table.

It doesn't matter what column the cursor is in, as long as it's in the row that you want to delete.

2 Right-click in the table and choose <u>D</u>elete from the QuickMenu, or choose T<u>a</u>ble⇨<u>D</u>elete from the Property bar.

The Delete Structure/Contents dialog box appears, as shown in Figure 12-8, giving you information about the table and enabling you to tell WordPerfect exactly what you want to delete. Instead of using a menu to display the Delete Structure/Contents dialog box, you can also select the row and press Delete (the Select Table Row button on the Property bar selects a row).

3 If <u>R</u>ows radio button is not marked, click it to mark it.

WordPerfect suggests that you want to delete row 1. If WordPerfect suggests a different number, change it to row 1.

If you raise the number of rows or columns, WordPerfect starts with the row or column that the cursor is in and deletes rows or columns below or to the right, until the requisite number is reached. If the cursor is in the last row or column, the number cannot be bigger than 1.

4 Click OK to delete.

The last row of your table blinks out of existence. If you've changed your mind, click Cancel instead of OK.

Deleting one or more rows is as simple as choosing T<u>a</u>ble⇨<u>D</u>elete from the menu bar and filling out the dialog box. The same method works for deleting one or more columns.

Table→Delete to delete rows or columns

Notes:

Table→Insert to add new rows and columns

Tip: Another way to delete rows or columns is to select the rows or columns that you want to delete with your mouse and then press Delete. WordPerfect displays the same Delete dialog box that you see when you use the preceding commands.

Inserting rows or columns

Whether you're inserting a row or column doesn't change the steps you take — just make sure to tell WordPerfect which you're doing.

Add an extra column for the poor neglected altos:

1 Put your cursor in the second *(Tenor)* column of the table.

Your cursor must be in a column that is adjacent to where you want the new column to be.

2 Choose Table⇨Insert from the Property bar or right-click in the table and choose Insert.

WordPerfect displays the Insert Column/Rows dialog box that enables you to tell WordPerfect that you want a column or row and where you want it to appear.

3 Click Columns to tell WordPerfect what to insert.

The number of columns to insert is already 1.

4 Choose Before to tell WordPerfect to insert the new column before (to the left of) the column the cursor is in.

If your cursor were in the first column, you would insert the new column After (to the right of) the current column.

5 Click OK.

A new, empty column appears in the table. The column is ready to be filled with an *Altos* heading, and the names of the poor altos.

6 Save the table.

The Table⇨Insert command displays the Table Insert Columns/Rows dialog box, which lets you tell WordPerfect what to insert and where to put it.

Table 12-6 lists other things that you may want to do with and to tables.

extra credit

Size Column to Fit feature

Instead of jiggling the column widths to get particular words or phrases to fit on one line, you can use the WordPerfect Size Column to Fit feature to set a column width to match the widest entry. Just follow these steps:

1. **Select the cell or cells that you want the column to be sized to fit.**

2. **Click the right mouse button to display the column QuickMenu.**

3. **Click Size Column to Fit.**

Table 12-6 Other Things That You May Want to Do with Tables

When You Want To . . .	Do This
Move a row or column	Select and then click and drag to new position
Copy a row or column	Select, press Ctrl+C, choose Row or Column, and press Ctrl+V where the new column or row will be
Join or split cells	Select the cells and choose Join Cells or Split Cells from the QuickMenu
Position the table	Choose Format from the QuickMenu, select Table, and use the Table Position part of the dialog box
Change a row height	Choose Format from the QuickMenu, click Row at the top, and use the Row Height part of the dialog box
Change a column width	Click and drag the column border to its new position
Delete the whole table	Select the whole table, press Delete, and tell WordPerfect to delete the Entire Table
Create a column header	A column header is text that will be repeated on the first row on each page of the table; select the rows, choose Format from the QuickMenu, select Row, and click the Header Row box

extra credit

Creating fancy-looking tables by using Table SpeedFormat

WordPerfect has a spiffy feature to help you beautify your tables: the Table SpeedFormat. Here's just a taste of the beautifully formatted tables that the Table SpeedFormat can help you create:

1. **Put your cursor in any cell of the table. Display the Table SpeedFormat by choosing Table⇨SpeedFormat from the Property bar.**

    You can also use the Table QuickMenu. With the cursor in the table, click the right mouse button and choose SpeedFormat. You see the Table SpeedFormat dialog box which displays a list of table formats and a sample table. You can also create your own formats.

2. **Choose a style from the Available Styles list.**

3. **Click OK to apply the style to the table in your document.**

    Poof! The table is formatted using the style you chose, including lines, shading, and text formatting. If it looks just terrible, click the Undo button on the toolbar, or press Ctrl+Z.

    If you want to play with borders and fills yourself, and not confine your choices to what the Table SpeedFormat has to offer, use the Cell Fill and Change Outside Line buttons on the Property bar. Neither button is hard to use. You do need to know, however, that the lines and fills that you change affect only selected text.

☑ Progress Check

If you can do the following, you've mastered this lesson:

❏ Create a table.

❏ Alter the widths of the columns.

❏ Add and delete columns and rows.

❏ Use the Table Expert to prettify your tables.

Notes:

F12 to convert table with tabs to real table

extra credit

Turning a tabbed table into a real, live table

You may find that you like the table feature so much that you never want to work with tabbed tables again. If you have old, tabbed tables, you can turn them into real tables by selecting the text and pressing F12. Here's how:

1. **Clean up the table, if necessary.**

   When you convert the tabbed table to a WordPerfect table, WordPerfect decides how to set up the new table based on where the tabs are, so it's best if there are no extra tabs or tab stops in the table (for example, if there's a tab stop at 0.5 inch but no columns start at 0.5 inch, the table will come out better if that tab stop is deleted). Use the View⇨Show ¶ command so you can see the tabs in the table. Delete tabs so that you have only one to separate text in each column. You may want to do a search and replace — search for two tabs in a row and replace with a single tab. (On the Find and Replace dialog box, choose Match⇨Codes and use the Left Tab code.)

2. **Select the text that makes up the table.**

   Include the column headings, but not the table title.

3. **Press F12 or choose Insert⇨Table from the menu.**

   The Convert Table dialog box appears. WordPerfect gives you the choice of making a table from the text in parallel columns or from a table that uses tab stops.

4. **The Tabular column choice should be check marked. If it isn't check marked, click it and then click OK.**

   Presto-change-o! WordPerfect converts the text into a table. WordPerfect knows that tabs separate columns, so it more or less takes out the tabs and replaces them with column dividers.

Unit 12 Quiz

For each of the following questions, circle the letter of the correct answer or answers. Remember, there may be more than one right answer for each question!

1. **It makes sense to use the WordPerfect column feature when you are...**

   A. Writing a newsletter.

   B. Creating a resume.

   C. Creating a table to compare features of two newspapers.

   D. Building a portico for your house in the Greek style.

   E. Creating documents and trying to figure out what to call 'em.

2. **It makes sense to use the WordPerfect table feature when you are...**

   A. Writing a newsletter.

   B. Creating a resume.

   C. Creating a table to compare features of two recipes.

   D. Serving dinner to a crowd of friends.

   E. Making something that looks like a spreadsheet.

3. **Balanced newspaper columns...**

   A. Work great when you want text in columns and text that isn't in columns all on the same page.

   B. Are columns that will all end at the same place on the page.

   C. Are articles that present both sides of an issue.

   D. Are newspapers that carry both Dear Abby and Ann Landers.

   E. Are a special type of newspaper columns in which WordPerfect adjusts the column breaks so that on the last page on which the columns appear, the columns are of approximately equal length.

4. **To tell WordPerfect to begin formatting your text into multiple columns, you...**

   A. Click the Columns button on the toolbar.

   B. Choose Format⇨Columns from the menu bar.

   C. Click the ruler bar with your right mouse button and then choose Columns from the QuickMenu that appears.

   D. Type *code: columns* in your document.

   E. Rub your computer screen until a genie appears to grant you three wishes. Use the first two wishes to wish for world peace and prosperity and for the Red Sox to win the World Series and then use the third wish to begin columns.

5. **To display the Columns dialog box...**

   A. Double-click the Columns button on the toolbar.

   B. Click the Columns button the toolbar and choose Format.

   C. Choose Format⇨Columns from the menu.

   D. Hire an architect to make some drawings of classical buildings.

   E. Double-click a column code in the Reveal Codes window.

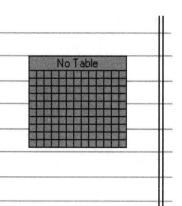

6. **This is...**

   A. A blank crossword puzzle.

   B. A way to create a tic-tac-toe game board.

   C. What appears when you click the Table QuickCreate button on the toolbar.

   D. A checkerboard.

   E. A method of creating a table, allowing you to select the number of rows and columns in your new table.

Unit 12 Exercise

In this exercise, you edit a real, live newsletter about a development project in far-off Guyana. Look it up in your world atlas; we're not going to tell you where Guyana is.

1. Open Guyana.101.WPD.

2. Add a title to the newsletter, maybe something like *Renee in Guyana*.

3. Make the text after the title into a three-column newsletter.

4. Turn off columns at the end of the newsletter.

5. Make the newsletter fit on one page by adjusting the fonts and the space between columns.

6. Create a table on the next page with dates in one column and where Renee was on those dates in the next. Add any comments in the third column.

7. Save the newsletter.

Creating Junk Mail (And Important Missives) with Mail Merge

Prerequisites
- Using commands and dialog boxes (Unit 2)
- Understanding WordPerfect codes (Lesson 9-1)

on the CD
- Addresses. 101.WPD
- Form Letter.101 .WPD
- Form Letter2.101 .WPD
- Sale Letter.101 .WPD

Objectives for This Unit

✓ Creating a file to contain information you want to use in a form letter

✓ Creating a form letter

✓ Merging the letter with addresses to create junk mail

So what's with this junk mail stuff anyway? Why do you need to know about it? Well, maybe you don't, but you may find the mail merge feature a good way to personalize material that is being sent to many people. We're a little tough on the issue — certainly all mail created with the merge feature is not junk. A mail merge is often a way to get information out to lots of people without a lot of hassle.

Mail merging doesn't require a lot of grunt work. You'll find the WordPerfect feature particularly useful if you often send letters to the same group of people. You can use the list of addresses over and over again to create new letters. For instance, you may send out an annual holiday letter to the same group of people every year — mail merge allows you to add a touch that makes the letter a little more personalized for each person it goes to.

use mail merge to create junk mail

the data file contains the information you want to merge into a document

Mail merge means that you take a list, often a list of names and addresses, and you merge it into a document, often a letter. Unfortunately, a brief break for terminology is necessary here. The list is called the *data file*. This is the information that you want to use to personalize the document. If you're creating a form letter, then the data file contains the names and addresses of the people you want to send the letter to. The document (most often a letter) is called the *form file*. You create the data file and the form file as separate documents. You then choose Tools⇨Merge to create a third file — the *merged document*.

Tip: The example in this unit consists of merging addresses into a form letter, but you may want to use WordPerfect's mail merge feature in other ways. Perhaps you want to merge order information into an invoice. The mail merge feature can handle that task, along with many other tasks, in addition to merging addresses into form letters.

These are the general steps to complete a mail merge:

the form file contains the document you want to add the information to

- Create the data file that will hold the list of information you want to merge into a WordPerfect document.

- Create the document you want to merge the data into — the form file.

- Associate the data file with the form file.

- Insert field codes into the form file to tell WordPerfect where to put the information from the data file.

- Merge the two documents to create the merged document.

Lesson 13-1   Creating the Data File

Before you start to create your data file, which is the personalized information that you want to use in your document, more definitions are in order. Your form file, which is the basic document itself, consists of *records* and *fields*. *Fields* are the categories of information you want to add to your letter, like first name, last name, and address. A *record* is all that information for one person. For example, your cousin's first name, last name, and address can be one record.

fields are catagories of information

The first thing to do when you create a data file is to decide what fields you need. For the example you see in Figure 13-1, the person's name, street address, city, state, zip, and product ordered appears in each record. When you create the data file, make sure that you define all six of those fields.

a record is one set of fields

Tip: You may want to put more fields in your data file than you need for the project at hand, thinking ahead to fields you may need for other projects. The time saved from mail merging comes when you use your data file for more than one project. For example, you may consider adding "Date sent" and "Type of payment" fields for use later, after the product has been delivered.

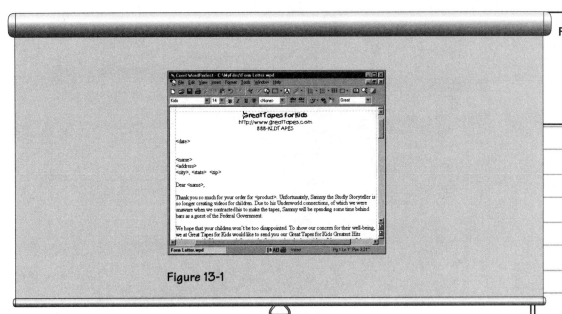

Figure 13-1

extra credit

You don't have to create your data file in WordPerfect. You may have your information in the Corel Address Book or somewhere else. If this is the case, you can skip directly to Lesson 13-2, where you create the form file. When you define the document as the form file, you will be asked to associate the data file. At that point you can choose the Address Book or another source that contains your data.

Creating a WordPerfect data file

Follow these steps to create a data file:

1 **Choose Tools⇨Merge from the menu.**

You see the Merge dialog box, as shown in Figure 13-2. This dialog box guides you through the three major merge tasks: creating the data file (Create Data), creating the form file (Create Document), and merging the two files to create the merged file (Perform Merge).

2 **Click the Create Data button.**

You see the Create Merge File dialog box. This dialog box enables you to create a new data file or use an existing data file. For this exercise, you'll create a new data file. For information on using an existing data file, see the explanation after the exercise.

3 **Click the New document window radio button and then click OK.**

You see the Create Data File dialog box. You'll use this dialog box to name all the fields you want to store in your data file.

4 **Click the Format records in a table button at the bottom of the dialog box, so that a check mark appears in it.**

This option enables you to see your data file in a table format, rather than in the ugly text-with-merge-codes format. Figure 13-3 shows the ugly form. Formatting records in a table means that the information you input for each field in a record appears on one row of a table.

Figure 13-2: The Merge dialog box leads you through all the steps for merging information into a document.

Figure 13-3: If you don't format records of your data file as a table, they end up in this ugly format.

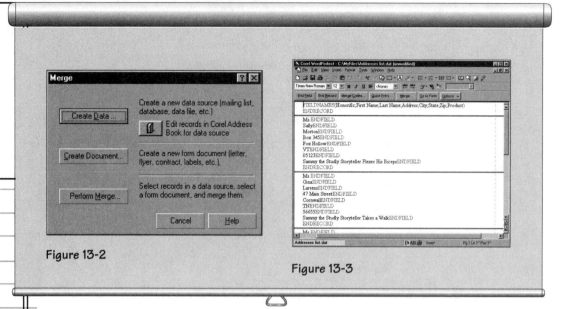

Figure 13-2

Figure 13-3

5 Create the first field name by typing *Honorific* in the **N**ame a field text box and press Enter.

The field name is inserted into the **F**ields used in merge box.

Notice that the **A**dd button on the Create Data File dialog box is highlighted, so pressing Enter is the equivalent of clicking the **A**dd button.

In the next step you'll enter the rest of the field names.

heads up

Entering field names in the same order as you want to enter the data is a good idea. The list in the Create Data File dialog box shows the logical order for entering the fields. If you enter a field in the wrong order, select it in the **F**ields used in merge box and click the Move **U**p or Move D**o**wn button to move it up or down in the list of fields.

6 Enter the rest of the field names: First Name, Last Name, Address, City, State, Zip, and Product. Press Enter between each field name.

As you press Enter, each field name appears in the **F**ields used in merge box.

heads up

You may wonder why we have so many field names. Why not just have one Name field, instead of three *(Honorific, First Name, Last Name)*? Having more field names gives you more flexibility. For example, splitting up the name enables you to put *Mrs. Sally Morton* in the address, but just *Mrs. Morton* after *Dear*. Splitting up the address into city, state, and zip code enables you to sort by zip code or any other field. Sorting by zip code makes bulk mailings cheaper.

7 Click OK to close the Create Data File dialog box.

You see the Quick Data Entry dialog box, as shown in Figure 13-4. You'll use this dialog box to enter the records you want to include in your data file. Notice that for each field you defined you now have a text box to fill in.

Now you're ready to input the data: the names, addresses, and product orders. You're going to put the following information into the data file. Remember — each set of fields is one record, so each time you fill in the fields on the dialog box you create one record in your data file.

Ms. Sally Morton
Box 345
Fox Hollow, VT 05123
Sammy the Studly
Storyteller Flexes His Biceps

Mrs. Henrietta Wallace
1771 Fourth Street, NE
Seattle, WA 98887
Sammy the Studly Storyteller
Does Sit-Ups

Miss Gina Larsens
47 Main Street
Cornwall, TN 56655
Sammy the Studly
Storyteller Takes a Walk

Mrs. Frieda Worth
45 Long Trail
Toronto, ON TF5 4E3
Sammy the Studly Storyteller
Flexes His Biceps

We'll lead you through the first record, and you can do the rest on your own.

8 **Type Ms. in the text box labeled Honorific and press Enter.**

The Next Field button is highlighted, so pressing Enter is equivalent to clicking the Next Field button. The cursor is now in the First Name text box.

9 **Type the rest of the information for this first record, pressing Enter after typing each field.**

When you get to the last field, the highlighted button changes from the Next Field button to the New Record button.

10 **Press Enter to start the next record.**

11 **Enter the information for the remaining four people.**

Remember to split the information up into the correct fields. Also, if you need to, you can return to a field by using the mouse, and you can move to a different record by using the four buttons at the bottom of the dialog box (First, Previous, Next, and Last).

12 **Close the Quick Data Entry dialog box by clicking the Close button.**

WordPerfect immediately asks you if you want to save the changes to disk.

13 **Click Yes to see the Save File dialog box, where you name the data file.**

You can see the Save File dialog box in Figure 13-5. The data file isn't saved as a regular .WPD file. Instead it gets saved as a .DAT file (notice the File type box on the Save File dialog box).

14 **Name the file *Addresses* and then click the Save button to save it.**

WordPerfect saves the file, and you finally get a good look at what you've created. Figure 13-6 shows the data file. Notice the Merge bar under the Property bar. These buttons give you easy ways to work with your data file.

You can edit the data file to make it look prettier, but unless you're going to print it, you may be wasting your time. We change the font size of our data file to 10 point to make the data fit in the columns a little better. We also have moved around the column borders to make the longer fields wider to fit all the information.

Once you've created the data file, use the Merge bar to edit and add records. The easiest way is to use the Quick Entry button to display the Quick Data Entry dialog box. Refer to Figure 13-4 for another look at the dialog box. You can then use the buttons on the dialog box to find, edit, and add records.

Notes:

use the Merge bar to edit and add records

Figure 13-4: Use the Quick Data Entry dialog box to type the information into the fields you defined.

Figure 13-5: Notice that the data file gets saved as a .DAT file rather than the usual .WPD file

Figure 13-6: Once you've saved the file, you finally get to see that it looks like this. You see your data in a table, with one record per row and one field per column. Also notice the Merge bar, which provides tools you use to work with the data file.

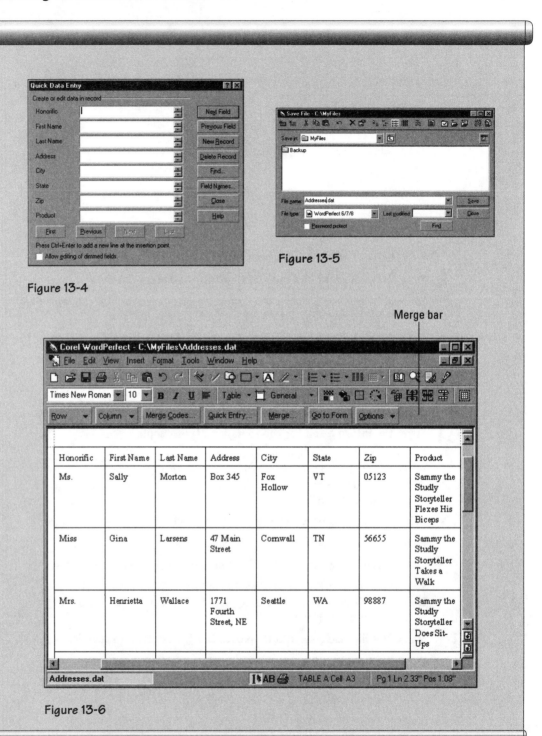

Figure 13-4

Figure 13-5

Merge bar

Figure 13-6

Adding a record to your data file

Back in the previous exercise, you put information for four people into your data file, but you need to send the letter to a fifth person. Here's how you do it:

1 **Open Addresses.DAT if it isn't already open.**

If you closed the file, make sure the File type box on the Open dialog box shows All Files or WP Merge Data (*.DAT). Otherwise, you won't see the data file with its .DAT extension on the list.

The Addresses file appears, as shown in Figure 13-6.

2 **Click the Quick Entry button to display the Quick Data Entry dialog box.**

You can use this dialog box to add another record's worth of data.

3 **Click the Last button.**

You see the last record in the dialog box. You're about to add a new record, which is placed after the displayed record. Displaying the last record ensures that the new record is added to the end of your table. If you want to add a record in the middle of the table, display the record that will be immediately before the record you want to insert.

4 **Click the New Record button and add the data below.**

Ms. Margaret Thorstens
127 Massachusetts Avenue
Boca Raton, FL 31134
Sammy the Studly Storyteller Flexes His Biceps

5 **Click the Close button to close the Quick Data Entry dialog box and see the additional data in the table.**

6 **Save the updated data file.**

After you've closed the Quick Data Entry dialog box, you can open it any time by clicking the Quick Entry button on the Merge bar. The Quick Data Entry dialog box gives you an easy way to edit the data you've already entered and add new data.

heads up

You can edit and add data directly into the table using the Row button, which enables you to add and delete records, and the Column button, which enables you to add and delete fields.

heads up

To delete a record, display the record in the Quick Data Entry dialog box and click the Delete Record button. You can also delete the row containing the record from the table.

☑ **Progress Check**

If you can do the following, you've mastered this lesson:

❑ Display the Merge dialog box to begin a merge.

❑ Define fields for your data file.

❑ Input data into your data file.

❑ Edit and add data to the data file.

Creating a Form File

Lesson 13-2

Once you've created your data file, you're ready to create the form file that will be personalized with the data file information. Often, the form file is a letter, but you may find many other uses for the WordPerfect merge feature, such as for contracts, lists, or invoices.

The form file looks more or less like a regular document with one important difference: You tell WordPerfect where to insert the information from the data file by adding *merge codes*. Fortunately, WordPerfect makes that easy.

Adding merge codes to the form file

Let's do a quick double-check here — do you know what the above heading means? Loosely translated, it means that in this exercise you're going to take the letter you need to send to the five people whose information you typed into the data file, and tell WordPerfect where to put each piece of information in the letter. The way you do this is by inserting *merge codes* in your form file. Ready?

on the CD

1 **Open Form Letter.101.WPD.**

This is the letter you saw back in Figure 13-1, but the bracketed information — <name>, <address>, and so on — has been deleted.

2 **Choose Tools⇨Merge from the menu bar.**

You see the Merge dialog box that you saw in Figure 13-2. This time you're going to click the second button, Create Document, which is the second step in creating a merged document.

3 **Click the Create Document button.**

WordPerfect displays the Create Merge File dialog box where you can choose to use the document that's in the active window, or you can create an entirely new document.

4 **Make sure the Use file in active window radio button is selected; then click OK.**

The Associate Form and Data dialog box appears, as shown in Figure 13-7. Use this dialog box to tell WordPerfect the name of the data file. Once WP knows the name of the data file, it knows the names of the fields you created and displays those names for you to use in the letter.

5 **Make sure the Associate a data file radio button is selected; then click the file folder button to the right of the text box.**

You need to input the name of the data file. The file folder button displays the Select Data File dialog box, which looks much like the Open or Save As dialog boxes. It enables you to navigate folders and select the file you want to use.

heads up

Notice that the File type on the Select Data File dialog box is set to .DAT, so you will only see .DAT files in the large box unless you change the File type.

heads up

The other choices on this dialog box enable you to choose a data source other than a WordPerfect data file — for example, you may have all the information you need in the Corel Address Book. Use the other choices on this dialog box when you want to use a data source other than a WordPerfect file.

on the CD

6 **Select Addresses.DAT (the file you created in Lesson 13-1). If you didn't do Lesson 13-1, select Addresses.101.DAT. Click the Select button.**

You again see the Associate Form and Data dialog box. The name of the file you selected now appears next to the Associate a data file option.

7 **Click OK.**

Now that you've chosen the data file and identified the form file (it's the open document), you're ready to tell WordPerfect where each field should appear in the letter.

You now see the document you opened in Step 1, along with a Merge bar below the Property bar that has different buttons than you saw in your data file.

8 **Position the cursor where you want the data to appear and click the Date button on the Merge bar.**

WordPerfect inserts a date code. Even though you're not in Reveal Codes mode, you still see these merge codes you're inserting. The code is big, red, and ugly, but don't worry: In the final document, you'll see the actual date, not the code.

9 **Press Enter at least twice to leave room between the date and the address. Click the Insert Field button.**

You see the Insert Field Name or Number dialog box, as shown in Figure 13-8.

10 **Select *Honorific* in the Field Names list box and click the Insert button.**

This action inserts the code for Honorific into the document without closing the Insert Field Name or Number dialog box. The code is FIELD(Honorific).

Instead of selecting the field name and clicking the Insert button, you can double-click the field name. The effect is the same.

11 **Type a space to leave space between the Honorific and the First Name.**

Even with the dialog box open you can still type in the document — the cursor is visible. You need to put the space between the *Honorific* and the first name.

12 **Complete the name: Select First Name in the Insert Field Name or Number dialog box, click Insert, type a space, then select Last Name and click Insert again.**

This inserts the merge codes you need to make this line of the letter read, for example, *Ms. Sally Morton.* Without the spaces, the contents of the fields would run together.

13 **Press Enter to move to the next line, and complete the address by adding the field codes for Address, City, State, and Zip.**

Make sure that you add the punctuation and spacing needed in the address.

14 **Repeat Steps 10-12, typing a space or comma or pressing Enter to start a new line when necessary.**

You can edit the document any time, even with the Insert Field Name or Number dialog box open. Just move the cursor in the usual way (with the mouse or with the arrow keys). If you're doing a lot of editing, close the dialog box and reopen it at any point to insert more fields into the document.

15 **Move the cursor to the line that reads *Dear*. Position it between the *r* and the comma. Insert the field codes for Honorific and Last name, adding spaces as needed.**

16 **Move the cursor to the end of the first sentence of the letter. Insert the field code for Product.**

17 **Select the code that you just inserted and make it italic.**

Making the Product field code italic in the form file will result in the product name appearing in italics in the final merged document.

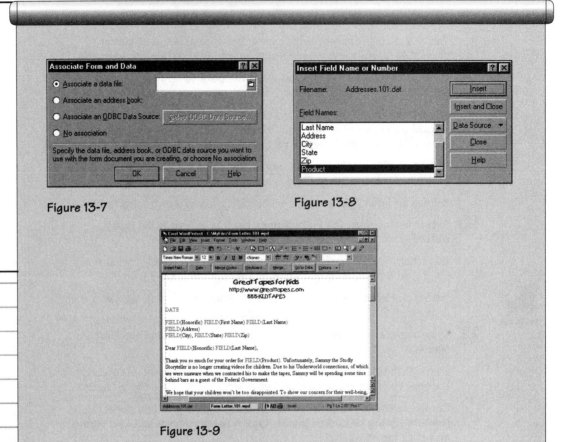

Figure 13-7

Figure 13-8

Figure 13-9

☑ Progress Check

If you can do the following, you've mastered this lesson:

❑ Create a document to use as a form file for use in a merge.

❑ Associate your data file with the form file.

❑ Insert field codes into the form file to indicate where the information from the data file will appear.

18 **Close the Insert Field Name or Number dialog box.**

Your document should now look like Figure 13-9, with lots of FIELD codes in it.

19 **Save the document.**

Once you've added the field codes, you're ready to merge the data file with the form file.

Recess

If you want, take a break now before you take the momentous step of merging the data file into the form file. Both files should be saved before you close WordPerfect. When you're ready for the big time, come back and open your form file.

Merging Information into a Form Letter

Once you've created the data file and put field codes into the form file, you're ready to merge the two files to create your junk mail. Before you do, though, check both the form file and the data file to make sure that everything is correct. You can always perform the merge again, of course, but you'll save time if everything is right the first time.

You can begin the merge by clicking the <u>M</u>erge button on the Merge bar in either the form file or the data file, or by choosing <u>T</u>ools⇨<u>M</u>erge and clicking the Perform <u>M</u>erge button on the Merge dialog box.

After all the work you've done to prepare the data and form files, the merge should go smoothly. Ready?

on the CD

If you've done the previous two lessons, you have the form file, Form Letter.101.WPD, open. If not, open it now. If you didn't do Lesson 13-2, you can use the form file we created for you — Form Letter2.101.WPD.

1 **Click the <u>M</u>erge button on the Merge bar.**

You see the Perform Merge dialog box, as shown in Figure 13-10. This dialog box enables you to check or choose three things: the name of the <u>F</u>orm document (the form file), the <u>D</u>ata source (data file), and where the result of the merge should appear.

2 **Check that the <u>F</u>orm document is the current document.**

If you clicked the <u>M</u>erge button from the form file to display the Perform Merge dialog box, this setting will be correct. If you clicked the <u>M</u>erge button from the data file, or chose <u>T</u>ools⇨<u>M</u>erge from the menu, you'll have to manually enter the name of the form document.

If necessary, you can change the location of the form file by clicking the <u>F</u>orm document button and choosing another source.

3 **Check that the <u>D</u>ata source is C:\MyFiles\Addresses.DAT or C:\MyFiles\Addresses.101.DAT.**

The file name was set in Lesson 13-2 when you associated the data file with the form file. If it is incorrect, click the File button and choose the correct file.

extra credit

Click the <u>D</u>ata source button to choose a data source other than a WordPerfect .DAT file.

extra credit

If you don't want to use all the records in your data file, click the <u>S</u>elect Records button to display the Select Records dialog box. In this dialog box, you can tell WordPerfect which records to use in the merge.

You can also choose the M<u>a</u>rk records radio button at the top of the Select Records dialog box and then click all the records that you want to use in the merge.

4 **Verify that the O<u>u</u>tput is New Document.**

By default the new merged document is created as a new document. When you create a new document, your form file and data file remain intact, so you can repeat the merge if necessary.

Notes:

Click the <u>M</u>erge button to merge the two files

☑ Progress Check

If you can do the following, you've mastered this lesson:

❑ Display the Perform Merge dialog box.

❑ Check the settings on the Perform Merge dialog box, and change them if they are incorrect.

❑ Merge the form file and the data file to create junk mail.

Although you'll usually want the merged document to be a new document, you can also choose to create it in the current document (the document active in the WordPerfect window) or send it straight to the printer. Click the Output button to choose another output option.

5 Click the Merge button to perform the merge.

The computer whirs while WordPerfect performs the merge. A merge of many records can take awhile, but merging only five records goes quickly.

When the merge is complete, you see the last page of the newly merged document in the WordPerfect window, as shown in Figure 13-11.

Because the data file contained five records, you now have five pages in the merged document, each with the same letter, but different name, address, and product information.

6 Look through the document to see what you've created.

Scroll through the document — you should have five pages, each with the information from a different record in your data file.

Ta da! You've created your merge document. What you do with it is up to you. You can print it, sign each letter, and send them. Or you may want to personalize the letters a little more. Perhaps you know some of the customers and want to add notes at the bottom of some of the letters. Remember that you don't have to save the merge document because you can recreate it. If you are likely to add or edit either the form file or data file, you probably shouldn't save your merged document. Instead, you should do another merge at a later date.

heads up

You may occasionally want to take advantage of merge options. By clicking the Options button on the Perform Merge dialog box, you can choose to add a page break between each merged document, make more than one copy of each merged document, or leave blank lines in the document when the field is empty.

Unit 13 Quiz

For each of the following questions, circle the letter of the correct answer or answers. Remember, there may be more than one right answer for each question!

1. **What is a form file?**

    A. The file you store addresses in.

    B. The document with field codes in it.

    C. The plastic model used to make a dress the correct size.

    D. The file you keep forms in.

    E. None of the above.

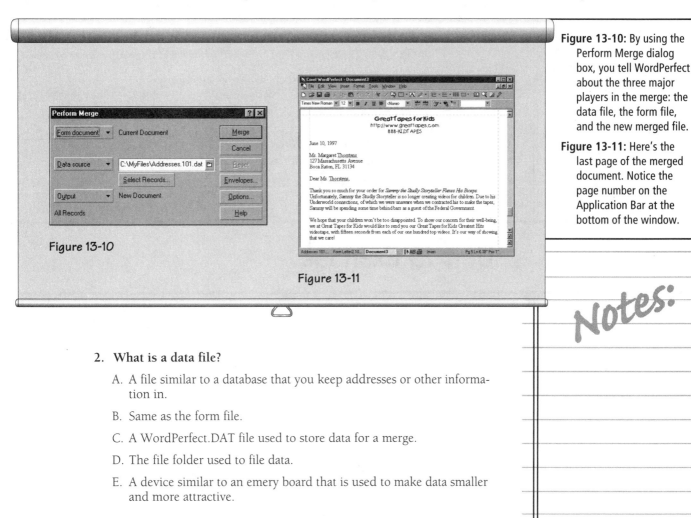

Figure 13-10

Figure 13-11

Figure 13-10: By using the Perform Merge dialog box, you tell WordPerfect about the three major players in the merge: the data file, the form file, and the new merged file.

Figure 13-11: Here's the last page of the merged document. Notice the page number on the Application Bar at the bottom of the window.

Notes:

2. **What is a data file?**

   A. A file similar to a database that you keep addresses or other information in.

   B. Same as the form file.

   C. A WordPerfect.DAT file used to store data for a merge.

   D. The file folder used to file data.

   E. A device similar to an emery board that is used to make data smaller and more attractive.

3. **Although you didn't learn how to use different data sources in this unit, data for a merge can come from which of the following sources?**

   A. The Corel Address Book.

   B. Quattro Pro.

   C. A database file.

   D. A WordPerfect data file.

   E. A pile of filed paper forms that you have on your desk.

4. **A record is...**

   A. An old-fashioned audio device that has since been replaced by compact discs.

   B. One row in your data table.

   C. A column in your data table

   D. A collection of information about one thing or person — for example, your cousin's name, address, and phone number.

   E. A collection of one type of information — for example, the last name of everyone in your database.

5. **What is a field?**

   A. A place to play Frisbee, soccer, or another sport.

   B. One row in your data table.

   C. A column in your data table.

   D. A collection of information about one thing or person — for example, your cousin's name, address, and phone number.

   E. A collection of one type of information — for example, the last name of everyone in your database.

Unit 13 Exercise

In this exercise, you'll use the data file you created in Lesson 13-1 (or the one we provide for you) to perform a new mail merge.

1. Open Addresses.DAT or Addresses.101.DAT and add a field, *Child's Name*.

   Hint: One way to add a field is to display the Quick Data Entry dialog box and click the Field Names button.

2. Enter a child's name for each of the five records (make them up).

3. Save the data file.

4. Open Sale Letter.101.WPD. Add field codes to the document.

5. Add a sentence (or more) to the letter that mentions the child.

6. Add the field codes for the child's name in the appropriate places.

7. Merge the data file with the edited letter.

8. Check the results.

Part IV Review

Unit 12 Summary

- **Creating columns:** To put text you have already written into columns, put the cursor at the beginning of the text, or select the text you want in columns. Then click the Columns button and choose the number of columns you want.

- **Ending columns:** To discontinue columns, put the cursor where you want the columns to end, click the Columns button, and choose Discontinue.

- **Changing the column definition:** To change the type of columns, number of columns, or the width of a column or space between columns, put the cursor in the columned text, click the Columns button and choose Format to display the Columns dialog box.

- **Create a column break**: To force a column break, position the cursor and press Ctrl+Enter.

- **Create a table**: To create a table, position the cursor where you want the table to appear, click the Table QuickCreate button, and choose the size table you want from the grid that appears.

- **Change column width:** To change the width of a column, click and drag the column border.

- **Deleting a row or column:** To delete a row or column from a table, position the cursor in the row or column you want to delete, right-click the table, choose Delete from the QuickMenu, choose the Rows or Columns radio button on the Delete Structure/Contents dialog box and click OK.

- **Adding a row or column:** To add a row at the end of a table, position the cursor in the last cell and press Tab. To add a row or column anywhere in the table, position the cursor in the row or column that will be after the inserted column, right click and select Insert from the QuickMenu, and choose the Rows or Columns radio button on the Insert Columns/Rows dialog box.

Unit 13 Summary

- **Creating a merged document:** To create a merged document, you need a data file that contains the information to personalize each document and a form file, which is the document the data will be merged into.

- **Creating a data file:** To create a data file, choose Tools⇨Merge from the menu and click the Create Data button on the Merge dialog box.

- **Creating a form file**: To create a form file, first create the text and format it. Then choose Tools⇨Merge from the menu and click the Create Document button on the Merge dialog box. Associate the form file with the data file, and add merge codes to tell WordPerfect where the information from the data file should appear in the form file.

- **Merging the form and data files:** To merge your form and data files, choose Tools⇨Merge from the menu and click the Perform Merge button. Check the information for the Form document, Data source and Output and click OK.

Part IV Test

The questions on this test cover all of the material presented in Parts I, II, III and IV, Units 1-13.

True   False

T   F   1. You can format a resume with the table feature.

T   F   2. It's a good idea not to put metal in a microwave oven.

T   F   3. The Undo key can undo your last ten actions.

T   F   4. Margaret and Alison's sweeties manage their computer networks.

T   F   5. Data in a data file is stored in records.

T   F   6. You can make a document look longer by making the margins larger.

T   F   7. The top of a newsletter is called the masthead.

T   F   8. Sammy the Studly Story Teller is a gangster.

T   F   9. 10 point Times New Roman is easier to read than 12 point Times New Roman.

T   F   10. You can't save your WordPerfect document in Microsoft Word format.

Multiple Choice

For each of the following questions, circle the correct answer or answers. Remember, there may be more than one right answer for each question!

11. If you want to undo formatting you added to a document you can:

A. Delete the formatted text.
B. Delete the formatting codes.
C. Click the Undo button.
D. Close the document without saving it and open the saved version.
E. Press Ctrl+Shift+Z to restore the text to the way it was.

12. Which of the following should you use to align text vertically on the page?

A. Spaces.
B. Tabs.
C. Columns.
D. Margins.
E. A table.

13. In this book you learned how to:

A. Put text into columns.
B. Restore deleted text.
C. Create a document merged from a data file and a form file.
D. Guarantee that your kids always have good manners.
E. Make sure headings stay on the same page as some of the text that follows them.

Part IV Test

14. It's a good idea to save your document often because:

A. The power might fail.

B. If you mess up, you can close without saving and re-open the document.

C. You don't manage to save money often, so you might as well manage to at least save your document often.

D. If you have to suddenly shut off your computer to protect your document from prying eyes, you won't lose too much work.

E. We told you to.

15. You can use the merge feature to:

A. Create a personalized Christmas letter.

B. Create invoices for different people who bought different products at different prices.

C. Create a letter to send to every one of your child's classmates.

D. Improve your marriage.

E. Write thank-you notes for all your wedding gifts.

Matching

16. Match up the following buttons with the corresponding tasks:

A.

B.

C.

D.

E.

1. Insert a row into a table.

2. Put text into columns.

3. Change the document zoom.

4. Display the Perfect Expert.

5. Create a table.

17. Match up the document with the feature you use to format it:

A. Newsletter.

B. Resume.

C. Term paper with multiple headings.

D. Form letter.

1. Quick format.

2. Mail merge.

3. Columns.

4. Table.

18. Match up the following keyboard shortcuts with the corresponding tasks:

A. Alt+F3.

B. Ctrl+S.

C. Ctrl+Z.

D. Ctrl+Shift+Z.

E. Ctrl+P.

1. Save.

2. Undo.

3. Reveal Codes.

4. Print.

5. Undelete.

Part IV Lab Assignment

Step 1: Create the text

Step 2: Edit and format

Step 3: Save the document

Great Tapes for Kids
http://www.greattapes.com
888-KLDTAPES

FIELD(Honorific) FIELD(First Name) FIELD(Last Name)
FIELD(Address)
FIELD(City), FIELD(State) FIELD(Zip)

DATE

Dear FIELD(Honorific) FIELD(Last Name),

Thank you very much for your order. The products we are shipping are listed below.

Product	Price
FIELD(Product 1)	FIELD(Price 1)
FIELD(Product 2)	FIELD(Price 2)

Sincerely,

Jonas Smith
Great Tapes for Kids

• • • • • • • • • • • • • • • • • • •

Answers

Part I Test Answers

Question	Answer	If You Missed It, Try This
1.	False — All files on disk must have a name	Review Lesson 1-3
2.	True	Review Lesson 1-1
3.	False	Just try it.
4.	True	Review Unit 2
5.	False, but only because most printers can't print them	Review Lesson 4-2
6.	We don't know, we're not writing comic strips	
7.	True	Review Lesson 3-5
8.	False	Review Lesson 4-1
9.	False	Review Lesson 3-1
10.	True	Review Lesson 3-2
11.	A, C	Review Lesson 1-3
12.	A, B, C, E	Review Unit 2 Introduction
13.	B	Take time to read *Peanuts*
14.	A, B, C	Review Lessons 1-3 and 2-2
15.	C	Review Lesson 1-1
16.	B, C works, though we didn't cover it, D	Review Lesson 1-1
17.	E	Review Lesson 3-1
18.	D	Watch more game shows (just kidding)

19.	A-3	Review Unit 1 and your Windows 95 knowledge
	B-5	
	C-2	
	D-1	
	E-4	
20.	A-5	Review Lessons 1-1, 2-1, 3-1, 3-3
	B-3	
	C-1	
	D-2	
	E-4	

Part II Test Answers

Question	Answer	If You Missed It, Try This
1.	True	Review Lesson 7-2
2.	False — WordPerfect always has at least three ways to do anything!	Review Lesson 5-1
3.	False — it helps with serious errors, but doesn't change your style	Review Lesson 7-4
4.	True	Review Lesson 6-3
5.	True	But he also hosts *Mr. Rogers Neighborhood* on PBS.
6.	Nah (just kidding) — True	Review Lesson 7-1
7.	True	Review Lesson 5-3
8.	False	Review the beginning of Unit 5
9.	False	Review Lesson 6-1
10.	True	Review Lesson 7-1
11.	A, B, D	Review Unit 2
12.	A, B, D	Review Lesson 5-3
13.	B (Trust us on this one)	
14.	A, B	Review Lesson 5-3
15.	A, B, E	Review Lesson 7-2
16.	A, B, C, D	Review Lesson 7-1

17.	B, D, E	Review Lesson 6-2
18.	A, B, C, D, E (It always pays to be open-minded!)	
19.	A-2	Review Unit 5, Lessons 3-1, and 7-1
	B-5	
	C-4	
	D-1	
	E-3	
20.	A-3	Review Lessons 1-2, 2-1, 5-2, and 7-1
	B-5	
	C-1	
	D-4	
	E-2	
21.	A- 2	Review Lessons 1-3, 3-4, 5-2, and 5-3
	B-1	
	C-4	
	D-5	
	E-3	
22.	A-2	Get out there and watch some television!
	B-5	
	C-4	
	D-1	
	E-3	

Part III Test Answers

Question	Answer	If You Missed It, Try This
1.	True	Review Lesson 8-1
2.	False	Review Lesson 8-1
3.	True — it is spelled wrong	Check your handy copy of *Strunk and White*
4.	False	Review Lesson 8-3
5.	False	Review Lesson 8-2

6.	True	Review Lesson 9-3
7.	True — but we concede that it's a matter of opinion	watch the movie
8.	False	Review Lesson 9-1
9.	False	Review Lesson 10-1
10.	False	Review Lessons 11-2 and 11-3
11.	A, D, E	Review Lessons 11-2 and 11-3
12.	C	Rent them all and watch the credits.
13.	D — but there are easier ways	Review Lesson 12-4
14.	B, C — it's pretty drab	Press Alt+F3 and have a look
15.	B — or just use Perfect Fit	Review Lessons 8-2, 10-1, and 10-2
16.	A, C — *StarTrek: The Next Generation* reruns are on at least once a day in most viewing areas. They make a good break from taking silly tests.	
17.	E	Review Lesson 9-1
18.	E	Click Format on the WordPerfect menu and see.
19.	A-2	Review Lessons 7-1, 8-2, 8-3, 10-1, and the "Making bullets" sidebar in Unit 10
	B-4	Review Lesson 8-2
	C-5	Review Lesson 10-3
	D-3	Review Lesson 7-1
	E-1	Review Lesson 10-3
20.	A-5	Review the parts of the window in Unit 2, as well as Units 9 and 10
	B-4	
	C-2	
	D-1	
	E-3	

21.	A-3	Review Lessons 3-1, 3-4, 5-3, 9-1, and 10-2
	B-1	
	C-2	
	D-5	
	E-4	
22.	A-5	Visit the Fantasy/Science Fiction section at your local library.
	B-4	
	C-2	
	D-3	
	E-1	

Part IV Test Answers

Question	Answer	If You Missed It, Try This
1.	True	Review Unit 12, especially the introduction
2.	True	
3.	True — but it can undo another 290 actions	Review Lesson 3-4
4.	True	Review Lesson 4-4
5.	True	Review Lesson 13-1
6.	True	Review Lesson 8-2
7.	True	Review Lesson 12-1
8.	True	Read Form letter .101.WPD
9.	False	Review Lesson 8-2
10.	False	Review Lesson 2-2
11.	B, C (if formatting was the last thing you did), D	Review Lesson 3-4
12.	B, C, D (align text against the left or right margin with justification), E	Review Unit 12 and Lessons 10-2 and 10-4

13.	A, B, C, E	Review Lessons 3-4,11-3, 12-1, and Unit 13.
14.	A, B, E (but you don't need to turn off the computer— just turn off the monitor)	Review Lessons 1-3 and 2-2
15.	A, B, C	Review Unit 13 introduction
16.	A-2	Review Lessons 3-5, 4-1, 12-1, 12-2
	B-3	
	C-1	
	D-5	
	E-4	
17.	A-3	Review Unit 12 introduction, Unit 13 introduction
	B-4	
	C-1	
	D-2	
18.	A-3	Review Lessons 1-2, 1-3, 2-2, 3-4, and 9-1
	B-1	
	C-2	
	D-5	
	E-4	

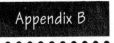

About the CD

heads up

Before you can use any of the CD files, you need to install them on your computer. But don't worry: The installation process is easy and fairly quick.

After you install the *Dummies 101: WordPerfect 8* exercise files, you can open them and look around as long as you don't save any changes. If you make changes and save them, the document may not look as it should when you open it to do an exercise. If you do mess up a document, you can go through the installation process again to get a fresh copy.

System Requirements

Before using the CD, make sure that your computer matches up to the minimum requirements listed below. If your computer doesn't have many of these items, you may experience problems in using the CD:

- ◗ A PC with a 486 or faster processor
- ◗ *At least* 8MB of total RAM (16MB recommended)
- ◗ Microsoft Windows 95
- ◗ WordPerfect 8
- ◗ At least 1MB of free hard-disk space available if you want to install all the items from this CD (you need less space if you don't install every item)
- ◗ CD-ROM drive — double-speed (2x) or faster
- ◗ Monitor capable of displaying at least 256 colors or grayscale

If you need more information on computer basics, check out *PCs For Dummies,* 4th Edition, by Dan Gookin, or *Windows 95 For Dummies* by Andy Rathbone (all published by IDG Books Worldwide, Inc.).

Putting the CD Files on Your Hard Drive

The exercise files are sample documents that you use while following along with the lessons in the book. Put these files on your hard drive where they'll be easy to access; then you can follow the steps in the exercises exactly. After you're done with the book, you can remove the exercise files.

Installing the exercise files in Windows 95

1 **Insert the Dummies 101 CD (label side up) into your computer's CD drive.**

Be careful to touch only the edges of the CD. The CD drive is the one that pops out with a circular drawer.

2 **Click the Start button and click Run.**

3 **In the dialog box that appears, type** d:\setup.exe **(if your CD drive is not drive D, substitute the appropriate letter for** d**) and click OK.**

A license agreement appears.

4 **Read the license agreement and click Agree.**

If you don't agree to the terms of the license agreement, you can't continue with the installation. After you click Agree, you see a message window telling you that the CD installation will be launched.

5 **Click OK in the message window.**

A message appears that asks you to wait a moment while the CD prepares itself. The Dummies 101: WordPerfect 8 For Windows installation window appears.

6 **Click Install Exercise Files.**

Another message appears, asking whether you want to go ahead and install the exercise files to your hard drive.

7 **Click OK to continue with the installation or click Cancel to stop the installation.**

If you click Cancel, you can install the files later by following these steps again.

You see a window asking where to install the exercise files on your computer. To make the installation and the exercises in this book as simple as possible, let the installer place the exercise files in the recommended location. If you really want to put the files somewhere else, follow the on-screen instructions to change the location (make sure that you remember where you put them).

heads up

If you change the location of the files, you will have to change to the folder each time you want to open an exercise file. If you install the files in C:\MyFiles, as recommended, and C:\MyFiles is the default WordPerfect directory (which it is unless WordPerfect is installed on a different drive, or unless you have changed the default folder), you see the exercise files automatically in the Open dialog box.

If you choose another folder, make a note of the folder name in the margin.

Click the Start button

8 **Click OK to install the files in the folder shown.**

The installation program copies the exercise files to your computer. You see a little window telling you that the installation is done and referring you to this book for instructions on using the files.

9 **Click OK to make the little window go away.**

The installation window reappears.

10 **Click the Exit button in the lower-right corner of the window.**

The program asks whether you are sure you want to exit.

11 **Click Yes.**

The files are now in C:\MyFiles (or the folder you noted in the margin next to Step 7) ready for you to use. You use the first file in Unit 2.

Tip: If at some point you accidentally modify an exercise file and want to reinstall the original version, just follow the steps for installing exercise files for your computer. If you want to save your modified version of an exercise file, either move the file to another folder before reinstalling the original or install the new replacement files to a different folder.

Remember that you need to have WordPerfect 8 installed on your computer in order to open and edit the exercise files — the exercise files are just documents, not software. WordPerfect 8 is *not* included on this CD; you need to purchase the program separately and install it to your computer before you can use the exercise files.

Tip: You can use the exercise files without installing them to your hard disk — just use the Look in option to navigate to the \lessons folder on the CD-ROM drive when the CD-ROM is in the drive (see Unit 2 for more details on the techniques of navigating folders and drives). Be aware, though, that you can't save back to the CD-ROM — instead, save to your hard disk or a floppy disk.

Removing the exercise files

After you're done with the lessons in the book, you might want to delete the exercise files.

To delete the exercise files under Windows 95:

1 **Double-click the My Computer icon.**

2 **Double-click the Drive C icon.**

3 **Click once on the MyFiles folder.**

If you used a different folder (as noted in the margin next to Step 7 above), you need to open (click on) the folder you copied the exercise files to.

4 **Select the exercise files (all the names have "101" in them) by clicking the name of the first file, and then holding the Ctrl key while you click the name of each of the other files.**

Because the exercise files are stored in the WordPerfect default folder, you should be careful about the files you delete — you may have created other documents that you want to keep and saved them in this folder.

Notes:

5 **Choose File⇨Delete from the My Computer menu.**

Depending on your Windows 95 settings, you might see a message asking if you really want to delete these items. Click the appropriate button to indicate Yes.

heads up

If you want to keep any of the installed files that were installed, move them to a different folder *before* you delete the exercise files. Depending on your Windows 95 setup, however, you may be able to restore accidentally deleted files from the Recycle Bin.

If You've Got Problems (Of the CD Kind)

IDG has tried its best to create an installation program that works on most computers with the minimum system requirements. Alas, your computer may differ, and some programs may not work properly for some reason.

The two likeliest problems are that you don't have enough memory (RAM) for the programs you want to use, or you have other programs running that are affecting the installation or running of the program. If you get error messages like Not enough memory or Setup cannot continue, try one or more of the following and then try installing the files again:

▶ Turn off any anti-virus software that you have on your computer. Installers sometimes mimic virus activity and may make your computer incorrectly believe that it is being infected by a virus.

▶ Close all running programs. The more programs you're running, the less memory is available to other programs. Installers also typically update files and programs. If you keep other programs running, installation may not work properly.

▶ Have your local computer store add more RAM to your computer. Adding more memory can really help the speed of your computer and allow more programs to run at the same time.

If you still have trouble with installing the items from the CD, please call the IDG Books Worldwide Customer Service phone number: 800-762-2974 (outside the U.S.: 317-596-5261).

Index

(continued)

▶ U ◀

IDG Books Worldwide, Inc., End-User License Agreement

READ THIS. You should carefully read these terms and conditions before opening the software packet(s) included with this book ("Book"). This is a license agreement ("Agreement") between you and IDG Books Worldwide, Inc. ("IDGB"). By opening the accompanying software packet(s), you acknowledge that you have read and accept the following terms and conditions. If you do not agree and do not want to be bound by such terms and conditions, promptly return the Book and the unopened software packet(s) to the place you obtained them for a full refund.

1. **License Grant.** IDGB grants to you (either an individual or entity) a nonexclusive license to use one copy of the enclosed software program(s) (collectively, the "Software") solely for your own personal or business purposes on a single computer (whether a standard computer or a workstation component of a multiuser network). The Software is in use on a computer when it is loaded into temporary memory (RAM) or installed into permanent memory (hard disk, CD-ROM, or other storage device). IDGB reserves all rights not expressly granted herein.

2. **Ownership.** IDGB is the owner of all right, title, and interest, including copyright, in and to the compilation of the Software recorded on the disk(s) or CD-ROM ("Software Media"). Copyright to the individual programs recorded on the Software Media is owned by the author or other authorized copyright owner of each program. Ownership of the Software and all proprietary rights relating thereto remain with IDGB and its licensers.

3. **Restrictions on Use and Transfer.**

   (a) You may only (i) make one copy of the Software for backup or archival purposes, or (ii) transfer the Software to a single hard disk, provided that you keep the original for backup or archival purposes. You may not (i) rent or lease the Software, (ii) copy or reproduce the Software through a LAN or other network system or through any computer subscriber system or bulletin-board system, or (iii) modify, adapt, or create derivative works based on the Software.

   (b) You may not reverse engineer, decompile, or disassemble the Software. You may transfer the Software and user documentation on a permanent basis, provided that the transferee agrees to accept the terms and conditions of this Agreement and you retain no copies. If the Software is an update or has been updated, any transfer must include the most recent update and all prior versions.

4. **Restrictions on Use of Individual Programs.** You must follow the individual requirements and restrictions detailed for each individual program in Appendix B of this Book. These limitations are also contained in the individual license agreements recorded on the Software Media. These limitations may include a requirement that after using the program for a specified period of time, the user must pay a registration fee or discontinue use. By opening the Software packet(s), you will be agreeing to abide by the licenses and restrictions for these individual programs that are detailed in Appendix B and on the Software Media. None of the material on this Software Media or listed in this Book may ever be redistributed, in original or modified form, for commercial purposes.

5. **Limited Warranty.**

   (a) IDGB warrants that the Software and Software Media are free from defects in materials and workmanship under normal use for a period of sixty (60) days from the date of purchase of this Book. If IDGB receives notification within the warranty period of defects in materials or workmanship, IDGB will replace the defective Software Media.

   (b) IDGB AND THE AUTHORS OF THE BOOK DISCLAIM ALL OTHER WARRANTIES, EXPRESS OR IMPLIED, INCLUDING WITHOUT LIMITATION IMPLIED WARRANTIES OF MERCHANTABILITY AND FITNESS FOR A PARTICULAR PURPOSE, WITH RESPECT TO THE SOFTWARE, THE PROGRAMS, THE SOURCE CODE CONTAINED THEREIN, AND/OR THE TECHNIQUES DESCRIBED IN THIS BOOK. IDGB DOES NOT WARRANT THAT THE FUNCTIONS CONTAINED IN THE SOFTWARE WILL MEET YOUR REQUIREMENTS OR THAT THE OPERATION OF THE SOFTWARE WILL BE ERROR FREE.

(c) This limited warranty gives you specific legal rights, and you may have other rights that vary from jurisdiction to jurisdiction.

6. **Remedies.**

   (a) IDGB's entire liability and your exclusive remedy for defects in materials and workmanship shall be limited to replacement of the Software Media, which may be returned to IDGB with a copy of your receipt at the following address: Software Media Fulfillment Department, Attn.: *Dummies 101: WordPerfect 8 For Windows*, IDG Books Worldwide, Inc., 7260 Shadeland Station, Ste. 100, Indianapolis, IN 46256, or call 800-762-2974. Please allow three to four weeks for delivery. This Limited Warranty is void if failure of the Software Media has resulted from accident, abuse, or misapplication. Any replacement Software Media will be warranted for the remainder of the original warranty period or thirty (30) days, whichever is longer.

   (b) In no event shall IDGB or the authors be liable for any damages whatsoever (including without limitation damages for loss of business profits, business interruption, loss of business information, or any other pecuniary loss) arising from the use of or inability to use the Book or the Software, even if IDGB has been advised of the possibility of such damages.

   (c) Because some jurisdictions do not allow the exclusion or limitation of liability for consequential or incidental damages, the above limitation or exclusion may not apply to you.

7. **U.S. Government Restricted Rights.** Use, duplication, or disclosure of the Software by the U.S. Government is subject to restrictions stated in paragraph (c)(1)(ii) of the Rights in Technical Data and Computer Software clause of DFARS 252.227-7013, and in subparagraphs (a) through (d) of the Commercial Computer–Restricted Rights clause at FAR 52.227-19, and in similar clauses in the NASA FAR supplement, when applicable.

8. **General.** This Agreement constitutes the entire understanding of the parties and revokes and supersedes all prior agreements, oral or written, between them and may not be modified or amended except in a writing signed by both parties hereto that specifically refers to this Agreement. This Agreement shall take precedence over any other documents that may be in conflict herewith. If any one or more provisions contained in this Agreement are held by any court or tribunal to be invalid, illegal, or otherwise unenforceable, each and every other provision shall remain in full force and effect.

Dummies 101 CD Installation Instructions

The CD-ROM at the back of this book contains the exercise files that you'll use while you work through the lessons in this book. See Appendix B for complete details about the CD (especially system requirements for using the CD).

heads up

This CD does *not* contain WordPerfect 8. You must already have WordPerfect 8 installed on your computer.

With Windows 95 running, follow these steps to install the exercise files:

1 Insert the *Dummies 101* CD (label side up) into your computer's CD-ROM drive.

2 Click the Start button and click Run.

3 In the dialog box that appears, type d:\setup.exe (if your CD drive is not drive D, substitute the appropriate letter for d) and click OK.

A license agreement appears.

4 Read the license agreement and click Agree.

If you don't agree to the terms of the license agreement, you can't continue with the installation. After you click Agree, you see a message window telling you that the CD installation will be launched.

5 Click OK in the message window.

6 Click Install Exercise Files to see another message window.

The Dummies 101: WordPerfect 8 For Windows installation window appears.

7 Click OK to continue with the installation or click Cancel to stop the installation.

(If you click Cancel, you can install the files later by following these steps again.)

You see a window asking where to install the exercise files on your computer. To make the installation and the exercises in this book as simple as possible, let the installer place the exercise files in the recommended location. If you really want to put the files somewhere else, follow the on-screen instructions to change the location (make sure that you remember where you put them).

8 Click OK to install the files in the folder shown.

9 In the next window that appears, click OK to return to the installation window.

10 Click the Exit button in the lower-right corner of the window.

11 In the window asking whether you want to exit, click Yes.

Unless you change the location, the exercise files are installed to C:\MyFiles. You use the first file in Unit 2.

If you have problems with the installation process, you can call the IDG Books Worldwide, Inc., Customer Support number: 800-762-2974 (outside the U.S.: 317-596-5261).

IDG BOOKS WORLDWIDE REGISTRATION CARD

Visit our Web site at http://www.idgbooks.com

ISBN Number: 0-7645-0189-5

Title of this book: Dummies 101 ® : WordPerfect ® 8 For Windows ®

My overall rating of this book: ❏ Very good [1] ❏ Good [2] ❏ Satisfactory [3] ❏ Fair [4] ❏ Poor [5]

How I first heard about this book:

❏ Found in bookstore; name: [6]

❏ Advertisement: [8]

❏ Word of mouth; heard about book from friend, co-worker, etc.: [10]

❏ Book review: [7]

❏ Catalog: [9]

❏ Other: [11]

What I liked most about this book:

What I would change, add, delete, etc., in future editions of this book:

Other comments:

Number of computer books I purchase in a year: ❏ 1 [12] ❏ 2-5 [13] ❏ 6-10 [14] ❏ More than 10 [15]

I would characterize my computer skills as: ❏ Beginner [16] ❏ Intermediate [17] ❏ Advanced [18] ❏ Professional [19]

I use ❏ DOS [20] ❏ Windows [21] ❏ OS/2 [22] ❏ Unix [23] ❏ Macintosh [24] ❏ Other: [25]_____
(please specify)

I would be interested in new books on the following subjects:
(please check all that apply, and use the spaces provided to identify specific software)

❏ Word processing: [26]

❏ Data bases: [28]

❏ File Utilities: [30]

❏ Networking: [32]

❏ Other: [34]

❏ Spreadsheets: [27]

❏ Desktop publishing: [29]

❏ Money management: [31]

❏ Programming languages: [33]

I use a PC at (please check all that apply): ❏ home [35] ❏ work [36] ❏ school [37] ❏ other: [38]_____

The disks I prefer to use are ❏ 5.25 [39] ❏ 3.5 [40] ❏ other: [41]_____

I have a CD ROM: ❏ yes [42] ❏ no [43]

I plan to buy or upgrade computer hardware this year: ❏ yes [44] ❏ no [45]

I plan to buy or upgrade computer software this year: ❏ yes [46] ❏ no [47]

Name: _____ Business title: [48] _____ Type of Business: [49] _____

Address (❏ home [50] ❏ work [51]/Company name: _____)

Street/Suite# _____

City [52]/State [53]/Zip code [54]: _____ Country [55] _____

❏ **I liked this book!** You may quote me by name in future
IDG Books Worldwide promotional materials.

My daytime phone number is _____

IDG BOOKS WORLDWIDE
THE WORLD OF COMPUTER KNOWLEDGE®

❑ YES!

Please keep me informed about IDG Books Worldwide's
World of Computer Knowledge. Send me your latest catalog.